D1407976

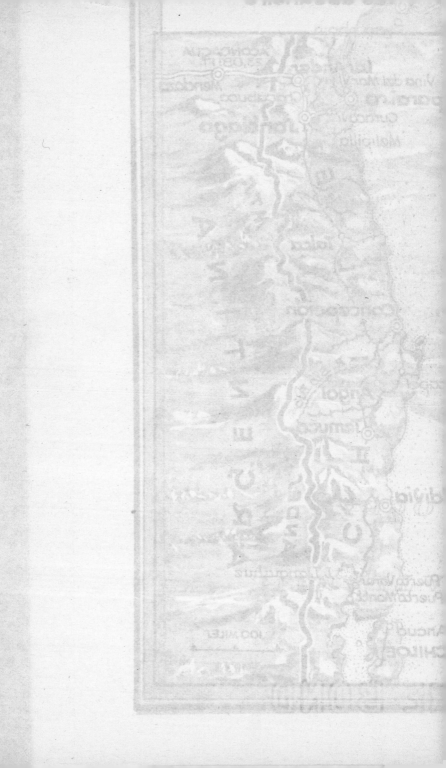

ALSO BY

ERNA FERGUSSON

" One of that small and honorable group of travel writers who combine appreciative observation, human interest and study with a sensitive and active literary conscience, and thus produce work of genuine value."

— *New York Times Book Review*

FIESTA IN MEXICO

DANCING GODS

GUATEMALA

VENEZUELA

OUR SOUTHWEST

OUR HAWAII

THESE ARE BORZOI BOOKS, PUBLISHED BY ALFRED·A·KNOPF

CHILE

CHILE

BY

ERNA FERGUSSON

NEW YORK: ALFRED · A · KNOPF

1943

This book has been produced in full compliance with all government regulations for the conservation of paper, metal, and other essential materials.

ACKNOWLEDGMENTS

IN WRITING such a book as this one becomes deeply indebted both to people and to books. Wherever advisable they have been named in the text. Often the representatives of government departments, of libraries, and of universities prefer not to be named. But I am grateful to them, not only for their practical aid in making published and unpublished material available to me, but for their unstinted kindness in helping me to understand what I read and what I saw.

Those whom I may mention and do, with appreciation, are Hubert Herring and the Committee on Cultural Relations with Latin America because they made it possible for me to take the airplane trip around South America which was such an invaluable introduction to Chile.

CONTENTS

CONTENTS

ILLUSTRATIONS

ILLUSTRATIONS

CHILE

CHILE AND THE CONTINENT

UCH MAY BE SAID AGAINST A QUICK, ALL-INCLUSIVE trip around South America, especially if it convinces the traveler that he knows the South American countries. But as an introduction to any one country it provides an invaluable background. It leaves one breathlessly conscious of the enormousness of the continent, the diversity of its populations, the inevitable conflicts among them, and the manifold complications of the job of being a good neighbor. A thoughtful person must, indeed, be quite chastened by the experience and ready to admit that he needs help and direction in trying to understand our America as a whole.

Three specific advantages of a trip made by air and fairly quickly occur to me — not to mention the inexpressible impression of that remote gliding (secure, smooth, and rapid) over and around such unimaginable beauty. No mind which has ever taken the impress of South America's grandeur from above, sailing in and out of whirling clouds or looking down on opalescent showers that fall from one cloud level to another, could ever again consider life — even at its pettiest or most horrific — without remembering the glory and the beauty and the wonder of the world. Or without remembering how much habitable earth there is — soft valleys and waving uplands, waters with fish and tall forests — where man could find fruitfulness and peace.

The three expressible advantages of seeing South America first from the air and as a whole are these:

One learns that South America is huge and multiplex. One country, Brazil, is larger than continental United States, and much of its Amazonian jungles are unexplored territory. South America is tropical and austral. Men die in humid jungles of wasting fevers or poisoned arrows; they freeze to death in glacial seas; they perish of thirst in deserts. They also possess vast untouched reservoirs of mineral, vegetable, and animal wealth, the most fertile lands on the globe, and waters that produce the finest fish. Out of it they have built up civilization in ten republics and three colonies. But ten republics, not one.

It was the ambition of Simón Bolívar, South America's great liberator, to unite the whole continent under one government which should not be a copy of the constitution of thirteen colonies in the far north, but a system based on the Latin genius, Spanish history, and Catholic faith of the people. Bolívar's dream was unrealized, though he himself freed more than half the continent from Spain and met the Argentine José de San Martín, who had done as much for Chile and western Argentina. Bolívar's other dream failed too. He tried to found a Pan-American union in 1826. He was too far ahead of his time. Not until the 1930's did Americans, North and South, begin to understand what a great American saw so clearly a century earlier.

Jealousy and blindness have held South America in separateness. Instead of a continental unit, there are ten bickering states, kept apart by artificial barriers; by misunderstandings which breed distrust; by conflicting interests which have caused wars, even until now; and by the hatreds produced by these conditions. For the second point that is made clear by flying fast from capital to capital is that the South American countries either do not know or do not like each other. This is denied, of course, in every public utterance, but admitted frankly in private talk and reflected in a hundred unconscious ways. Generally the difficulty is a disagreement about borders.

The Spanish Empire had three viceroyalties in South America: New Granada, consisting of Venezuela, Colombia, Panama, and part of Ecuador; Peru with parts of Ecuador and Bolivia and all that was known of Chile; and Buenos Aires or La Plata, which included modern Uruguay and enough of Bolivia to breed future disputes.

Brazil stood apart as a Portuguese possession, and her later history was very different from that of Spanish America. For when Portugal fell into Napoleon's hands, the royal family emigrated to Brazil and placed its Empire's capital at Rio de Janeiro. Brazil thus skipped the revolutionary period which tore the rest of the Americas from Europe, and drew apart from Portugal late in the nineteenth century and very peacefully.

The Spanish colonies, inspired by France and the United States, won their independence in the first decades of the century; and when Bolívar's hope for a general federation failed, the new nations formed themselves around their capitals. Caracas, Bogotá, Quito, La Paz, and Santiago claimed autonomy; but the borders between states were undetermined. Surveying was an unpracticed art; the vast stretches of mountain, jungle, or plain probably seemed hardly worth the claiming. Only later, when they were explored and wealth was discovered in nitrates and minerals, forest products, and oil, did each country remember that its frontiers properly included all the riches on every side.

Our first South American capital was Bogotá, magnificently set among green mountains and pearly peaks at the perfect altitude for coolness and comfort in the tropics. Bogotanos are as loftily cool as their capital. They claim to speak the purest Castilian in the world, including Spain's Castilian, and are upstage with all their neighbors on the ground that Colombia is a true democracy and " a white man's country." Venezuela, on the east, counters with the charge that Colombia covets her eastern counties; they would certainly provide a desirable way out for Colombia's oil. Bogotanos, who entertained us lavishly and sent round baskets of orchids, like to refer to our high-handed grab of their erstwhile province of Panama. But they quickly pour another glass of wine and add: " It's lucky for us that the Canal is there. We may all need it some day."

Leaving Bogotá, the plane soars grandly out of the bowl-like valley, around the silvered purple peaks, and drops soon into the port of Cali, a flowery place with soft heavy air. All along that shore are tiny smooth green patches. " Japanese truck farms, all ready to be converted into landing fields. To say nothing of submarine bases." Always some oil engineer or North American who has lived there for twenty years occupies the next seat and whispers fearsome hints.

Quito is just below the equator, as Ecuador's name indicates. Warned by the solicitous steward, we were all prepared for the pilot's salute to the Line, but it was a thumping, stomach-shaking drop all the same. The Southern Hemisphere. From there on, winter is summer, summer is winter, up, for all we knew, was down. It needs a mental wrench to move July over into midwinter.

Quito is a gem of a place, and from it one sees the most stupendous display of volcanoes in all South America. Chimborazo, just under 20,500 feet in altitude and the only slightly lesser Cotopaxi and Pichincha. There Bolívar first saw his truest love, Manuela Saenz, tossing him roses from her balcony as he rode in triumph through the streets. The streets are still narrow and the same exquisite churches raise perfect towers aloft and glow with the same gold, silver, and finely wrought woods inside. The same Indians in the same blankets beg piteously on the Cathedral steps, throng the arcades, or huddle in palace doorways, still hopeless of the freedom the Liberator tried to bring them. Young Quiteños entertained us with Ecuadorian music and liquor and speeches in English at their institute dedicated to bettering relations between Ecuador and the United States. Their best ally is the United States Ambassador, Boaz Long, whom they call " mas Quiteño que los Quiteños " (more of a Quiteño than the Quiteños).

Ecuador, being among the smaller nations and without any developed wealth the whole world needs — like oil, nitrates, or copper — feels put upon by both Colombia and Peru, and describes her nearest neighbors in words which make any South America reference to Yankee imperialism sound almost affectionate. The war of 1941, fought over a rich Amazonian province, seemed to her a high-handed and unjustifiable grab on Peru's part. The country seethed with rancor against the stronger neighbor which the later settlement of Rio de Janeiro has probably only deepened; Ecuador felt that she was unfairly forced by the imminence of general war.

From Quito's fifteen thousand feet of rarefied air, where

one must move slowly and never climb stairs, it is only an hour's drop to Guayaquil on the sea. And then along the coast — still unexcelled for enemy plane or submarine landings — to Lima, not on the sea, but connected with her port of Callao by a wide tree-shaded boulevard. Everything about Lima is queenly, as befits Spain's vice-regal capital: magnificent churches, the oldest university in all the Americas, palaces with overhanging balconies; the country home of a famous mistress and one where Bolívar lived; shaded alamedas; modern avenues of wealthy homes; and marvels of Inca handiwork in stone, metals, and textiles, now in museums. Lima lacks no splendor of nature or of man. Peru would seem to have no cause to envy any country.

Yet Peru is torn with strife between her government and a strong undercover democratic movement. And, overbearing and powerful as she seems to Ecuador, she still nurses resentment against Chile for the nitrate and copper deserts that country won in 1879 from both Bolivia and Peru. In Lima they ruefully show the empty chambers which housed the vice-regal library before the Chileans carried it off to Santiago, where it is now. The treaty Chile and Peru signed in 1929 is hopefully considered the end of the " Tacna-Arica Dispute," a hangover of that same war of '79. By it Peru got the province of Tacna, and Chile Arica. Bolivia lost all her coast line but was partly compensated by railroads between her capital La Paz and the Chilean ports of Arica and Antofagasta. In 1921 Bolivia appealed to the League of Nations for restitution of her lost provinces of Antofagasta and Atacama, but the League declined to be drawn into so American a dispute, and Bolivia remains hemmed in away from the Pacific.

So Bolivia hates Chile and has no more affection for her eastern neighbor Paraguay, with which she fought the long and exhausting Chaco War for that tropical selva, immensely rich in hard woods and potentially rich in oil. In La Paz, fourteen thousand feet high, where a constant sandy wind rasps the nerves, they showed us on a map how hapless Bolivia is surrounded by grasping neighbors. The settlement of the Chaco War gave her an outlet to the sea through the Plata basin, and her mines, the world's greatest source of tin, assure her an income. But Bolivia trusts nobody. At the moment she fears that Argentina may (or actually is) draining off her oil reserves through hidden pipe lines. In La Paz they point hopelessly from the map of their vast unexplored tropics, so difficult to exploit, to the gnome-like brown Indians in their streets, so far from an intelligent and democratic citizenry. Bolivia is full of potentialities. And of distrust.

The flight from La Paz to the sea is one on which most travelers take surreptitious drags of oxygen through the handy little rubber tube. But it is short. The Andes here crowd in on the sea, and one has scarcely eaten lunch from a tray before the plane dips one wing as it swerves toward the surf, creaming along a rocky coast, and alights at a shining airport. The polite steward reminds travelers to keep their seats until the captain has left the ship, and he comes quickly through with no self-importance but as though aware of his responsibility to report bringing us safely through so far. Men in coveralls have already wheeled out the supplies, placed the gangway, and swarmed up onto the plane to service it.

This is Arica, the first Chilean port and the northernmost town of that uniquely situated country. In fact, no country in the world boasts so strange a configuration: a two-thousand-six-hundred-mile strip of land between the Andes and the Pacific, seldom more than a hundred miles wide. Every writer on Chile has dwelt on its singular geography. "*Faja, larga y estrecha,"* is the phrase everyone uses in quotation; I have never run it back to its maker. *Faja* might be translated scarf, sash, or belt; *larga y estrecha* is unquestionably "long and narrow." Others have compared Chile with a sword, suggesting that its point is the stern unconquered Araucanian Indians in the south. For its entire length Chile clings precariously to the continent's edge in seeming danger of being sloughed off by the cordillera or eaten away by the sea; but between them mountains and ocean have made her wealth and formed her character. In the north the frozen Andes send no streams down, and land winds blowing coolly over the water force the clouds to disgorge their moisture before they reach the land. So the deserts have been stored with nitrates, which otherwise would have washed out to sea. This northern third, the Atacama Desert, was inhabited by Indians before the conquest; it is now the home of the dispossessed and of the Yanquis who can live anywhere they find wealth. Farther south the Andes have opened wide valleys to pour down rich volcanic soil and water it with numberless clear streams made of snow.

The central region was country the Spaniards knew and could utilize: good soil, mild, semi-arid climate with plenty of water for irrigation, and good harbors. The River Bío-Bío, on to the south, was the point at which the Araucanians said: "So far and no farther." That might not have been enough to stop the conquerors. But what lay beyond had no charms for people from Spain's dry and sunny warmth. For Chile's southern third is one of the cloudiest, chilliest zones on earth. Only aborigines inured and immunized to it through many generations or immigrants from a similar clime would choose it for a home. And such is its population still: Indians and northern European immigrants, who began to come a century ago.

10

North of the center the cordillera stands on sheer hard cliffs against which the waves bite and foam and make no headway. But in the far south the ocean has gnawed the coast into a tattered series of islands, peninsulas, estuaries, bays, and straits, beyond counting; it has drowned the coastal range so completely that only its peaks poke up as islands. Between them sea and cordillera have given Chile another fantastic dimension — height. South America's tallest peak, Aconcagua, holds its crest of perpetual snow 22,385 feet above sea level, and Aconcagua is only one of many volcanic peaks almost as high.

Chile has an undersea reach as well. The coal mines at Lota have opened a tunnel four miles wide and more than a mile under the ocean; and hundreds of miles of coal are known to underlie Chile's shore. " A crazy geography " indeed, and one bound to affect anyone who looks upon it even casually. How much more, then, must it have marked the people whose home it is!

Chile seems the friendliest nation of them all, except perhaps Brazil. She, at least, is serenely satisfied with her settlements with Bolivia and Peru, and both Chile and Argentina are justifiably proud of the adjustment of their ancient boundary difficulty. In colonial days Chile's map crossed the Andes and took in large stretches of pampas, but a treaty of 1881 named the " division of the waters " as the frontier. That is, each country was given control of the source of its waters. But Argentina's diplomats, sedulously seeking, found also some mention of the " highest peaks " which divide the waters. The two nations then agreed to accept the arbitration of the King of England and in honor of the peaceful solution of their differences they erected the noble " Christ of the Andes " with its inscription:

*" Sooner shall these mountains crumble to dust
than the people of Argentina and Chile break the
peace which they have sworn to maintain at the feet
of Christ the Redeemer."*

Nevertheless Argentines joke about that early day when
the Pacific will have washed Chile quite away and left the
Andes as a palisade to protect their pampas. Chileans react as
one would expect them to. They find Argentines hard, grasping, and far too Italian to be trusted.

The flight from Santiago to Buenos Aires is not as altitudi-
nous as others I had made. Planes fly Uspallata Pass at only
fifteen thousand feet. But its splendor is unexcelled. We rose
before the sun did, but a sinking moon showed us the city and
marked out the Rio Mapocho in silver. The landscape flattened
out, as it does from the air, and Chile's rich farming land was
spread below like a carpet of smooth green patterned with
lines of trees, meanderings of streams, and criss-crossed roads.
Then we flew the length of the Aconcagua Valley, and the
Andes were shouldering us into the pass between the peaks of
Aconcagua and Tupungato, 22,385 and 19,500 feet in altitude. Down, infinitely below, between forested slopes we
glimpsed flashing lakes, roofs of ski lodges, and tiny towns
in squares. Now and then we could trace the daring grades
and curves in which British engineers had laid the *Ferrocarril
Transandino* many years ago. Often snow puts that railroad
out of use for months at a time. That was true when we crossed
so quickly the barrier which has kept Chile and Argentina as
far apart as though they were on different planets. A motor
road and air traffic are bringing them closer now.

Aconcagua is often smothered in clouds; we were vouch-
safed the grace of seeing it clear, as noble a cone as exists.

The Plane's Wing Brushes the Peaks

Llamas

Just as our plane's wing brushed its shimmering snowy tip and our eyes were strained trying to record an image that would never fade, the steward summoned us to see the *Cristo de los Andes* out the other window. It is too small to be impressive from the air. One should, I am sure, stand below and look up at that benign countenance above the noble words.

Then we were dropping, leaving the mountains behind, seeing the Argentine pampa spreading away in soft hues as limitless and as flat as the ocean. At about the tropic of Capricorn the Andes, which have been plunging eastward into steaming tropical jungle, suddenly find themselves set on the flattest, widest grazing land on earth. Not a hummock, not a hillock, not a pebble breaks its 250,000 square miles of even slope to the Atlantic. With a rich black topsoil eighteen inches deep, cattle fatten on grass to stupendous size, and fertilizing is unknown. Critical Argentinos say that some of their people are underfed, but the ones one sees are as sturdy as their cattle. Even Buenos Aires' poorer streets are alive with rosy children, their school aprons tucked up over well-muscled legs, their whole bodies bursting with health. And the stately stone houses with wrought-iron gates and magnificent motors speeding along great boulevards and streets of solid banks and stores jammed with luxuries! No wonder Parisians used to say: " As rich as an Argentine! " Quite naturally little love is lost between her and less favored lands.

Argentines (who have the way of the powerful of minimizing their neighbors) find Brazilians Negroid, Paraguayans Indian and degenerate, and Uruguayans a thorn in the flesh because perky little Uruguay is quite as white as anybody, quite as rich as Argentina, more democratic than most, and correspondingly difficult to make feel inferior in any regard. Uruguay has been called the Sweden of South America, her schools are so modern, her literacy so high, her social laws so advanced and well enforced. Homogeneity has helped, of course; people of the same culture work best together. But Uruguay's well-placed few, aware of the backward drag of concentrated wealth and landownership, have patriotically put the general good before their personal aggrandizement. Uruguay, too, was the first American country to realize the full extent of the Nazi menace and to stamp it out at home. An Uruguayan, Hugo Fernández Artucio, who first brought it to his government's attention, then made a study of the situation throughout the continent, which was published in English as *The Nazi Underground in South America.* Americans, North and South, owe much to Uruguay.

Brazil, like the others, has had border brushes with other countries, but except for a prevalent resentment against Argentina, Brazilians seem to have little awareness of their neighbors and less knowledge. The Andes and the Orinocan and Amazonian jungles make the rest of South America much more remote from Brazil than Africa, Europe, or North America — in that order.

Lovely Brazil! Everyone who has known her even slightly must forever carry the memory of her infinite and lazy charm. With fabulous wealth in everything, from iron to diamonds, by ways of nuts, sugar, mahogany, coffee, vanilla, cocoa, cotton, and rubber, Brazil stretches languidly from deep tropics to comfortable temperateness, and slumbers peacefully on her inestimable wealth. Brazilians, pale and wispy, move with careful calculation, as though the effort of any gesture might prove too much. They blame their national lassitude on climate and on Indian and Negro blood; and they come alive only for Mardi Gras, which is so important that even breaking relations with the Axis was not allowed to interfere with the sacred week of masque and frolic.

No, South America is no unit — in any sense. And this brings us to the third point that occurs to the rapid traveler: the South American countries are better known to the United States than to each other. Because of both heritage and culture South Americans have gone to Europe whenever they left home; seldom to the United States, almost never to other South American countries. But, for a century or so, business has taken many North Americans to South America to visit or to live. And our predilection for travel and for discovering new lands to vacation in has given many a North American at least a view of the southern continent. This is not to say that we know the southern countries well or truly, but that we know them better than they know each other. What a historical irony if the function of the United States should be that of introducing Latin Americans to one another!

Certainly the present effort toward hemispheric unity and understanding comes from North rather than from South America. Its motives may be discounted as selfish, inspired by fear, or otherwise bad. They may be credited to an American named Roosevelt who saw as clearly in 1933 as an American named Bolívar did in 1826, and to the winning friendliness of " Hull of the United States," who is said to pronounce correctly only one South American diplomat's name (Benjamin Cohen of Chile), but whose basic nobility and natural courtesy speak straighter to their hearts than the most polished Castilian. Whatever the cause, the result of the Good Neighbor policy is to bring all Americans together as never before. We are learning to appreciate our fundamental unities. The gratifying response to the need of the United States after Pearl Harbor reflected, of course, confidence in Roosevelt and Hull. But deeper and far more significant than that lay the fact that

15

all Americans, North and South, are forever dedicated to the same ideals of independence for nations, freedom for individuals. The conference at Rio proved the basic oneness of the Americas more than it proved any diplomatic skill or power of propaganda.

II

GABRIELA MISTRAL

OCCASIONALLY ONE PERSON SEEMS TO EMBODY AN era, a people, or a country. For me Gabriela Mistral, whom I knew in Brazil, typifies Chile and the Chileans. As a poet she has drawn her country and her people with deep feeling and fine images; but her personality expresses more than even she can say. She is strong, profound, and tragic as are her native cordillera and ocean, her heritage is Spanish, and some inexplicable quality of her nature is unconquerable Indian. In *Panorama y Color de Chile* she sums up her country in phrases which might as well express her life.

" Something like a synthesis of the planet is realized in the geography of Chile. It begins with the desert . . . a sterility which has no use for man: it is humanized in the valleys of the transition zone; makes a complete home for itself in the agricultural region; takes on a heroic forest beauty at the continent's end as though to finish worthily; and it finally crumbles away, offering equally life and death in a sea which vacillates between its liquid quality and the Buddhic nature of eternal ice. . . ."

17

With a truly Latin appreciation of the arts, the Chilean government makes it possible for Gabriela Mistral to live abroad, generally as consul. So she has known many significant men and women of our time. Everywhere her lofty spirit and her wide mental reach have brought her the friendship of great thinkers. Gabriela Mistral is of that small but potent band that stands for the highest and most unattainable human values.

We met for lunch at the Lido on Copacabana Beach. Gabriela had appointed the place. " Being Chilean," she explained, " I have to live in the mountains and come often to the sea."

We lunched on shrimps and Brazil's rich and savory stew, with Chilean wine and papaya with squeezed lime for dessert. For hours we sat over clear black coffee, talking while the tide went out and the lowering sun altered the outlines of Sugar Loaf across the bay.

Gabriela is a large woman with a noble head topped by iron-gray hair cut short, but too vigorous to lie still. Her features are strong — the nose might be Indian — but the effect is never heavy because of the large, lucent hazel-green eyes and sensitive mobile mouth. Under the quick interest in the eyes and the ready sympathy of the smile sadness, even tragedy, always lie. Her voice is low, of thrilling timbre, and everything she says is enhanced by the gestures of her mobile hands. Beautiful hands: delicate, they are most notable for strength; constantly moving, they never seem futile, but reaching, like antennae, for some imponderable she is sure to catch.

When we parted, Gabriela said: " Come to Petropolis for a week so we can talk." What a Chilean gesture! " I like you; come for a week."

Petropolis, the summer home of the imperial family before Brazil became a republic, is now frequented by diplomats and

Gabriela Mistral

the wealthy. A leafy, flowery town. But Gabriela lives above it on a cliff. On clear days the view spreads out over valleys and plains to Rio's white buildings on the shining Atlantic like an Italian painting of what Satan showed Jesus. But during my visit we suffered almost constantly from *los rusos,* a damp and chilling mist which rolls in from the sea to overwhelm the heights and seep into the houses.

Every day I went to Gabriela's house for lunch, generally to find her digging with a trowel in her garden and trying to instill some sense of responsibility into the mulatto lad who assisted her. She has a need to touch the earth after hours of mental work, and she has, too, the teacher's need to touch some seed in everyone she knows and to help it germinate.

Later, at lunch, Yin-Yin would join us. He was a nephew of Gabriela's, born of a Chilean father and a Spanish mother, educated in France until the age of fourteen.

We talked about people and war and money, and the distant hoped-for day when the world might consider people more important than the other two. We talked of books and Indians, of what makes South Americans differ so and have so many differences. We talked of the cataclysm in Europe, which Gabriela, living in Nice, had seen coming. We talked of a new world which might accept the truly American doctrine of a fusion of races into a real democracy. And that brought us again to Indians, and to Gabriela's background.

She claims Indian blood and points to her features and her dark skin as proof. This is the story she tells. Two generations ago a countryman came down from the Chilean hills. His name was Godoy, and Gabriela's relatives deny that he had Indian blood. But he may have had, and the importance of that, as of the gentleman himself, is that he was Gabriela's grandfather. He married Isabel Villanueva, a lady of high degree, and later left her and their four children and disappeared again.

Doña Isabel trained her two daughters to such piety that they both took the veil as nuns. Her son, Jeronimo, was to follow his father's example. But first he qualified as a teacher, with the title "maestro," and married Petronila Alcayaga, a widow with a twelve-year-old daughter. Of this marriage was born a fair, hazel-eyed daughter whom they named Lucila. She later chose the name Gabriela Mistral. She was her sister's charge. The two sisters speak of each other with lively affection; the mother seems to have retreated into her grief and her religion, leaving little mark on their lives. For Jeronimo Godoy left her when their daughter was two years old — perhaps like his father impelled to return to the hills. Gabriela, as a mature woman, came to understand him. But the hurt to the sensitive child is plain in her poems about children.

One of her first memories is of a visit to her grandmother, who lived in La Serena. Young Emelina dressed little Lucila in her best ruffled dress, curled her hair, and even dusted her face with powder. Both sisters remember how Doña Isabel received them, standing poker-stiff, and gave her hand to be kissed. She then coolly looked at Lucila's finery, remarked: "How worldly!" and produced a handkerchief to remove at least the powder.

Poor little Emelina was crushed as she took her adored baby back home to Vicuña. Lucila saw Doña Isabel now and then. She remembers her as "a Biblical woman, almost a Quaker," who taught her to repeat the Psalms from memory.

Lucila attended her sister's school. She learned readily everything except to play. Her sister teacher was distressed to see her stand aside during recess. Lucila remembers that she was saddened by her fatherless home; there was an episode of an unjust accusation which she did not report to the sister so eager to help her.

When Lucila was twelve her father came home. She found him charming, but her joy in that and in having a proper family was soon lost. Jeronimo Godoy was drinking then, and his wife was unable to cope with his complicated nature. He had spells of unreasonable violence, he wrote poetry, he was given to going off alone. Perhaps he was not kind to Lucila. Soon he disappeared for the last time. During those dark days the mother and her two daughters were devoutly dedicated to the Holy Virgin of Succor. The image they prayed before had remarkably beautiful hands: the hands, so her sister says, which Gabriela has now.

When she was thirteen Lucila wrote her first poem, *Flores Negras,* " Black Flowers."

> I cannot sing because verse will not spring
> From my saddened soul.
> Do you wish the broken harp to sound?
> The wounded soul to sing?

The thirteenth stanza concludes:

> Therefore I beg that you will never peruse
> These lines which are black flowers,
> Scentless and lifeless because they were born
> Within the autumnal valley of a sick soul.

It is easy to laugh at a child of thirteen who mourns her life's dusty end. But the sensitive Lucila had suffered more adult grief than many long lives hold. The years before her thirteenth had given her the understanding of sorrow, the appreciation of children's needs and tragedies that have marked her work and her life.

When she was fifteen, Lucila went to work as a primary

teacher. Three years later she had advanced to the secondary schools (an almost impossible promotion under Chile's system) and to the post of *directora*. It was a brilliant career which produced its quota of envious enemies. But it was a happy time for a young woman who found her greatest joy in children, her truest expression in working with them.

Pictures of Lucila Godoy as a teacher show a plump girl, not much older than the pupils laughing with her. Such a girl would be expected to marry, raise a large family, and perhaps be a teacher too. The scars of her unhappy childhood might have been erased by her fine health, sense of fun, sane love of nature and of human nature. But her poems reflect later tragedy, especially *Interrogaciones*. The questions it asks are the unanswerable queries a suicide leaves behind him.

> How, Oh Lord, do the suicides sleep?
> With a blood clot in the mouth, the temples fallen,
> The eyes' crescents whitened and enlarged,
> The hands outstretched toward an invisible anchor?
>
> Or dost Thou come after men have gone
> To lower the lid over the blind eye,
> To straighten the limbs without pain and silently,
> And to cross the hands over the silent breast?

These are the first two stanzas; the last shows how she was finding reconciliation with the tragedy and bitterness of life.

> Thou art the vase from which are sponged
> Sweetly clean
> All the wounds of earth.

Lucila's suicide was a young man who worked in a railroad station. Perhaps he did not mean much to her; one cannot imagine that such a weakling could long have commanded a mind and spirit like hers. But when his accounts were found confused if not falsified and he killed himself he left some indication that his love for Lucila had made him ashamed to face her with his guilt. She does not speak of this experience, but it infuses all her later work — not as grief for one pitiful youth, but as motherly tenderness for all unfortunates. And as a mature acceptance of responsibility for so much tragic human waste.

Very soon, then, Lucila Godoy became known in Chile as a poet. She took the name Gabriela Mistral because, she says, of her passion for the tempestuous northern wind of that name. Her first public appearance was in 1924 when her poems, *Sonetos de la Muerte*, were read before the writers' society of Santiago. She did not read them herself because she did not like " literary-mundane fiestas." She sat instead in a back seat, her cold hands tightly clasped, her eyes shining in a pale face. When the *Sonnets on Death* were published they were hailed throughout the Spanish-speaking world as among the finest lyrics in all Spanish literature.

That ended Lucila Godoy the school teacher, opened the whole world to Gabriela Mistral. She went first to Mexico to dedicate a school which bore her name and to work in the Mexican school system, then in its brilliant inception under José Vasconcelos. Then on to New York. There her collected poems were published as *Desolación* under the auspices of the Hispanic Institute and the American Association of Teachers of Spanish of New York. We may be proud that her worth was immediately recognized by the Spanish-reading public of the United States.

Federico de Onís, Director of the Hispanic Institute and Professor of Spanish Literature at Columbia University, has evaluated Gabriela Mistral as a poet and a person as follows:

"In whatever she does she shows a natural superiority and on all that she touches she leaves a deep impress. She moves with an air of age-old repose and serenity; her voice sounds plaintive, monotonous, and faraway, with shades of severity and sweetness difficult to imagine; the sorrowful droop of her mouth can become a smile of infinite gentleness. A tremendously impassioned soul, great in all its aspects. After pouring the grief of her personal tragedy into some of her best poems, she has filled this void in her life with concern for the care of children, the redemption of the lowly, and the destiny of the Hispanic peoples. All this is only another way of expressing the basic sentiment of her poetry, her unsatisfied maternal desire which is at once feminine instinct and religious longing for eternity.

"The sources of her literary art — perhaps overly close and apparent — are unimportant compared with the greatness and intensity of her passion: who knows what hidden awareness leads her always through the most intimate and universal reaches of the Spanish tongue to the precisely right expression."

So this critic recognizes Gabriela's pre-eminence as a person. Though her poems rank among the greatest of modern Spanish lyrics, she has published little poetry since that first volume. Her prose is very fine, but it is scattered throughout magazines and newspapers in many countries; she has never bothered to collect and republish it.

In 1926 Gabriela Mistral went to the League of Nations as cultural representative of all Spanish America; and later to Paris and Rome in various cultural posts, representing Chile and other countries. After that she began her service as consul. During the dictatorship of Ibañez, whose administration she openly opposed, she was without a post. All other Chilean governments have been proud to be represented by Gabriela Mistral.

Much of this I did not know as I studied her at Petropolis, but nobody could have had that experience without recognizing a great woman. She sits at the head of her table, long after the dishes have been removed, following a line of thought which reflects her reading (the Bible, Dante, Tagore, Bergson, Maritain, the Spanish mystics, and her two namesakes, d'Annunzio and Mistral). She vibrates most thrillingly to her love of her own country and her deep conviction that our only way out of this sad world's mess is through democracy. And religion.

Gabriela is a mystical Catholic. That is, she is a mystic by nature, and her early training has brought her surely back, after twenty years of a Christianized Buddhism, to the Catholic Church. That does not mean that she needs its outer forms; she seldom, I believe, goes to Mass. But the Catholic expression of spirituality is so natural to her that long excursions into Indian mysticism have only led her back to the saints and the Mother of God. Her poems are so full of Catholic images that the North American reader must often translate more than the Spanish to get the true feeling of Mistral.

During my visit our company often included Yin-Yin, a half-French Peruvian lad, and a young Jewish refugee. Yin-Yin doubtless answers Gabriela's need for maternity; he responds with easy devotion, touching her hand to attract attention, kissing her hair in greeting. The French-Peruvian regretted the Indian heritage which would forever prevent any American country from reaching the heights he lived on. The Jewish refugee was particularly scornful of the people who had given him generous sanctuary from Europe's horrors. Gabriela would sit, regal and still, her calm wisdom dwarfing them until they felt it and begged her confirmation.

To the Peruvian: " You are Indian, as we all are — Indo-Americans. And it should be your pride that the blood of such a magnificent people flows in your veins."

To the young Jew, smiling superiorly under his nose, she said little. Her motherliness surely knew that his ugly screaming came from a hurt too deep and too recent for curing. She had once written a poem about his people:

> Jewish race, body of sorrow,
> Jewish race, river of bitterness;
> Like the skies and the earth you endure,
> And your numbers grow even from wailing.
>
> Trembling your women suckle their babies,
> Trembling your men harvest their sheaves.
> Into your dream the nightmare is thrust
> and your speech is only Miserere. . . .
>
> In your woman, Mary still walks,
> Over your face lies the profile of Christ . . .
> Over the hillsides of Zion they have seen him,
> Calling you vainly as the day dies.

Those young Europeans were like three light straws, dry before they had matured, with no force of their own, blown out from that hideous conflagration they had escaped; unaware of the splendor of the new world they had chanced upon.

Gabriela was like America, deep and vast, offering them everything, but without insistence, waiting to see if they could understand and take it.

Gabriela is all America — not what we too often take it to be: white, Nordic, and Protestant; pushing and optimistic. She loves the universal American ideals — independence, equality of opportunity, and tolerance. But she sees life from a Chilean viewpoint very different from ours. There is first that deep sense of life as tragic. Is it Indian, Spanish, or Catholic to accept suffering and evil without revolt, but with despair or resignation? Gabriela thinks it is Indian: the ages-old pessimism of a people hopeless under Inca rule long before the Spaniards conquered and enslaved them, and always helpless before overpowering nature, whose violences may be endured but never combated.

" We are Indian," she said. " Even those who have no Indian blood — or will not admit it — are Indian. Indo-American."

She finds the Spanish influence less potent in Spanish America than that of all Latin-European culture, especially that of France. She hopes for increasing influence of the Nordic and English — that is, North American — culture in South America.

" Our culture is colonial, except for a few vigorous young writers who have recently risen from our submerged classes. Chile is only beginning to feel her individuality, to dare to express her own soul. . . .

" You will understand us only if you remember always that Chile is Catholic. Even Chileans who are not Catholics are Catholic of the soul. Do you understand that? "

I was not sure I understood any of it, that I could ever understand Chile. But if I did, it would be, I knew, because of knowing this woman who so completely expresses Chile's rugged strength, magnificent in its heights and profundities, but with serene valleys where quiet simple human needs are understood and met. She has also her country's mysticism, the conviction that life is too complicated, too tragic, and too terrifying to be faced without superhuman aid.

A North American poet, singularly appreciative and sensitive, said of Gabriela: " She is one of the greatest poets living, perhaps the very greatest. But I find her persistent gloom hard to bear." Herein lies one of the stumbling-blocks to inter-American understanding. How can we, brashly ready to take on nature and conquer her, understand the Indian's stoic endurance of suffering or the Catholic acceptance of it?

We can hope better to understand the new Chile which Gabriela also represents. She is of the class which knew poverty and paucity of opportunity. Her genius has set her apart, but she is quick to recognize in her people gifts that will make the future Chile worthy of her finest ancestry — Indian as well as white.

III

THROUGH THE CHILEAN LAKES

ONSIDERING WAYS OF GETTING FROM BRAZIL TO Chile impressed me again with South America's vast extent. One could go to Panama and down: six weeks or so, not counting layovers. One could ship on a Chilean steamer for Valparaiso by way of the Straits of Magellan: a month at least, with the likelihood of impenetrable fogs and intense cold so early in the spring as November. Flying is expensive, though a blond young man in a tourist agency assured me that the German Condor Line was much less expensive than anything American. Gabriela advised ship to Buenos Aires, train across Argentina to Bariloche, and the journey through Chile's fabulously beautiful lakes. I decided on that.

Argentina's pampas, which look from the air like water petrified in ripples, are Texas to the life when seen close to. Or Texas is Argentina to the life. Same plate-shaped earth with a bowl of blue above; same shanty towns with false-fronted buildings, horses at hitching racks, and people in buggies and Fords down to meet the train. Women and children might be Texans, but the men! These robust, red-cheeked, booted and spurred gauchos are masculine in the extreme. But their trousers are just what Mrs. Amelia Bloomer designed in 1850 to preserve feminine decorum while permitting some leg action. On heavy masculine legs, in stuff light enough to flutter, they seem all too incongruous with the vicious spurs below, the manly sombrero and short poncho above.

Our train was crowded with Catholics going to a great Eucharistic Congress in Santiago de Chile. Priests said Mass in the dining-car before breakfast could be served to anyone. Giggling girls read their prayers while waiting for their coffee; older women exchanged gossip, sitting stately erect among their young charges. I shared my compartment with a young woman who wept for two days because she was leaving home for a position as social worker in Bariloche. To the Latin, leaving one's family for any reason whatever is only less tragic than death. Happily her friends had supplied her well with candies and train letters, so she munched and read as she sobbed, and finally she was strong enough to write replies. At stations we walked together because she felt it was not quite correct for a young girl to appear alone.

Just before Bariloche the train began puffing up the Andean slopes along dry rivers where thorny growth had taken root. The lakes, which we think of as Chilean, cross the international boundary, and Argentina owns Lake Nahuel Huapí, one of the loveliest. Bariloche is a tidy town with a solid stone civic center opening on the lake, a couple of travel agencies, and hotels for every taste.

The Hotel Parque repels the visitor from the first. Its entrance, down a cement stairway between stone walls, suggested an underground dungeon. Indoors a small stern woman stood waiting, her hands folded under a stiff white apron, her demeanor harsh and unwelcoming enough for the wardress of a prison. I thought I heard the clank of keys as she moved.

To my request for a room she made no reply; just widened her gaze to include others who had filled the lobby behind me, speaking Spanish, French, and German. Suddenly a couple of British came stamping through in heavy boots, steered by a slighter man who spoke a word to the wardress and led his charges up the stairs beyond. How childishly endearing the British are in their utter unawareness of the less aggressive folk they shove aside!

Later, made aware of me by a travel agent, these very Britishers allowed me to share their car on jaunts around Bariloche and proved themselves as considerate and as much fun as their people always are once one has penetrated the chilling fog in which they shroud themselves.

The hotel, too, proved friendly in its servants, the food was good, and many windows gave on Lake Nahuel Huapí, lapping its shingly beach and mirroring sky and mountains in its clear surface. Driving out we found that Nahuel Huapí is only the largest of a string of shining blue or green lakes, strung together by streams and colored by the wooded hills or snow-capped azure peaks between them. They all offer " the world's finest fishing," for the government has stocked them with fresh-water salmon imported from Maine. We visited the hatchery and stopped for tea at a lodge on a ski run, decomposing into mud under the spring sun. And we walked through the still-empty corridors and salons of the great summer hotel which is Argentina's pride.

When we were asked to register, the lady looked at her husband questioningly. " Shall I write ' Argentina '? "

" Why not? " he teased. " You were born here. Aren't you an Argentine? "

His own "British," written heavily below, seemed to carry extra weight.

This couple's sons, born Argentines, had been excused from military service in that country to serve with the British armed forces. The lady herself, trained by an English governess, had never learned Spanish. Certainly this is dual citizenship, though so one-sided as to make even the word " dual " dubious. I remembered how different such things seem in the case of Japanese born in Hawaii or in California.

In answer to my query, Sir William said: " Oh, there could be no question about our loyalty in case of trouble between our country and Argentina. We are British, of course."

Another day we saw a glacier, my first and very disappointing. Instead of brilliant white or blue ice, it was a mass of brown-black volcanic stuff, melting into a stream as foul as the drainage from a mine dump. It came from El Tronador, a peak in Chile. The Thunderer was silent that day, though the spring thaw would later break off enormous chunks of ice and send reverberations of their creaking and crashing across many miles of country. On the other side, too far away for an afternoon's jaunt, another glacier, uncorrupted by soluble ash, sent down a blue-green stream as transparent as glass. When the two brooks met, the foul one muddied the pure, but in time the impurities sank away and a decent little river followed us for miles of grassy valley. So much unoccupied land, ready to produce all the best foods of the temperate zone.

The day before I set out for Chile, Sam Wagner of Texas came in to take the Britishers on a fishing trip. After twenty years in Argentina, Mr. Wagner was as Texan as his drawl, and as amusing to Sir William as that gentleman and his accent were to my compatriot. What a lot of entertainment will be lost if a standard English pronunciation is ever used by us all!

" Is the shovah theah? " inquired Sir William.

" Ah reckon so," replied Sam Wagner. " Are you-all ready to shove? "

One meant " chauffeur " and the other meant " start," but they understood each other perfectly.

Embarking next morning on the *Modesta Victoria*, I found among the passengers people I had known at the hotel: three Brazilians, three Argentines with Italian names, and two Uruguayans. The morning was misty, and clouds hung below the peaks which should have been reflected in the lake. But we assured each other it would clear after lunch and stayed shivering on deck lest we miss a view.

There I fell into talk with a young woman with red-gold hair, milk-white skin, and English accent with Continental overtones. I could not guess her nationality. I had even less idea when her husband added his English with a strong German accent.

His opening remark caused us a good deal of amusement later: " I'm surprised to see so few *Yanquis*," he remarked. " I thought every place would be thick with them. . . . Of course, the fewer I see the better I like it."

It is fun in a case like that to wait awhile and then refer to oneself casually as a Yanqui. Without waving the flag exactly, one can show that no offense is taken from Europeans who cannot know just what that flag stands for. Later, when we had made friends, I learned that even the scornful European's greatest ambition was United States citizenship.

Nahuel Huapí is a large lake, but by noon the hills were narrowing in to a strait at Puerto Blest, where we should lunch.

It was a desolate, cold, gray day. Benjamin Subercaseaux complained, in his *Chile, Una Loca Geografia,* that in the country of the lakes " each phrase of admiration is followed by a ' what a shame that! ' " In my case it was what a shame that I could not see it.

Benjamin Subercaseaux is an irreverent young modern who called his book a *Crazy Geography* and then wrote wittily and intelligently about his country. Luckily for foreigners who dare to write about Chile, Chileans have said everything needful about their country and their people with striking effect, cool objectivity, and humor. What I could not see through the muffling mists of Chile her writers lit up for me. I make no apology for quoting or paraphrasing them. Subercaseaux, who might have been writing of that very day, complains:

" This is the precise point where all the geographies of Chile show themselves vulgar. The worst bad taste which tourist advertising produces makes it speak of ' the best climate in the world,' although the climate is rainy and detestable. . . . We . . . call the region *of the blue mirrors* when, in fact, gray and foggy tones predominate and . . . blue is only an exception."

If for me the Chilean lakes were less than the extravagant wonderland I had read about, it was my own fault. I had come along before the season opened, deliberately taking a chance on unseasonable clear days, with a few views through the left-over clouds of winter. It was a gamble and I lost.

The only thing to do was to turn to the company, and that was charming and bright enough to compensate for all the outdoor cold and wet.

The Brazilians, muffled in furs, were ready with cameras if the sun ever came out. The older couple had lived abroad,

but did not know the United States. The girl, slim and graceful, spoke the English of a British governess, thickening certain sounds as the Portuguese do. She was engaged to a young
diplomat who hoped soon for a post in Canada; meanwhile
they were building a completely modern house, " all American in style and conveniences," and she had ordered her
whole trousseau, linens and all, from a New York house.
" They were so kind; they appointed me a shopper and she
made my selections and we wrote back and forth just like
friends."

The Argentines, speaking no English, helped me with Spanish, giving me colloquial phrases. Uncle was a mine of legends
and stories of the old days in Patagonia.

Nephew, an engineer, longed as all South American engineers seem to do for a trip to the United States. His señora,
politely regretting that " her *compatriotas* were not developed
and public-spirited like Mrs. Roosevelt," comforted herself
by saying: " But our home life is so beautiful! When I remember how our family was always together for meals with
Papá at one end of the table and Mamá at the other; how we
talked of everything, the jokes we had! "

I knew it would be futile to tell her that we too had family
meals, that not all mothers worked away from home, that she
had read in English and not North American books about
lonely little boys sent away from home at eight or nine. In
any case our conversation was interrupted at Puerto Blest.

In hooded raincoats we filed across the soggy pier and into
a frame house where there was a blessed sheet-iron stove to
huddle round and a friendly welcome better than the indifferent lunch. Outside the *Modesta Victoria* gave a farewell
hoot and started back to Bariloche.

After lunch a small rattling bus carried us across a soggy

isthmus to the next lake. In the midst of a moss-hung and
dripping forest, at the risk of bogging down permanently in
the oozing leaf mold underfoot, we stopped to see a giant
coigue. This *Nothofagus dombeyi* is an evergreen, native to
the region, and the grandfather and great-grandfather, so the
Argentine uncle said, of all trees. It may be related to the
California sequoia and, though not so large nor perhaps so
old, it was worth plunging through the wet to see. Subercaseaux again expresses my thoughts:

" And the humidity — which is healthful in this region —
but which we see in the pool, in the moss, in the rotting leaf,
in our spongy footsteps, becomes an obsession which clamors
for dryness, for a hot climate, for the desert, even for devour-
ing thirst. Here one ends by hating water and rivers, and
lakes, and rain."

Afternoon was no better. Tiny Laguna Frias could only
offer us an echo in lieu of the beauty that should have enthralled us, but we had begun to think it funny and to make
polyglot jokes. Also the traveling South Americans were
showing their true colors as tourists. The North American
tourist is the fellow *par excellence* who is scornful of all other
countries, especially for their lack of comfort and efficiency.
But our Brazilians complained bitterly of cold, wished they
had spent their vacation at Petropolis; the Uruguayans
yearned for the clear skies of Bariloche; and the Argentines
resolved to go straight back to their own sunny country if
Chile could do no better than this.

In the next portage bus I found myself beside a young man
whose Mussolini jaw, football shoulders, and free and easy
Yanqui gait had baffled me. But a Brooklyn accent became
apparent as his deep gray eyes brightened with someone to
talk to. He was tired of traveling alone. His scholarship was

taking him all round the circle "to compare educational methods," though he had neither Spanish nor Portuguese enough for casual conversation. But it soon appeared that, whatever he had learned about educational methods, his Y. M. C. A. ethics were having difficulty with South American mores and morals.

"Funny," he said, "how little those boys know of what they miss. They begin their sex life at thirteen, usually with the maid in the house, and nobody minds. Their fathers even encourage it. So they think of girls in only one way and they can't imagine that anybody else ever had a decent idea about them."

Suddenly he laughed. "I almost got in a jam at a dance. I danced with a pretty girl and she danced well, so I asked her again. I noticed one of the fellows glowering at us, but I thought he was peeved because I was beating his time, so we danced again. But three was too many. He came over and said:

"'You've danced three times now with my sister, and it's getting conspicuous. What are your intentions?'

"Intentions! Gosh! I just went over and sat in a corner and looked at a magazine all the rest of the evening.

"But look at what they miss! Never to know a nice girl in a nice way! No studying or playing together; nothing natural or easy. They never even know their fiancées until they marry, and by that time they've got such false ideas of sex that they can't treat their wives decently. They think they're so sophisticated, but gosh, see what they miss!"

This troubled young Yanqui might have had more to say if we had not just then stopped at Paso, where Chilean officials took our passports. So this was Chile, with deep snow in a heavy leafy forest, weirdly incongruous in the tropical vegetation. The driver stopped so our South Americans, who have no snow at home, could play in it. They plunged and fell, threw up huge white feathery puffs, laughed and got red-faced, and forgave Chile her lack of sun and bright color in their joy of the dry white snow. While they built a snow man and photographed each other, the Argentine uncle and I discussed the forest's strangeness.

Those fugacious trees hung with silvery moss and especially the big-leaved ferns looked all wrong where one would expect evergreens and naked trees in time of snow. It was so strange it seemed anything might appear: antediluvian beasts or even humans left over from an age long gone. Subercaseaux suggests a change of climate so quick that the flora could not keep abreast of it. Sixteenth-century explorers, he says, found the lands along the Straits of Magellan well wooded and of relatively mild climate. But the Chilean's comments seem less scientific than peevish, with the resentment of a person from a sunny clime who takes wet weather as a personal affront. I was like him, and grateful when we rode out of the forest and looked across a wide sun-flecked valley.

Descending the Peulla River we entered a land of many flowers. Even in early spring the yellow retamo, a cassia, was in bloom, a few daisies, and a vine with a large purple flower and a way of sending tendrils out from the edge of its leaf. We stopped to look out over a valley with cultivated fields and a few farmhouses; the touch of man was pleasant after that snowy tropical forest. There the Argentine uncle showed me a cane, delicate-seeming, but so hard the Indians had used it for lances. And beyond we encountered many ciruelas, small hardwood trees with flamelike flowers as cheery on a gray day as a crackling fire on the hearth.

At Peulla the human touch warmed into efficient hospitality. Two nice Germanic-looking youths made out our customs declarations, assigned rooms, sold postcards and horse-hair flowers, and suggested that we have tea while the baggage truck caught up. After tea we performed according to our kind. The young Europeans set out for a walk in the rain; the Brazilians found a stove and clung there; the Argentines disappeared; and I discovered a big pile of old *Sateveposts*, *Lifes*, and *Times*.

Life offered just what I needed for the Argentine señora: the pictured day of a typical housewife in a small Illinois town. Her early rising to cook breakfast for her family before she got out the car and took them all to office and school. Her marketing, and dash home again to wash the dishes and scrub the tub, to sweep and dust before cooking lunch. There was a most useful photograph of that family around the table, and another of a company meal served from a side table with no maid. And one of mother resting while she mended and darned.

The señora looked, amazed, but seemed convinced at last that this was a typical North American home. One fact struck her especially: that a high-school, if not college, graduate should do work that any South American above the lowest rank has a servant for. Another came out after she had summoned her husband and uncle and reviewed it all for them.

" Imagine," she sighed with weariness. " They must be very strong, those *Norte Americanas*."

Peulla was the spot of all others where we should have found Chile to be " the Switzerland of America." But the peaks which, in the pictures, rise out of the very garden were hidden, and the chestnut trees wept sadly over flowering shrubs and grass and graveled paths. The young people came in glowing from their walk, and the husband who did not like

Yanquis handed me a bouquet of wild fuchsias in giddy pinks and purples. Our Europeans were then revealed as Swiss. He was an oil geologist working with a Dutch company in Venezuela. So we were all accounted for; among us we commanded six languages and represented five nations; we had become a happy polyglot family, fortified by friendship against unsympathetic nature.

Next day set in just as rainy as we embarked to cross *Lago Todos Santos*, which is also known as *Esmeralda*. Whatever emerald it may show in happier times, it was a murky jade that day and the name All Saints seemed more appropriate to the occasion. Only all the heavenly hosts could have reconciled us to another dark day. But we mustered our spirits, pinned up a postcard picture of the magnificent cone of the volcano Osorno, which should have dominated the view, and joked weakly about sheets of water pouring down over window panes.

At Petrohue the Argentines turned back, hoping to find Bariloche as sunny as they had left it. The rest of us lunched at Ensenada and there ran head on into Germany. A long two-storied house of weathered shingles and a well-planned garden with azaleas, lilacs, calla lilies, and peeping crocuses and violets. It looked so friendly, and the thick-necked manager was so domineering. The question was should we take his bus to Osorno or go another way round by Puerto Varas and on to Osorno by train. The tourist company had made a mistake in all our tickets.

"We have decided," announced the petty führer, "that all who hold tickets for Osorno have to go in this bus."

The Swiss decided to do so. The Brazilians, Uruguayans, Yanquis, Brooklyn and New Mexico, got their dander up. So after much talk two cars were provided to take us along Lake

Crossing Lake Todos los Santos, Osorno in the background

Chile's Strange Pines

Llanquihue's southern shore to Puerto Varas. Doubtless we left one more Aryan convinced that these ill-bred undisciplined Americans, both North and South, need a firm foot on the neck.

At every little lake port we saw them loading produce for Puerto Varas, Puerto Montt, and so by sea to distant markets. And the produce was that of a temperate clime: wheat, oats, potatoes, apples, and pears. The men directing the work were tall heavy-set Germans with bright blue eyes in pink faces, bulbous necks above their long, heavy, shaggy ponchos. That Chilean wrap against the cold and damp is a handsome, most masculine garment. The hole through which the head protrudes is fortified by a high collar, the arms are free under stately folds, and it swings low enough to protect everything that high rubber boots do not cover. The men who swung the crates and manned the launches were Chileans.

On a grade we passed a team of oxen hauling rocks on a sledge. The men who lifted the stones and the man who guided the team by a slender rod laid on the heavy yoke were barefooted, their clothes were rags, their faces dull and weary. Only their square orange ponchos seemed comfortable and added color. Chile's *rotos*, ragged ones, tattered, landless, and overworked. And the oxen, with heads so weighted that they can be guided with the touch of a bamboo rod. Get the head low enough, with the eyes on the ground and a heavy enough burden on the neck, and any creature is easily led.

As we swung round the curves of the lake we passed one farmhouse after another looking fat with their mansard roofs and bay windows and prosperous with freshly painted scrollwork on porches and shining windows with lace curtains inside. Every house had a garden packed tightly with pansies, iris and bleeding hearts; banked with azaleas, snowballs, and lilacs; and adorned with a pond where fat ducks and geese waddled between forget-me-nots and violets or sat under calla lilies on the banks. Beyond the house was always the plethoric barn and farther off brown fields with turned, even furrows and meadows newly green with fat cattle, pigs, and sheep all washed to immaculateness.

" Gee! " crowed Brooklyn. " This is swell! I am glad I came. It's just like upper New York State. Just look at those Holsteins! Good stock, that! And the big barn! Just like farms at home! "

But it was not like home in one important particular. This was German Chile. Perhaps Nazi Chile. An American land where foreigners remained unassimilated, un-American.

IV

GERMANS

THE EXCELLENT GRAND HOTEL AT PUERTO VARAS, owned and operated by Chile's National Railways, was a vast emptiness where seven of us watched one another disappear down wide halls and dine in spacious salons which hundreds should have thronged. But even out of season the place was fully staffed with solicitous and courteous Chileans. This was doubly impressive as a contrast with the bossy Germans we had been combating and because tips were discouraged by a bilingual sign in the lobby.

In courtly Spanish " the gentlemen travelers " were " respectfully informed," and in curt English it was brusquely stated that no tips would be accepted, ten per cent having been added to the bill. Another sign announced that the Café Simón offered not only tea but " a homelike atmosphere, fine kuchen, foreign and national reviews." It was the only place for tea. In fact, all businesses in Puerto Varas seemed to bear German names — bookstores, a printing shop, dress shops, men's stores, and groceries.

The proprietor of the Café Simón, ruddy and bustling,

handed me the latest air-mail edition of *Time* even as he seated me and bellowed my order to a Chilean maid. As a safe opener I asked what was the best book on Germans in Chile.

He named one in German, which unfortunately I could not read, and *Recuerdos del Pasado* by Vicente Pérez Rosales, who had supervised the first German colonists.

"The first settled around Valdivia in 1848. That was the year of revolution, when so many went to your country too. Others came later. Many came from Westphalia, many Catholics. We have here a German Catholic school."

"Why," I asked, "have Germans not been absorbed here as they have been in the United States?" It is the obvious question for us, considering how completely our Germans have disappeared as such, though German names and German blood appear on every list from the Supreme Court to the sand-lot baseball team.

"Here," he explained, "Germans had to live apart because in the south there were only Indians and a few Chileans, but mostly bad ones, even criminals banished from the north. Like in your country where bad men drifted west. Decent people could not mix with them. There was no intermarriage. Of course not! Many women of that time did not learn Spanish. I know old ladies now, back in the country, who speak only German.

"No, very few children have gone from here either to Santiago or to Germany. It is costly, here are few wealthy ones. From Valdivia, rather, they send to Germany their children. But that is not good; they come back with silly notions."

I was agog to learn what the silly notions were, but he found duties elsewhere just then. Later I got his own story. An immigrant from Germany to the United States, he was a

salesman for a U. S. firm in Chile in 1917. He had not completed his naturalization; nothing for it but to stay in Chile.

"Would you rather have lived in the United States? "

" But of course," he said. " Who wouldn't? " Then, quickly:
" But I am grateful to Chile. I have had a happy life here."

As I left I mentioned that if it did not rain I might go to
Puerto Montt next day. He greeted that with the comfortable
chuckle German men save for childish women. " Never wait
in southern Chile for a sunny day. Here it rains thirteen
months in the year. Only that can you count on."

So I went to Puerto Montt in a downpour. The bus was
loaded with Teutonic-looking men: fat and masterful or meek
and clerkly, all smelling of wet wool. A poorly-clad Chilean
held two seats for a couple of prosperous-looking Germans
who ignored him as he slid out and dropped off the bus. We
drove past gabled and shingled houses set in gardens of dripping flowers; plump blond children were scampering into a
German lyceum and stout matrons puffed on and off with
umbrellas and baskets. At our left the lake was a gray sheet
dimpled with rain, and clouds that could not rise hung in the
wet air.

Puerto Montt is built round a plaza, but little else looks
Spanish. The architecture suggests a woodsy northern country; the names on the stores are German, though with Spanish
phrases: " *Kunstermann Hermanos, La Tienda de Hermann.*"
Blonds seemed to predominate, though the men were muffled
from head to heel in the black wool ponchos, and women
and children were indistinguishable in hooded raincoats and
rubber boots. Unmistakably Chilean were the tatterdemal-
ions, who splashed wetly along in broken shoes or none, with
inadequate coats and shawls or none. They are said even to
sleep in wet clothes without complaint. Walking the length

of the main street, I noted show windows full of what prosperous people buy — watches, mechanical aids for kitchen and farm, modernistic furniture, books, cameras, and radios. The buildings, strongly constructed of stone or faced with stone, bespoke a solid permanence.

In the Hotel Miramar, Germans predominated among the men at lunch.

" There are many Germans here? " I asked the waiter as he poured the good dark German beer.

" Everything is German here."

" But these people came long ago; they must be completely Chilean now."

" Descendants of Germans."

When I pressed my point: " Surely they are loyal Chileans now? " he reiterated: " Everything is German here," and went hurriedly away.

That predominance of Teutonic types in the good places and of German names on the best stores is general throughout southern Chile. Some writers, generally following the German Carl Martin, cite figures to prove that Germans are ten or twenty times outnumbered by Chileans even in the south. They estimate a mere 8,000 Germans in all Chile. If so, one can only conclude that the well-drilled Nordics march constantly in and out like a stage army. As others estimate as many as 200,000 Germans and as there are no reliable statistics, it becomes a matter of guessing. Hubert Herring, who seems to have judged sensibly, states in *Good Neighbors:* " Today there are in Chile some 20,000 Germans, non-Jewish and born in Germany. In addition there are about 40,000 German-Chileans, born in Chile of one or two German parents. There are about 9,000 German refugees, mostly Jews."

Much more important is the German influence in Chile,

Puerto Montt Looks like a German Village

Hotel at Peulla

which, though not calculable from census reports, is widely evident. It is best understood through a knowledge of the peculiar history which has tended to insulate Germans from their new country and to keep them culturally connected with the Fatherland.

Whether it was because sun-loving people would not live in a perpetual fog or because the conquering Spaniards found all the land they needed in genial central Chile, neither Spanish colony nor Chilean Republic undertook to exploit the southern region, which could be developed only by hard living and unremitting toil. Until the middle of the nineteenth century they had only made dashes into the Araucanian country. There the Indians lived their roving forest life, proudly defiant of white men, claiming the River Bío-Bío as their northernmost frontier. But if Chilean Spaniards would not colonize those dripping chilly forests they knew how to get it done. And by whom. They wanted northern European stock, preferably people with money enough to buy land, and families who would be sure to stay. In 1824 the government first invited foreign colonization by offering land for factories or plantations, exemptions from taxation for twenty years, and other inducements.

But it was not until 1846 that the first Germans arrived at Corral, the port for Valdivia. They were seventy men, ten women, and five children in the barque *Hermann,* which had taken a hundred and twenty days from Hamburg. Most of them were men of property who had paid their passage and who expected to buy farms or to go into business.

The whole story is best told by Vicente Pérez y Rosales, the immigration agent at Valdivia. Reading his *Recuerdos del Pasado* one becomes downright fond of the little man. His character demands that he should have been little. He bustled out at once to board the ship, because " the impressions which this most important vanguard of the future progress of Valdivia receives must correspond with the hopes . . . they had conceived of the hospitality which awaited them. . . ." He found the newcomers low-spirited, but in no time: " to timid discouragement had succeeded the liveliest content." Refreshments were served and temporary quarters were provided for the travelers. Señor Pérez then sped back to Valdivia to see that the citizens took advantage of their opportunities. Valdivia was about to have a boom, and no town ever had a more efficient official greeter than our author.

The first move on the part of the colonists was the presentation of eighteen questions which show clearly that they expected to become Chileans altogether. They first asked how they might become citizens. They inquired if non-Catholics would be required to abandon their religion, if their marriages would be recognized and their children considered legitimate. They were curious also about what military service they would owe, the validity of contracts made in Germany, and whether or not land would be available for a thousand families. Some of the colonists were considering promoting Chilean real estate back in Hamburg.

Señor Pérez was inspired. " Nothing exalts the importance of living in a free republican regime like being born and having to live under the more or less despotic tyranny of a monarchy. It is not strange, then, that the idea of becoming citizens of a republic where the names ' master ' and ' servant ' have no meaning, where virtue and work are noble, where the only taxes are levied by those who will pay them should be the first aspiration of the immigrants." And more of the same.

Carlos Anwandter, for the Germans, declared: " We shall

be Chileans as honest and industrious as those who are most
so. United with the ranks of our new compatriots, we shall
defend our adopted land against all outside aggression with
the decision and the firmness of a man who defends his country, his family, and his interests."

They then separated to face the less inspiring problems of
actual settling. Not enough land was available until a public-
spirited citizen sold them the whole island of Teja at a reasonable price. Señor Pérez found two advantages to this deal:
" the moral and material effect which would be produced on
this melancholy and apathetic village by the example of German activity, work, and industry; and that the immigrants
should find, at their disembarkation point, that cordial recep-
tion which nationals always dispense among themselves in a
strange country." But outside of this haven real-estate prices
soared; and while Señor Pérez was distractedly trying to
persuade his compatriots to be reasonable, another ship
docked at Corral, the *Susana*. And then the *San Paoli*. The
promoters in Hamburg were doing good business. Fortunately
all these land-seeking Germans brought a solution of the
problem they created. Among them were many skilled workers in leather, wood, and metal. Valdivia was overjoyed " to
buy, good and cheap, at home, what formerly she had had to
buy dearly and . . . of bad quality, from outside." Within
four months eight German houses had been built in Valdivia.
" Immigration was for Valdivia the benign guest which
brought the light, the crafts, and the material wealth to pull
her out of the prostration in which she had been."

Señor Pérez, always far-seeing and energetic, bestirred
himself to find other lands where he might settle his colonists.
He said that Chile knew of the province of Valdivia only that
it was big and unpopulated, and that it rained 370 days out

of the 365. He found all that to be true, as he plunged along a river marveling at the " exuberant vegetation which rises from the water without leaving an inch of beach whereon to set foot." He rejoiced in the occasional open glades among the forests, in the thickets of wild apple trees, and scolded because nobody had bothered to dig out the beds of coal he saw within easy reach.

Before returning to Valdivia, Señor Pérez instructed his guide to fire the forest, which that Indian did so successfully that he only saved himself from cremation by digging a cave into the damp roots of a friendly coigue. " This frightful blaze, whose flames could not be stopped either by the trees' foliage nor by their shaded and always soaked trunks, nor the torrential and almost daily rains which fall on them, lasted three months; and the smoke . . . so blurred the sun that during most of this time it could be seen at Valdivia with the naked eye."

As unperturbed by this holocaust as any Yankee conquering the West, our hero returned, when the cinders had cooled, and pushed his way southward to Lake Llanquihue, which he decided was the place for colonization. He was pleased to note that most of the land around the lake was flat and that a divine hand had left certain patches of woodland unscathed by his fire. A port was needed, so the site of Puerto Montt was chosen, and a road cut through the forest from there to the lake. It was a three months' job to clear twelve miles through such sodden land that two men lost their lives in the mud. The first year of the Llanquihue colony, 1853, was tragically hard. Supplies which should have been sent from Osorno failed, and the Germans were apparently not so good with a rifle as our Western pioneers. Many Araucanians sold them land for which they could not show title. But the immigrants stuck it out and in time they cleared the country and forced the Indians back.

If ever a people won a land, those Germans won southern Chile. They hewed it out with axes, grubbed out the stumps, imported seeds and planted them, built log, then frame, and finally stone and cement houses. Knowing the forests of northern Germany, they utilized every open glade, planted where the drainage was best, imported good stock, made good business out of everything they touched. Within twenty years they had built six towns in country formerly considered uninhabitable, and the new provinces of Arauco and Llanquihue had been admitted to the Republic. The towns, naturally, were as Teutonic as pumpernickel. The Germans, many of some education and money if not wealth, brought a highly developed culture; and they had practically no contact with the Spanish culture of central Chile. So every town had German schools and churches (both Protestant and Catholic), *Turnvereine*, and *Kaffeeklatsche*.

The only Chileans they knew, as the German in Puerto Varas had said, were escaping outlaws, drifters, and other misfits from the highly organized society farther north. Many of them had married or otherwise mixed with Indians, they had taken what land they could, and held it as they could. If they had no titles to it, they had guns. They were the tough, courageous, self-reliant, and aggressive frontiersmen such as took our own West from the Indians. Chile is full of legends about them. Unfortunately she never established them on properly surveyed lands, or gave them enough strength to absorb and Chileanize the Germans. After the Pacific War, Chile's Army succeeded in forcing the Araucanian line at the Bío-Bío and throwing the Indians back. A liberal government had some idea of giving ex-soldiers free land — some 6,000 of them were located on farms — but, as George McCutcheon McBride states it in *Chile, Land and Society:* " an hacienda-controlled government was more interested in keeping laborers on the estates than in attracting them to new regions." So Chile lost her opportunity to establish a strong frontier population out of which to build a future democracy. What she got instead was a powerful German state within her own.

It is still German. McBride found that in the commune of Valdivia all property valued at more than 40,000 pesos belonged to men with foreign names, chiefly German. " As late as 1925 only five of the 36 important fundos in that commune were not owned by men with foreign names." Germans still own the lumbering and brewing companies, the large stores, the hotels, and banks.

Many thoughtful Chileans are fully aware of the menace of a strongly integrated minority, alien in language and thought, and blown up with baseless superiority. I translate, loosely but not inaccurately, from *Intuición de Chile* by Mariano Picón Salas, a Venezuelan who has served Chile long enough as university professor and government official to express a thoroughly Chilean point of view:

" The German has been so praised in the colonization of the south that it is fair to ask if, believing himself superior, the German has not isolated himself too much and, drinking his Valdivia beer and singing his songs, neglected to have his children learn the language of the country and become sentimentally attached to the land. . . .

" Some southern dailies and magazines, when . . . Germany accomplished the plebiscite of the Saar, followed the affair with excessive Germanic fervor. *' Deutsche ist die Saar!'* those provincial papers told us amid great and Teutonic acclaim. In cities and towns the German continues to form his exclusive circle, his social, sports, or athletic club where he scarcely — and as a sign of grace — receives the Chilean. Only rarely the German child attends a national school . . . when his mentality and language are already set in their hermetic German idiosyncrasy. Thus of Chile or of the Hispanic spirit he receives only those particulars necessary to obtain his degree." Does such training make patriotic Chileans of undivided allegiance? Dr. Picón Salas thinks not.

Dr. Picón Salas also notes the Germans' curious political ineptitude, which he finds partly responsible for their faulty Chileanization. He writes: " In the political combat the gringo [meaning in this case the German] collides with the quicker and for him more tricky imagination of the Chilean. They have not produced a statesman, an orator, or a writer worthy of attention. Recently they have found their political expression in certain military organizations, of very simple ideology, which the recent crisis and the example of a hysterical Europe have precipitated in Chile. These institutions where they carry on healthful gymnastic exercises, which offer the plumed and Prussian burghers military titles and where they talk little, well express their limited imaginative skill and their still green political inexperience. ' Much administration and no politics,' these gentlemen seem to say to those who produce efficient leaders. But the government of a country is something more than a confederation of leaders; the leader can make gardens and aqueducts, but history is not made of public works alone, but with faith and a national will which animates the present and looks toward a future. This does not appear among our powerful friends of the south, who take so obstinately the duties which their militarized institutions impose on them."

Their entire history in Chile has produced *Germanized* Chileans. The question of universal importance is: How Nazi are they? Answers vary from the statement — generally from well-placed conservative Chileans — that all German-Chileans are patriotic and loyal Chileans, to the conviction that their loyalty is to Nazi Germany, whether through honest belief or equally honest fear. One clever Chilean answered my question by touching his teeth with a finger. " All Germans," he said, " are loyal Chileans from here out."

Both these points of view are doubtless true — of certain German-Chileans. Lines which divide the loyal from the disloyal are unfortunately difficult to follow.

Incontrovertible facts are that most, if not all, German-Chileans have been educated in German schools; those who were able have sent their children to Germany. This applies also to many Chileans of Spanish blood, for the German schools are thorough and efficient; and Nazi Germany has been generous with scholarships and invitations to students and professors. Graduates of German universities, warmed by German *Gemütlichkeit* and admiring German efficiency, have returned to Chile convinced that her best hope lies in Nordic domination.

Other quainter concepts emanate from the Reich. A *Profesor del Estado*, who had topped off his Chilean university education with two years in Germany, was discussing the marvels of Nazi science.

"Determinable racial differences have been proved," he averred. " In Germany they brought hens' eggs from Italy and from Scandinavia. Under laboratory conditions where no confusion was possible they were hatched out."

"Under a completely neutral hen? " I ventured, but was unheeded.

" Then those chickens were offered colored corn — red and blue." He paused for effect. " And actually the Nordic chicks chose the blue, the Sudics the red. Positive, scientific proof! "

I offered myself as a Nordic, even Aryan according to his Führer's definition, who prefers red. He brushed that aside. " But you are an intellectual, and no proof."

The proof of the chicks led to the conclusion that Nordics must rule. " Europe must be dominated by Germany, the Americas by the United States, Asia by Japan. This is undeniably true, this will be." The suggestion that there might be a world in which there was neither domination nor submission won me prompt demotion from the intellectual class. " Women," he assured me, " cannot understand matters of state."

Such beliefs may not be widespread; the lack of humor indicated surely is. And German-educated men and women wield an influence in Chile out of all proportion to their numbers. Educated and often wealthy, their associates are the conservative aristocrats, inclined in Chile as elsewhere to hope that totalitarianism may save their property.

Since the last war the Chilean Army has been trained by German officers. Many Chilean officers have been sent to Germany for training or observation, and returned dazzled by Nazi efficiency and munificent hospitality. Other officers, sincere patriots, are convinced that Chileans are unfit for real self-government and must be ruled by a stern upper class. They believe so deeply that this is not incompatible with true patriotism that they will state it to a wandering Yanqui like me.

The *Carabineros*, Chile's military police, are also German-trained, though their German leader disappeared in 1940. Picked for superb health and physique, and intelligent and educated above the average, they are experts with sword and lance as well as pistol and rifle, with tear-gas bombs, and in the technique of riding down and dispersing mobs. A high-class Chilean told me that their greatest value lay in their ability to put down incipient revolution.

Nazi propaganda in Chile has been appallingly efficient — newspapers which slant the news one way, radio stations bringing loud cheers from Germany, movies which picture German successes on all fronts and happy scenes from occupied countries. Weeklies, like *Acción Chilena*, which are frankly hostile to the United States, carry cartoons which brutally, viciously attack President Roosevelt and Yanquis generally. A monthly, *Veinte Naciones*, not only counts the United States out as an American country, but is cried on the streets as " *Contra el imperialismo yanqui* " (" Against Yankee imperialism ").

Nazi success in organizing and militarizing Chile's Germans is convincingly detailed in *The Nazi Underground in South America* by Hugo Fernández Artucio. He names German diplomats who, under cover of diplomatic immunity, have organized bunds and directed the military training of youths in sports clubs. The usual pattern. But in Chile, as in Argentina, Nazi propaganda has reawakened ill feeling between the countries. An old dispute over the Beagle Channel has been revived, Nazi newspapers in each country accusing the other of designs on the vast unoccupied regions of Patagonia and the Straits of Magellan. The purpose, of course, is the establishment of a German state at the tip of South America with control of the alternative passage between the Atlantic and the Pacific in case anything should happen to the Panama Canal.

This Chile of the Germans makes one ponder. These are people the world needs and always will: women whose houses smell of cleanliness and wholesome food cooking; whose children are well nourished, rosy, and strong; men who can use their arms to fell trees and build houses, and their intelligence to direct others, to build up internal trade and external commerce; peasants who, with a generation or two of opportunity, become men of wealth, professional men, scientists, artists, thinkers, musicians.

Yet what can the world do with people who repeatedly permit themselves to be pushed around by their most unworthy sort? People who never smell on the wind the distant scent of coming oppression, who never stand together to protect themselves against political exploitation. Individually fine, each German seems to live within his own small orbit, doing well what he does, but unconcerned about the general welfare. With no gift for politics, he is the foredoomed victim of any cheap politician. This must not happen again. Somehow the world must use the German's fine powers without permitting his fatal weakness to destroy him and threaten us all. How? Out-marriage seems to be the answer. Germans married to less regimented folk, more aware of their fellows, able to cope with them, politically-minded, produce good children. Comparing Chilean Germans, so purely German, so stupidly blind to the dangers of the Nazi menace; with hyphenated Germans in any country where they have married out, the answer is plain. Spread them thin. Marry them out.

Perhaps the natural concomitant to this program should be to give Germany to the Jews. Akin to all Europeans, with centuries of experience in adjustment to all cultures, and naturally pacific, they would create a center of understanding and decent relationships just where Prussianism has forever fomented resentments and hatreds. A Jewish state would not howl for *Lebensraum;* it would need no colonies. It would be too busy trading with all the world and promoting exchange of every kind, cultural as well as commercial. For this people excels most in the arts of urbanity and peace. As bankers, business men, scientists, and practitioners of every art, the Jewish people might be expected to make of Germany a wealthy, civilized, and peaceful center as useful to Europe as London is to England, as Paris was to France.

V

THE AUSTRAL REGIONS

BEFORE STARTING NORTH FROM PUERTO VARAS through the German towns and the Indian country into central Chile of the Chileans, I had toyed with the notion of journeying south. One should see the island of Chiloé and the complicated labyrinth of channels, fiords, and straits where ice-green and beryl-blue glaciers slip into the sea and icebergs float like snowy sails against the sky. But a day in Puerto Montt, watching the sullen rain pour down the windows, had washed that ambition quite out of me. I was ready to take Chile's austral glories on hearsay, which would, after all, be as good as looking without seeing.

Fortunately Chile's southern third has intrigued all writing Chileans. Benjamin Subercaseaux expressed its mystery in the title: *The Country of Crespucular Night,* where, he says, "the light diminishes as one sails southward; an opalescent penumbra veils the landscape and the outlines of things as though they were submerged in the atmosphere of a dream."

Puerto Montt faces south across the Bay of Reloncaví, beyond which the long Gulf of Ancud is divided from the Pacific

59

by the island of Chiloé. This body of land, deeply cut into by the sea toward the south, is Chile's last effort to hold up her western coast line. The rest of the coastal range appears above water only as a highly irregular archipelago running all the way to Cape Horn. The longitudinal central valley has disappeared under water.

The island of Chiloé consists of 12,000 square miles of swampy forest so impenetrable that men have succeeded in occupying only its northern and eastern tip. There its only towns, Ancud and Castro, hold mossily on to a strip between sea and wood. Spain founded both these towns, but, as Subercaseaux says, " Spain is not a wooded country and Spaniards do not like these complications." So they left Chiloé to its Indians, though they did somewhat modify its indigenous blood stream. Subercaseaux found the Chilotes " soft and docile," and described them as " short, active, smiling, good sailors, and lovers of peace; a sort of Japanese, which, as I see it, is the best we have in the way of a homogeneous, moral, and efficient race." Señor Subercaseaux may have changed his opinion.

Agustín Edwards, on the other hand, found the Chilotes " cold and indolent, captious, with an underlying vein of mysticism and fancy." I quote from *My Native Land*.

The conditions of life would hardly make for geniality or neighborliness. The island's only railroad connects Ancud and Castro, and the only roads through the forest are logs laid on bogs which jiggle under ox-drawn sledges hauling potatoes to market. Most Chilotes live in tiny clusters of wooden shanties set on piles. Back of them is the forest, so thick that McBride found neighbors living close enough to shout at each other who had to travel two days to meet. The forest resembles a northern one with its elms, larches, hazels, oaks, and cypresses.

60

Useful trees, but difficult to fell and impossible to burn, damp as they are.

Edwards finds Chiloé " like Ireland for dampness, verdure, and piety." The people, he says, " raise pigs and potatoes and live in dire poverty under the towers and bells of many churches." They fish, of course, and like the Irish their superstitions, their folk tales, and their character are deeply marked by the sea. The dying go out with the tide. Sea bathers are in danger of being pulled under by Manta, a sort of mystical octopus. And fishermen find allies in the lovely fairy Pincoya and her husband Pincoy, who have the virtue of attracting fish and shellfish in abundance.

Every Chilote knows, too, the ship *Caleuche,* which Subercaseaux suggests may be a heritage from Dutch pirates who, along with fair hair and blue eyes, left the legend of the Flying Dutchman.

Gabriela Mistral, quoted also in *Panorama y Color de Chile,* sees no connection with the Flying Dutchman. She writes:

" The *Caleuche* is a pirate ship — a noble outlaw of the seas, which . . . runs miles and miles under it, so well hidden that for weeks and months all trace of it is lost, and it seems to have . . . left the sea of the Chilotes for some other. . . . But suddenly on the loneliest of those southern nights the *Caleuche* emerges . . . and runs a long course in full view, navigating at full steam, almost flying, without permitting herself to be overtaken by any whaleboat or poor fishing launch which might try to follow her. The fleeing thing, in the sight of fear-crazed fishermen, is a phosphorescent mass . . . whose deck swarms with sea devils and a tribe of witches very like them. . . .

" Let its pursuers approach their illuminated prey and before they glimpse or catch the secret, the burning palace of the

Caleuche simply stops, goes out like a great firebrand, and leaves a dead hulk, dark cinders which drift with the waves and mock those who had already pictured their victory. . . .

" The *Caleuche* cannot be exactly described because it resembles nothing except — the *Caleuche*. Pushed to define it, one can only stammer negations. It is not a whale although it appears so in its knack of overturning fishing boats, and it is not a ship although it is so called for no other reason than that it always navigates."

Nor are the *Caleuche's* demon masters described. But the crew, those captured careless dreamers, are creatures with their heads on backward and their left legs so twisted that they hop awkwardly on one foot. Few return to land; those who do never lose that backward look or that habit of hopping. And their memories are forever lost, lest the *Caleuche's* secret should be known to mortals. It seems a happier fate to stay aboard, where life is a perpetual kermis. As the *Caleuche* is eternal, so are her masters and crew. Always young, they sleep by day and play by night. But in the nicest possible way. It is not related that they ever captured maidens at play or clam-gathering on the beaches.

The *Caleuche* is more than a legend of the past. Even now she occasionally carries bewitched fishermen down to the treasure houses at the bottom of the sea. Mistral says: " Fishermen benighted at sea behold her if they keep watch; those who sleep relaxed on shore lose her; lighthouse-keepers watching the sea see her sometimes or often, according to whether they are dull or given to miracles. . . . In fact, most Chilotes have seen the *Caleuche* at one time or another, and those so fortunate carry all their lives the memory of the lighted ship ' like something from another life.' "

The *Caleuche's* most modern appearance is as the name of

Santiago's smart yachting club, which has a painting of the phosphorescent witch ship over the mantel, but whose members most likely lack the seeing eye which would let them vision her in full flight across the ocean.

No legend could be too fantastic for these stretches of land-fretted water which mark the southern reach of Chile and the continent. Diego de Muñoz, quoted from the same volume, pictures it:

"A sculptor of a brutally vigorous madness formed the inexhaustible diversity of this austral landscape. Immense moles of rocks rise twisted and contorted, now tall and extensive, now overthrown by a force which must have been gigantic. We sail through a road of tranquil waters which widen at times to narrow again between black rocks. Then the canal shuts in and opens again on a new perspective. The mountains, black to start with, fade into purple, violet, and ten tones of gray until it is fused in the distance into snow-capped glaciers. The ship sails steadily on, and the mountains seem to go along in virtue of some movement of their own. . . ."

Most mariners, and the regular Chilean steamers which ply between Valparaiso and Rio de Janeiro, stay well off shore. Subercaseaux traveled with a daring captain who ran the Canal Moraleda — inside the archipelago of islands which lie like spilled peas all the way to the continent's tip. Every description makes one shiver with the sensation of loneliness, ice, and darkness. Even Subercaseaux, young and avidly interested, moans that " there is no town, no refuge, where man can feel the nearness of man. . . . Nature appears to know nothing of man nor to care. There is no hut, no mark of an axe on a tree, no pilot who remembers an ancient landing."

There are a few settlements. Now and then a huddle of Indian huts or the sheep ranch of an intrepid Scot or Yugoslav.

But the sub-human population is large and varied. Formally dressed penguins bob like Japanese ambassadors at the sleek luxurious seals on the rocks. There are aquatic birds in infinite variety, gulls, cormorants, and petrels, and the flamingo, whose fiery flash must be a sight against the white and black of snow and ice. In the hills are pumas, huemules (*Cervus Chilensis*), foxes, and guanacos, the ancestors of both alpaca and llama.

Beyond those channels is country marked unknown on all the maps. As late as 1940 it was first explored by an expedition of Chileans named Federico Reichert, Walter Ihl, and Ernesto Hoffmann. They crossed from the Isthmus of Ofquí, which cuts Laguna San Rafael off from the sea, to Lake Buenos Aires; the first white men, probably the first men of any race, to tread fields which are unique on the globe for their obelisks of ice. The Spaniards call them *los Penitentes* (the penitents) and scientists find their slow melting proof of the approaching end of a glacial age.

In spite of its fringe of islands the continent has here run down into a thin white tail, the caudal extremity of the backbone of the Andes. On the map it is neatly divided between Chile and Argentina, but because of faulty definitions they have here too a disputed frontier. Useless as it seems for ordinary human needs, each country dreams of the gold it may contain and one hears whispered hints of oil wells capped for future use. Perhaps it signifies something that the three Chileans who so lately explored it all bore German names.

It was the Portuguese Magellan who gave his name to the stormy strait through which he fought against a terrifying rush of icy waves higher than his little vessels. His passage was one of the most stupendous triumphs of human endurance in history. Naturally he named the cape he made at last *Cabo*

Deseado, the Desired. Magellan and his immediate followers took the land to the south for another continent and they spread the belief that ships could make that passage only westbound, so strong was the current. Perhaps Spain, jealousy guarding her Pacific empire, deliberately fostered the notion.

But before the century's close England's sea rovers were testing all theories for themselves, and the most daring navigator of them all, Francis Drake, took the plunge at Magellan's strait. Met there by a furious sea, his three small craft were spun round, lost each other in fog, and never came together again until two met in England years later. Drake's *Golden Hind*, running from the storm, found a passage between glacial mountains and so rounded Tierra del Fuego and discovered that it was an island. He left various place names, as did other English, Dutch, and French sea rovers who followed him. Mostly their names are those of kings or heroes or nostalgic names like Londonderry or Horn, which Captain Schouten, who rounded it in 1616, called for his town of Hoorn in the Netherlands.

As long as Spain held her empire these northerners were pirates, attacking Spanish galleons wherever they were found, raiding the coastal towns all the way to Mexico. Later, when England dominated the sea and lost her American colonies, Yankee skippers appeared in the fastest and most beautiful ships that ever sailed: the birdlike and shining clippers. Beating round these dangerous reefs, they carried China tea and willow ware to New England, which shipped back calico, tinware, and missionaries bearing the Word. In '49 the United States was to send gold-seekers rushing — in a sailing ship, for months, all round a continent — to California.

Curious that down there, at man's last outpost against the frozen antarctic, should be one of Chile's largest towns: modern, bustling, progressive, and prosperous Punta Arenas. One would expect the southernmost town on earth to be a hamlet, or queerly picturesque like an Eskimo village. But Punta Arenas has a population of 30,000 people and is dominated commercially at least by Chileans of Scotch and Yugoslavic origin. Their business is sheep and cattle and they make money even now that the world's trade misses them and tourists no longer come along in luxury liners. They say Chile continually forgets Punta Arenas and that Punta Arenas is reminded of Chile only by the flag over the immigration station and the portly officers around the barracks.

Beyond Punta Arenas, which is 53 degrees south, Chile goes on with scattered bits of land like puffs of hair from the tail. Tierra del Fuego, the largest one, would be an important island in any other clime. Perhaps it will be some day when they find gold or oil. Meanwhile it supports only a sparse population of Indians known generally as the Fuegians.

One of the most exciting accounts of this world's end was written by a young Englishman who sailed along here in 1835 making notes which were published as *The Voyage of the Beagle*. What a pity that most of us have known Charles Darwin only as a steel engraving with a beard; he was such an engaging young man! He saw everything, was interested in everything, tried everything: navigation, mountain-climbing, running rapids, horseback riding, shooting, and whaling. People, plants, rocks, and climate attracted him equally, and his comments on them were equally trenchant. The Strait of Magellan he found " a forge of storms," wherein he " never saw a more cheerless prospect."

Darwin and later explorers found the Fuegians simple in the extreme, with religious beliefs tied in with their clime. Evil was bad weather, and their climate must certainly have confirmed a belief in widespread depravity. Their gods were beneficent or malevolent demons, and one of them was Setebos, he whom Shakespeare made Caliban's deity. Naturally such beliefs necessitated many sorcerers, both men and women, who killed and cured, and told legends to explain natural phenomena. One told of the cataclysm which had cut Tierra del Fuego off from the mainland. One scientist, trying to trace sun-worship (which appears little if at all), was told that the sun and moon were very old indeed and that some old men who knew their maker had died without leaving information on the subject. This is told by Hartley Burr Alexander.

Beyond Tierra del Fuego are more islands, lesser and lesser in importance and size. Men gave out long before land did. At last land let go to disappear forever under the austral seas of the Antarctic Ocean. Forever, that is, until a Yankee naval man came along and discovered a polar continent where he could raise the Stars and Stripes.

VI

NORTH TO THE CENTER

[OSORNO]

BOARDING THE TRAIN FOR OSORNO, I WAS SEATED IN A day coach with leather-covered reversible seats, a tiny toilet and water-cooler at one end, and racks for baggage. The Chilean railroad, *Ferrocarriles del Estado*, is excellently administered; all trains are immaculately clean and well served, and they run on time; a few are streamlined and elegantly luxurious.

The Brazilians and Uruguayans were aboard too, and just as we were getting settled the young Swiss joined us. He had been to Puerto Montt, leaving his señora to rest in Osorno. He was full of a story he insisted I must write.

" I met a fellow on the way down — an educated man and rich enough to own a *fundo*, a farm — and he showed me pictures of his *four* families. Yes, four, and all at once. Very pretty women, and each with several children. He says he doesn't marry because it is cheaper this way. Imagine! He has invited me to visit on his *fundo*, where one of the ladies lives. The favorite, I presume."

The porter came along then with the baggage man, who

68

charged us all excess, but in a spirit too friendly for resentment. Then a waiter came to find out who wanted lunch and at what hour. Chileans do this much better than we do. You name your hour, you are given a ticket, and when you reach the dining-car you are seated and served at once. Waiters, swaying expertly with the train, balance piles of plates, handfuls of cups, or huge trays and expeditiously serve thirty people a five-course meal without spill or clatter.

I had already learned to skip at least two courses in a Chilean meal, but that abstemiousness greatly distressed the waiter.

" No roast? Then may I not serve the señora an omelet? "

It is this personal concern, which could spring only from pure friendliness, that makes Chileans so endearing.

We had been traveling along the shores of Lake Llanquihue, so this is the place for a legend which Benjamin Subercaseaux relates. He warns against believing it and hedges to say that all legends are formed around a nucleus of truth.

Some years after the conquest a detachment of Spanish soldiers guarding the frontier (which then crossed Lake Llanquihue) were suddenly attacked by a force of Indians. Surrounded and outnumbered, they were facing surrender when help came. Men wearing old-fashioned armor and helmets of the time of the conquest, had fallen on the enemies' rear and were forcing them to give ground. The friendly reinforcers were white men and they were heard to use Spanish. But they did not stay to explain themselves. When they had routed the Indians, they disappeared again into the dark forest as mysteriously as they had come. Some of their weapons, fallen on the battleground, were identified as of Spanish manufacture. And Indian captives told of the *City of the Cæsars*, far in the interior, where Spanish and Indian people lived together.

69

The colonial government was sufficiently impressed to send an expedition out in search of the unaccountable city. They did not find it. But later, in 1563, two Spanish soldiers showed up in Concepción with the report that they had seen the City of the Cæsars. It consisted, so they said, of seven villages along a lake, and had been founded by seven Spanish survivors of a shipwreck. Spanish colonial history, like our own frontier story, is dotted with tales of white men who preferred life among the Indians to that of their own people. Unfortunately the location the soldiers described turned out to have a lake, but no city. Ricardo Latcham, a serious student, seems to rest on this. But Subercaseaux, younger and more addicted to wonders, suggests that old maps are notoriously inaccurate and that myths are still formed around a nucleus of truth.

This one is supported, at least, by the two who came to Concepción. Young men who like to explore might, in happier times, find ruined walls of Spanish construction, pieces of armor, or traces of Spanish features and Spanish words among the Indians. In any case here is material for a good yarn.

The Hotel Burnier at Osorno is altogether modern, with baths, radiators that are heated, if not hot, and an elevator. The baths, throughout Chile, offer an unexpected sporting hazard. Water let out of the tub comes bubbling up through a grating in the floor. In no time the unwary bather may find slippers, bath mat, and towels afloat. Nothing serious ever occurs, for the management has provided a slat raft on which to make shore, and the water soon subsides gurgling into the drain. Why it does not run directly into the drain without this upsurge onto the floor is not explained.

The town of Osorno, listed as having a population of over 20,000, is fresh, clean, and square, with geometrical flower beds in the quadrangular plaza and all the architecture in box-

Osorno Is a Clean Little City

*The Spanish Type
of Chilean Appears*

like lines. Every prosperous-looking business house seemed
to have a German name and solicitous German clerks. The
Brazilians and Uruguayans, complaining still of the cold,
chartered a car and departed in the rain for the nearest lake
and waterfall. The Swiss couple had gone to visit the virile
estanciero of the four mistresses. I decided to explore the bookstores and drive around in one of the conveyances which stood
on the plaza with horses and coachmen equally a-droop.

The number of bookstores in Chile is astonishing. In the
United States a town of fifty thousand may offer only a few
badly chosen books among the drugs or the furniture. In
smaller places one is lucky to find a detective magazine and a
popular weekly or two. In Chile even very small places boast
several shops owned by Santiago publishing houses and dis-
playing not only Chilean books, but translations of North
American best-sellers too. It may be said for us that our libraries are going concerns; librarians try to keep books in
action, a large circulation is the desired end. In Chile a library
is a place to keep books; only the privileged few may ever
carry one home. So to have a book at hand, for reading at
one's lazy ease, it must be bought.

For my drive I chose a brougham, which offered more protection against the rain than a victoria. Its windows had not
operated for many decades, but its broken springs were plush-
covered and an ornate lantern had been newly polished. The
coachman had gently fitted the door into place and mounted
his box before I remembered that I had only a fifty-peso note,
so I suggested stopping at a bank to change it. He kept on,
however, shaking the reins over the bony haunches of his team,
whose clump was the weariest sound I ever heard. Not until
we were well beyond the business houses did he stop at a wine
shop labeled *El Sin Rival,* The Unrivaled. Taking my bill, the

driver descended and offered it to the proprietor, who shook his head, goggle-eyed at such wealth. But a ragged one loitering near offered to have it changed at a corner shop.

I sat comfortably, glad of such a good opportunity to study a group of Chile's rotos. They looked very Spanish. Unlike the opaque eyes, heavy features, and swarthy skins one sees in Indian countries, their eyes were clear with definite pupils and many were hazel or gray; but it is the narrow, almost pinched nose, small lips, and slender neck that mark the Chilean type. And a prevailing expression of alert intelligence.

In time it dawned on me that our roto was not coming back. I summoned the driver from his chat. He referred the matter to the wineseller, who advised patience; perhaps our emissary had had to go farther than he planned. So I waited, but with growing doubt, which soon blossomed into the conviction that that roto had run off with my fifty pesos. The entire concourse agreed that it must be so. The driver inquired at the corner store. Nobody had been there. I suggested the opposite establishment, where charcoal and wilted vegetables were offered. No hope. We then agreed that I should inform the police, and the assembled citizens gave me the delinquent's name: Manuel Alvarado.

My coachman proposed that we go to Manuel's house. So we clattered through cobbled streets and down a slippery road to the river's edge, where he disappeared into a forlorn-looking hovel. Was he, I wondered, making an honest search or collecting his share? He came back to report that Manuel's " woman " suggested the *Bar Tinto*. But the bar knew nothing of Manuel; it was lunch time; and I was either bored or ashamed to be hounding a poor roto for what was near wealth to him and only a bit more than a dollar to me. I compromised by leaving it to the coachman to locate Manuel, promising not to notify the police until he had had time to recover my wealth.

At the hotel, to my surprise, I was advised to do no more about it.

" You get yourself mixed up with the Chilean police," said a Yanqui traveling man, " and you'll never get away from here. They'll hold you to give testimony or call you back. It'll be worth a lot more than fifty pesos to you to keep away from the police."

So I left Osorno and my fifty pesos, divided between a conviction that one should take a stand for law and order and a lazier one (perhaps) that there is something vulgar about a superiority founded on anything so extraneous as an exchange rate of thirty to one.

[VALDIVIA]

If I had known how I should yearn for the Hotel Burnier with its warmth and good food, I should have stayed. But one never knows these things in time. I settled myself again in a clean coach for Valdivia.

There were more Germans now; the young Swiss pointed out one as the Nazi district führer. He looked it with a head which sloped back from his eyebrows, his thick neck, and his way of puffing out his lips. All day he was conferring with one or another Teuton who rode for a station or two.

This is the great central valley of Chile. We crossed many streams which the map showed were rushing from clear mountain lakes to the sea. They are Chile's vacation land, for every one of a string of lakes is well stocked with fish, the forests offer game, and during Santiago's hot summer the days are cool and the nights cold. The whole countryside was fresh and green, and though the heavy virgin forest is gone, we saw plenty of fine trees, and at every station there were piles of boards or railroad ties, smelling of wet, cut wood. Men were carrying wood on cushioned shoulders or sitting huddled under sacks folded into hoods against the rain. For the rain continued and only yellow wild flowers — of which there were thousands — seemed to promise future sunshine.

At Antilhue, where our branch for Valdivia left the main line for Santiago, we waited a long time. The platform was filled with people, dressed for holiday, and when another train steamed in from the north we knew why. This was the President's special bearing back to Buenos Aires His Eminence Cardinal Capello, who had been presiding at the Eucharistic Congress. In no time among the village crowd were well-dressed and impeccably groomed clerics, their high rank indicated by pipings of red or purple on black cassocks. I watched one whose red probably connoted a bishop munching a banana while his foot rested on a bootblack's box. He looked Irish, with keen face and clear eyes that flashed blue as he laughed and chatted with the youngster kneeling before him. Then His Eminence, surrounded by other Church dignitaries, was pacing the walk while the crowd pushed up respectfully to kiss his ring or to be photographed with him. Soon the train pulled out with the Cardinal on the rear platform, raising three fingers or dropping blessed objects into upraised hands.

The Brazilians and Uruguayans left us there, discouraged by the continuing rain, hoping for amusement if not clear days in the capital.

Of two German hotels at Valdivia we chose the one reputed to be least Nazi. Its porter at the station promised *calefacción central,* but whatever heat there was kept so close to center that the Hotel Palace was too cold for staying in. Fortunately the little city is worth looking at. Everything seemed very German, with Teutonic types on the streets, German names on the stores, and residences with the fresh paint which is said to be sure indication of German ownership. And taking tea in the place recommended by a driver as best, I heard only German; at not one table was Spanish being spoken.

Valdivia is beautifully set where several rivers join to make a long bay with an island in the center and on the sea the port of Corral, where the first German immigrants were received. Valdivia was an old town then, for it was founded in 1552 and named for Pedro de Valdivia, the conqueror and first Governor of Chile.

Chile was entered from Peru; first by Diego de Almagro, who returned to report no gold and a killing desert to cross. But Valdivia was a glory-seeker and determined and energetic enough to raise and equip a hundred and fifty Spanish soldiers and three thousand or so Indians to carry the impedimenta. For he planned settlement as well as exploration and conquest. Pedro de Valdivia was of the race of giants Spain was breeding in those days. Like Cortez, Alvarado, Pizarro, and hundreds of lesser men, he led a small force across unexplored country that the best-equipped modern expedition finds almost impassable, fighting Indians and maintaining itself by conquest. But Pedro de Valdivia was surely unique in one regard. For on his saddlebow he carried a small wooden image of the Blessed Virgin, and beside him rode his mistress, the beautiful and intrepid Inez de Suárez. Surely few conquerors were ever so assured of comfort in this world and salvation in the next!

Within a year of leaving Cuzco, Valdivia had founded *Santiago de Nueva Estremadura* in honor of the patron saint of Spain and of his native province. In spite of every disaster — Indian uprisings, troubles with rivals, and upsets in

Peru — Valdivia pushed southward as far as the island of Chiloé. He founded six cities all together, though they were little more than garrisoned outposts against the ever belligerent Araucanians. Among them was Valdivia.

A year after its founding, in 1553, Don Pedro was summoned from there to put down an Indian uprising at Tucapel. Feeling that a sharp lesson was needed, the Governor himself went with forty men. But the lesson went the other way. Tucapel, according to Augustín Edwards, means " taken without permission," and the Araucanians were determined to have it back. They were led by Lautaro, then only twenty years old, but one of the greatest Indian generals of history. He had been a servant in Valdivia's own household; he knew Spaniards. Wilily he led them on, letting them believe that the Indians had fled after burning the fort at Tucapel. Then, when he had them off guard, he fell on them with one small band, yelling, and brandishing lances. When that band was destroyed a second advanced, and a third, and more and more, until the Spaniards were forced to retire. But more Indians came, harrying the last survivors until all were killed or taken, including Pedro de Valdivia himself. The tradition is that he was killed under the most dreadful torture. But no one escaped to bring back the details of his end.

During most of the colonial period Valdivia was a frontier town of dusty or muddy adobe, of narrow unlighted streets, of soldiers resting between their unending and unsuccessful campaigns against the Araucanians, and of occasional flurries of liveliness when a ship put into the port of Corral. The port was fortified in the middle of the seventeenth century, but that did not put an end to contraband trade or the raids of pirates. At the close of the eighteenth century Ambrosio Higgins put through the first road from the capital to Valdivia.

Higgins, an illegitimate Irishman from County Sligo, proved to be one of the best administrators Chile, and then Peru, ever had. His rise began as a fighter against the Araucanians, but he rose rapidly to be General, then Governor of Chile, and finally Viceroy of Peru, the most important post in Spain's colonial empire. His public works were many, and he fathered the great hero of Chile's independence, Bernardo O'Higgins. He had a Chilean mother and somebody had added the indication of nobility to his patronymic.

The wars of independence divided Chile, as they did all Spain's colonies, between loyalty to the royal family and desire to break free of Napoleon's Spain. Valdivia was held by the royalists, and the Spanish squadron took refuge in its harbor while the whole coast, from Ecuador to Chile, was harried by Chilean patriots, who were commanded by another brilliant drifter from the British Isles.

Thomas Cochrane, Earl of Dundonald, was a liberty-loving, radical, popular, and much hated member of Parliament and Admiral in the British Navy. He was popular with the people, but anathema to his peers, who finally brought charges against him which might have been motivated by fear of his radical ideas. In any case he left home to fight for freedom wherever a free fight was going on. His crowning achievement was the capture of Valdivia, where he performed a feat of impudent daring which only shining success saved from charges of inexcusable rashness. Cochrane has been quoted as saying that " where calculation is well-founded, rashness disappears." He calculated on taking, with his sailors and marines, a series of fortified islands held by a Spanish force that outnumbered his two to one. And thanks to his almost hypnotic powers of leadership, his personal courage, and the stunned surprise of the Spaniards, who in the confusion fled from their own men, he did it. Later, up the coast at Callao, he captured a Spanish frigate in Lima's very port and ended Spain's domination of the Pacific. So this errant Scot ranks with the Irish O'Higgins and the Argentine San Martín as Chile's great revolutionary heroes. The name Admiral Cochrane is so proudly and unalterably remembered in Chile that when a descendant of his recently visited there, she was generally called " Miss Admiral Cochrane."

Neither Higgins's road nor Cochrane's victory made Valdivia an integral part of Chile. Long after independence was won, it was a perilous outpost on the edge of the vast uninhabited Indian country. As late as Pérez Rosales's time Valdivianos spoke of goods from Santiago as " from Chile." Only after the Germans settled the region and the Araucanians were finally driven back did the town begin to maintain a close and vital connection with Chile's capital and the outside world.

At Valdivia the Swiss and I definitely decided against visiting any of that string of perfect lakes at the head of the streams and under the peaks. Natives assured us that such rain as we were having was unprecedented so late in the spring. Perhaps. But unusual weather is so usual in the life of a confirmed traveler that I listened less than I looked at the moss-stippled frame houses and picket fences and the umbrellas, rubber ponchos, and overshoes in the shop windows. I noted too that the well-dressed señorita was wearing a colored and transparent raincoat and knee-high rubber boots. Neither nature, merchants, nor the general public was surprised by the weather. So we took the morning train which would get us to Temuco in the late afternoon.

[TEMUCO]

At Valdivia a few men on the plaza showed Indian blankets for sale, the German photographer's shop had the Araucanians' silver jewelry among the Agfa films, and on postcards Indians were beginning to outnumber scenery. But Temuco is definitely Indian. As in an Ecuadorian or Peruvian town, the streets are brightened and given character by Indians in red, gray, and green ponchos, the women with heavy silver necklaces and smoothly wound braids. These are Araucanians, who prefer to be known neither as Indians nor as Araucanians, but as *Mapuche,* a word which in their tongue means " people of the earth."

But Temuco is not only Indian. Mariano Picón-Salas describes it as one of the southern towns of " zinc and painted wood [with] the sawmill near the railroad which in '96 had already reached Temuco. From the beginning they were distinguished from those other towns of dusty adobe . . . of the central zone; towns strangled by the too near and voracious feudalism of Santiago."

Señor Picón-Salas is clearly of the younger generation of writers who resent the dominance of the ancient landowning class and look forward to a day when small holdings will replace vast fundos. For he goes on: " Over the regional economy pressed the clutch of those Santiago gentlemen who in the '80's . . . acquired on paper ranches of four thousand cuadras [about 15,500 acres].

" It detests Santiago, the distant city which charges taxes and that terrible two per cent on sales; and although great industry has not yet appeared, there is a certain painstaking and beauty of craft in the . . . furniture of Traiguén . . . the leatherware of Temuco made in saddle shops; the sweet

79

apple chicha, bubbly as the best champagne . . . the delicious rosy beverages of currants and raspberries.

"The stranger, who brought superior techniques, does all this and, as throughout the south, is beginning to outrank the poor Chilean who stays in the country and does not manage to become part of the bureaucracy or professional life of Santiago."

Despite these handicaps, Picón-Salas foresees an interesting future for Chile, whose great wealth so far has been found in the northern deserts of nitrates and copper. He prophesies:

"When nitrates are done for, the great new Chilean economy will have to be founded in these southern lands, vaster and rainier than those central lands worked for three hundred years of patronage *(encomienda)*. In the new plans this useless *latifundismo* (system of great estates) will be extinguished and the Mapuche, who is not a consumer now, will be incorporated into modern economic life. The forests and lakes give the land a certain look of cultivated Sweden, although the wide, flat grain fields are golden and hot during the brief but ardent summer. The Germans whose *quintas* (villas) adorn the environs of Temuco find here . . . a horticulture where the largest cabbages of Chile fatten, where the raspberry and red currant flower and give off scent as in a northern spring. And the conifer for making paper — as in Sweden; the ulmo, whose bark gives the red parchment for tanning, a tree superior to the oak; the *pellín*, which grows stronger near the sea . . . serves for furniture, girders, and ships: everything in this land offers the hope and the resources for civilization."

We saw all this in Temuco as we made dashes from the frigid hotel through the flooded streets to shops where leather goods and woodwork, blankets, and rough but interesting silver jewelry made us calculate not only spending-money but packing-space. Between purchases we called at a Baptist mission, a Capuchin mission, took tea or cocktails, or just gave up and went to bed in an effort to fend off that insistent cold. Our hotel had declared it spring and given up completely its *calefacción central*.

Temuco shows not only the sadness of the Indian, but the close juxtaposition, as Ernesto Montenegro expresses it in *Panorama y Color de Chile*, " of two groups of people, two ways of life, and has a tart and picturesque flavor. . . . One feels, as at the confluence of two rivers, the friction of two currents and the contrast of two human streams."

For the northbound traveler Temuco is the last town from which to see something of Araucanians as they live.

VII

ARAUCANIANS

HILEANS ARE PRONE TO SAY THAT CHILE IS A WHITE
man's country with no Negroes and no Indians. " We are very
fortunate," they put it, " because we have no Indian problem."

Only once I heard this statement contradicted, and that at
second hand. Ernesto Maes, a young Yanqui studying South
America's Indians, heard an Araucanian say: " I suppose all
these Chileans have told you that there is no Indian problem
in Chile? "

Mr. Maes nodded.

" Well, if they don't stop robbing us of our lands, they'll
find out that they've got an Indian problem. We fought them
once, for three hundred years or so, and we can do it again
if we have to."

As the Araucanians, some 200,000 of them, are organized
in several associations headed by intelligent and politically
conscious men, they may well win their rights without recourse to arms.

The Araucanians were first celebrated by Alonso Ercilla y Zuñiga, who was both soldier and poet. As a page of Philip II he had heard such tales of the gold of Peru that he left the ease and luxury of the court for Lima and went on from there to the uttermost end of Spanish exploration in Chile. By that time, 1557, Valdivia had been killed and García Hurtado de Mendoza had been appointed Governor of Chile at the age of twenty-two. Spain's giants in those days were young as well as powerful. Hurtado de Mendoza pushed the conquest vigorously, and under his command Spaniards founded the town of Mendoza in what is now Argentina and explored much of Chile's interlaced land and water to the south. Young Ercilla was one of ten who volunteered to cross the channel from the mainland to the island of Chiloé. He had then already begun to compose his epic *La Araucana*.

Ercilla drew enduring portraits of Chile's Araucanian heroes: Lautaro, Caupolicán, Galvarino, and the heroine Fresia. Edwards says: " It is certain that these indigenous figures would not have become legendary if Ercilla's pen had not immortalized them with . . . a fantasy which raises to sublimity the heroic acts of barbarians who were following their instinct in defending their lands and homes."

But, sentimentalized or not, Ercilla's Indian heroes have taken their place in Chilean history and been presented in prose and verse, in paint and bronze and marble, from then until now.

Lautaro, Valdivia's escaped groom, after that leader's death at Tucapel, swept on with his conquering hordes, forced the Spaniards to abandon Concepción, raised another army when his first refused to follow farther, and was threatening Santiago when his flame failed. Instead of forcing his advantage he hesitated and the Spaniards under Francisco de Villagrá cut down his forces in a fierce battle. Lautaro himself was killed.

The leadership then passed to Caupolicán, whose legend has been most strikingly perpetuated by Nicanor Plaza in a bronze statue which won high praise in Paris. Caupolicán fought successfully for four years. Then he was captured by the Spaniards and tortured to death, unquailing to the end. Edwards describes it: "submitted to the torture of impalement, which consisted in seating the victim on a sharpened pole which ruptured the intestines. Caupolicán died with the same phlegm and indifference with which shortly before he had received Christian baptism. . . ."

Authorities seem agreed that the Araucanians were magnificent fighting men, the best possible prototypes for a people of fiercely proud and independent spirit. Nobody claims much more for them. Alberto Cabero, in *Chile y los Chilenos*, writes: "They had no creative imagination; their limited fancy did not permit them to produce delicate fabrics or artistic arms and jewels; to populate their magnificent nature with mythological gods; to give their rude combats the proportions of legends; or to build monuments or even comfortable homes. . . . Their crafts were rude, their huts miserable, their skill was limited to insipid tales and a music indicative of the habitual sadness of their character, developed on a scale of a few hoarse notes, a sort of a soporific melody, complaining, anguished, music more suitable to the dead than to the joyful."

He sums them up: "Because of his mental instability the Araucanian was versatile; because of his limited memory and his difficulty with generalizing and association of ideas, improvident; because of his lack of meditative faculty and

Araucanians Wear Their Warm
Wool Ponchos

Araucanian Jewelry Is Crude but
Interesting

Coming into Town to Trade

Some of the Old Ceremonies Persist

knowledge of the law of cause, superstitious; because of his inability to distinguish between good and bad, a thief; because of his scorn of life, brave. They have shown themselves incapable of evolution." Not a very attractive picture.

In these modern days Araucanians, like so many peoples complacently considered inferior, are producing individuals quite equal to whites in creative imagination and ability to conceive abstract ideas, produce works of art, maintain moral standards, and develop in all directions. There are in Santiago, as doubtless in other Chilean cities, men and women of pure or almost pure Araucanian descent who daily disprove their compatriot's judgment of them by presiding as judges, arguing cleverly as lawyers, making keen diagnoses as doctors, by teaching, writing, and painting. They have evolved a long way in comparatively few years, and in spite of every handicap that the white race could place against them.

The origin of this race that is at once so admired and so misprized is little known. Presumably fighting people from the Argentine pampas filtered through the Andean passes between the Toltén and Bío-Bío rivers and conquered and mingled with the aborigines of the Chilean valleys. *Araucano* is said to mean people from the east. History discovered them in seven tribes, extending from central Chile down into the southern archipelago. They operated under a loose federation which was strong enough to stop both Incan and Spanish invaders. They speak related languages and their beliefs and customs are still very similar.

Though the Mapuche — the Araucanians prefer that name — have been called people without religion, they had a worship which they still practice. Cabero calls it an ancestor cult, and its chief figure, Pellín, the race's founder. Hartley Burr Alexander, in *Mythology of All Races,* describes him as a deity of fire and war, but a sort of pantheistic divinity which all dead warriors and chiefs went to join. His name, Pellín, meant thunderer or mysterious power. He lived on the volcanoes, many of which still keep his name.

Inevitably the fearsome natural cataclysms of the volcanoes with their related earthquakes and tidal waves were considered acts of offended deities, whose wrath could reduce the most valiant warrior to a state of superstitious timidity. Numberless minor deities were everywhere, in fish or animal form as vampires or incubi. Some were good but most were evil, and Mapuche religion was more concerned with beguiling a malevolent spirit or removing a bad spell than with worship. The few helpful genii were feminine: forest or water nymphs who served men. And the shamans were often, if not usually, women.

Much of this information may be put into the present tense. Every group still has its *machi*, soothsayer, who studies the clouds, the flight of birds, and dreams for omens; who cures disease by exorcizing the spiritual cause, and who locates and combats witches.

During the nineteenth century Chile's Indians, like ours, were the enemy on the frontier. In time Chile overcame them, as we did, with superior arms and numbers, but also with alcohol, diseases, and bad habits. True, chicha, the national drink, antedated the Spanish conquest; but as the white men's pressure increased they drank more and more.

The government ordered the eradication of the Araucanians in 1823, but that was easier decreed than done. Many a general won his spurs against the Araucanians before final military submission came about as by-product of the War of the Pacific, fought by Chile against Bolivia and Peru. While the Chilean troops were off in the northern deserts, the Indians had their last fling. But once the war was won, Colonel Gregorio Urrutia, put in command of the army of the frontier, soon had the towns fortified and new lands awarded to ex-soldiers and under cultivation. By 1883 the warrior race had been reduced to a few miserable natives, as gloomy as their dense, dark forests. Alberto Cabero describes them: " Of phlegmatic character, taciturn aspect, no excitement animates their indifferent mien, a mask which conceals strong hates, rancor, and revenge."

True to the belief that there is no Indian problem, the Chilean government has never dealt with Indians separately. As they laid down their arms they were accepted, theoretically at least, as full citizens of the Republic and took their chances with politics, land laws, and schools of general applicability. Only the Church, also typically, considered Indians as a group apart with special aptitudes and needs. From the earliest days of the conquest, Franciscan and Dominican friars went into the pathless jungles to carry the gospel to the savages. And they are still there. Bearded Capuchin monks, mostly Germans, conduct a school and trading post at a place near Temuco which is appropriately called Padre de las Casas for the great humanitarian apostle to the Indians, and several other establishments far back in the forests.

Mariano Picón-Salas describes a Capuchin mission: " They bring these German Capuchins from Bavaria with their reddish beards and very blue eyes; friars who take to the climate and love the woods and who ride out among the *rucas* (huts) on their native nags and even split with their own sturdy arms the tree trunks from which they make their church and their school. Among these men have been those who compiled dictionaries and grammars of the Araucanian tongue, who have written it and collected and translated its poems."

Regarding the religious success of the mission Picón-Salas has some doubt. " If the Mapuche pays for a funeral and asks baptism, in his moment of necessity, when man is alone before the cosmic mystery — he prefers his own [gods]. The machis keep on exorcizing evil, and rain falls where the gods are invoked in the howling ceremony of the harvest. The mission to the Mapuches . . . has perhaps to content itself . . . with teaching them to air out their rucas, so dense with smoke and parasites, to improve their rudimentary agricultural technique, and with transmitting to them that universal prayer, Our Father, which expresses only the primary need of peace and of bread which all races have.

" But the Catholic missions are stimulated by Protestant missions, for along with the bearded German Capuchins Protestant missions have appeared with their shaven Yanquis and their eccentric misses."

This author is sharply critical of educational methods which, following the general scheme, disregard the Indian's greatest needs, which he lists as agricultural training, health measures to offset the machi's superstitions, and soap. Of the land problem he writes:

" It is not that the Indian lacks sufficient lands for working. . . . Around Temuco . . . there are for example a wide zone of good Mapuche lands. Naturally they were taken from other lands and still are taken. There is an almost epic struggle in some regions between the Indian and the Chilean adventurer or colonist who also wants lands." The technique is the one so familiar from south of the Araucanians to the Eskimos. The ingratiating stranger, the fiesta, liquor, the proposal of immediate money, cash in hand, the ill-understood transfer of property.

" It is a combat between the ruca and the tiled house, between nomadism and sedentariness; a combat which will find neither solution nor truce as long as the Mapuche is not an agricultural worker as apt as the stranger or the Chilean."

For three hundred years the Araucanian kept the Chilean mindful of him. For the last fifty years, since he laid down his arms, concern for the Araucanians as a race or as individuals has disappeared from the national consciousness as completely as Indian blood has merged in the ethnic group known as Chilean. To Chile the Mapuche is not a person who needs food, education, medical care; he is a symbol.

[THE MAPUCHE AT HOME]

The mud was too deep to get far by motor; even horseback riding would be a dreary drag through sheets of rain over seas of mud. But we could visit an Araucanian village not far from Temuco and meet an old woman who was reputed to be a machi.

We slithered along slowly, gingerly easing out onto the road's shoulder while a wide wain passed us, and took several wrong turns. This made it possible for us to visit several rucas while the driver asked his way.

At the first one a couple of small boys ran out to take our measure with beady black eyes. They ducked inside again. The driver talked with the man — a well-formed person hoeing a ridge of sweet-smelling brown earth. There was no frenzied speed in his movements certainly, but a steady going that promised a long row done by night. When a woman appeared in the doorway I ventured to approach her. The ruca, shaped rather like a Navajo hogan, showed a dark interior, but after a little talk I was invited in and could see that the light was enough for any activity. The usual entering wedge of talk about children, and a proffer of candy led to easy chat.

The ruca, they explained, could be put up in little more than a week. Say six days to get the materials ready: wood for the frame, grass for the roof, and the fiber for tying it together. Nails are not yet plentiful in Araucania. Ten men or so can erect a ruca in a day. Finished, it is a circular lodge, about eight by ten yards, with a central pole and a sloping thatched roof. Generally an uncovered fire provides cooking heat and Rembrandtesque effects of smoke and flame. Other times there is a separate cooking lodge; and as the family grows, other apartments are added. The old lady showed her jewelry: a long silver spike with roughly worked head to fasten her blanket; a sort of breastplate of linked silver with dangling medals; earrings, and rings. It is all the crudest sort of work, interesting, but with no real beauty.

This home typifies the fierce old Araucanian's adaptation to the modern world. Living still in the prehistoric thatched hut, they guide their lives by what old women read in clouds, the course of birds across the sky, dreams, and other signs from beyond. We had been told that our wrinkled old hostess with all the jewelry was a machi. Yet her grandchildren attended a school — Catholic, Protestant, or government — her daughters carried their woven ponchos to tourist shops in Temuco, and her sons sold their produce in the white man's market.

Some Araucanians are prosperous, if not actually rich men; and like so many examples of suppressed groups, they are often found squeezing their poorer neighbors even more cruelly than do their white models. But the Araucanian average income and mode of living is very low indeed. Though they farm and own cattle, few families produce more than enough for a meager diet; surplus to sell is sometimes altogether lacking.

When our driver had got his bearings and I had satisfied myself that our hostess, who might be a machi, was not going to act like one, we set off for the Baptist school. Its teacher was Alberto Nahuelán, a devout graduate of the Baptist training school in Temuco. He met us on the sagging porch of his frame schoolhouse. Inside, fifteen children rose to greet us from long benches behind high desks. The enrollment, Albert said, was thirty-eight. Fifteen in attendance was very good. They all looked Indian with the exception of two little girls with pinched white faces. One of an Oriental cast of features looked thoroughly miserable as though she were struggling stupidly against pain. The boys, all dark, seemed sturdier, though one was lame. They sang, dreadfully, with voices all out of tune, forced, and hard. They did not know the national anthem when we requested it, but sang Spanish words to familiar old hymn tunes. Then they read, very well, in rapid singsong. Three grades were represented and Albert pointed out, with justified pride, how much better the third grade could read than the first.

We went out then for picture-taking and to meet Albert's family, who emerged from two rucas in gala attire. The grandmother had woven a green ribbon into her braids, and her heavy black shawl was striped with magenta. Albert's wife, too, wore Indian dress and heavy old silver plaques. But the youngsters, Victorino and Isaias, wore manufactured rompers of dull blue. They were as brownly rosy, as plumply robust, as anyone could wish. Victorino would soon be in school; he already cherished a book he could not read and showed its pictures. Albert was aglow with pride in his family and his school.

"I am," he explained with the dignity of perfect simplicity, "doing a work for my country as well as for my God."

Mud precluded our visiting either the Episcopal or the Catholic missions. They would doubtless show as single-minded devotion on the part of the teachers. But what of the mass of Mapuches? What happens when they gather from these assorted missions in a general meeting? No reports on these people suggest such a sardonic humor as that with which the Navajos regard the whites. But their comments would surely make good eavesdropping. How would a totally immersed Araucanian Baptist, say, discuss the religion of Jesus with a convinced Catholic Mapuche while they waited together for the old machi to complete her divinations? Perhaps we shall never know.

VIII

IOWA IN CHILE

ROTESTANT MISSIONARIES IN TEMUCO INSISTED THAT I must visit the Methodist mission farm and school, El Vergel, near Angol. It is an experiment in agricultural education and Middle Western farming methods which is having notable success in rural Chile.

The school was founded in 1917 as the result of the dream of Ezra Bauman, a Methodist missionary in Chile. His hope was that the Church, along with evangelization, would offer practical training in farming, with the by-products of education in self-reliance, diligence, and economy and generally enlarged concepts of life's possibilities and wants. "Their needs," said Mr. Bauman, in urging his scheme on his Bishop, "are greater than they themselves know." Other by-products would inevitably be growing discontent with the Chilean latifundian system and the production of men capable of owning and managing their own small farms: aid, in short, to the developing middle class in Chile.

A teacher from El Vergel met me at the train. Luckily we had to wait for Mr. Reed, the school's director, and that gave me a chance to watch the town's gaiety. It was November 15, the day of Chile's spring festival. Schools were closed and youngsters swarmed the streets dressed as Spanish cavaliers, prehistoric Araucanians, Chilean *huasos*, or mythological characters. It was before noon, and the clouds were not too lowering for a faint hope that the afternoon might clear for the parade. A couple of little angels with pink wings scuttled across in front of the car, and two big boys in red sashes came up to talk importantly about the arrangements.

Then Mr. Reed joined us: brisk, matter-of-fact youngish man and a graduate of the Iowa State College of Agriculture at Ames. Before we got out of Angol several men stopped Mr. Reed, who is a director of the Fruit Co-operative and clearly a person of consideration and prestige. Once we stopped while the pretty Chilean girl on the back seat, the farm's resident nurse, picked up a bundle for a new baby at El Vergel. Out on the country road we were hailed by two men driving horses loaded with a queer brownish mass. Seaweed, Mr. Reed explained, which they sell for fertilizer. The men make a regular route bringing seaweed inland and taking manufactured articles back to their coast villages. It is almost the only survival in Chile of a regular commercial route covered afoot by peasants such as are so common in the Indian countries.

As we drove along, skirting puddles and breathing in the damp earth scents from fresh brown furrows, Mr. Reed told me something of the history of Angol and El Vergel. Angol is an old town, one of the many frontier forts which Pedro de Valdivia himself built against the Indians. Many times its stockades and straw-thatched huts had been burned and rebuilt before the final pacification of the Araucanians; then this rich valley of many streams quickly developed into a flowering agricultural region. Its flower is the apple blossom, for soil and climate are as suited to that fruit as those of Oregon. The first commercial orchard in Chile was El Vergel, planted by Manuel V. Bunster, an English-Chilean who gave it the name which means Garden of Paradise. The Methodists kept the name, though they insist their farm is a safe Eden which harbors no Eve and produces no snakes.

The original purchase of 900 acres included over 500 acres of flat land under irrigation. Of that 250 acres are now in orchards and nursery and 15 acres in vegetable gardens. Later purchases have added Los Alpes, hilly uplands without irrigation. Parts of it are being planted to forest trees at the rate of fifty or sixty thousand annually, which even now provide firewood and some building timber. Some of it produces grain, some pastures a Holstein herd which supplies milk for all Angol, and Hampshire sheep and Duroc Jersey hogs. Formerly a major crop was lentils, but as their best market was Germany, their production is being kept low until Chileans may learn to eat that rich source of vitamins. The farm raises a wide variety of other vegetables for local consumption. There are experimental groves of olives, almonds, and figs; but this climate lacks the hot California sun. Its prime crop is apples — Delicious, Rome Beauty, Yellow Newton, Jonathan, and Winesap — which are shipped not only all over Chile, but to neighboring countries as well. El Vergel is also an experiment station, conducts a thriving business selling trees, and is an active member of the National Apple Producers Association, a government-sponsored organization.

By that time we had stopped at a wide gate to let a truckload of boys pass. But they hauled up. It had been decided, they said, to give up the afternoon's program because of the rain. They were going to an indoor meeting at the gym. Nobody could have missed the ease and confidence of their manner with Mr. Reed. We passed huge silos, gable-roofed barns, beds of many-hued tulips and rhododendrons in pink, lavender, and white. We crossed a stream under wide trees and were in a wide clean compound surrounded by large well-kept farm buildings and the Reeds' house.

Mrs. Reed welcomed me into Iowa. Curious down there in the Southern Hemisphere, in a Spanish-speaking, Latin, Catholic country, to step into the typical Middle Western home. Nothing was lacking of that, nothing suggested Chile. The house itself with its narrow front hall and long stairway and the family bathroom with towel racks marked with the children's names. The sitting-room with its base burner, rocking-chairs, and table laden with English books and magazines. The family meal opened with the English grace which, with reverent familiarity, told God all about the family affairs.

Mrs. Reed was born in Bolivia of missionary people. Mr. Reed left excellent opportunities in the States for the mission field. Evangelization was the moving spirit of their lives; no doubt of that. But their daily living was made up of stirring mundane activity; the big business of a huge hacienda, the exacting task of a house and children, with schools and mothers' meetings on the side. Their good sense appeared in planning the day's schedule so the sixteen-year-old daughter could stay in Angol overnight for the spring festival dance. The daughter of Methodist missionaries dancing!

"We don't dance," Mrs. Reed explained, "but we want our children to be a part of the social life of the town, so she often stays with a Chilean family and does as their daughters do. We have tried to bring up our children so they can make their own decisions."

El Vergel was planned as an agricultural mission which

should be a self-supporting plant. Everything that happens there is an outgrowth of one of these root ideas. As an apple orchard it not only produces prize apples, but has presented Chile with its most valuable parasite. When Mr. Reed reached Chile in 1920 its entire apple industry was threatened by the woolly aphis, which was destroying the orchards alarmingly. The *Aphelinus mali*, a minute wasp which generally flourishes along with the woolly aphis and preys on it, was lacking. So Mr. Reed imported the *Aphelinus mali* from Uruguay, where in had recently been acclimated from the United States, and a merry war was on. In a couple of months the *Aphelinus mali* had bested the woolly aphis at El Vergel and jumped to the neighboring orchards. Since then hundreds of colonies have been shipped to all parts of Chile; the elimination of the woolly aphis has put apple-raising on a sound commercial basis. As El Vergel has never charged for this useful parasite, the Methodist mission may be cited as one telling refutation of the charge that Yanquis are forever and only money-grubbers.

El Vergel's crops and herds produce almost enough foodstuffs to supply its resident population of about eight hundred people. Besides eight missionaries, all of whom hold secular jobs as farmers, office workers, or teachers, there are Chilean skilled employees and unskilled laborers, who are paid the usual Chilean wage. They work from dawn to dark, as is customary in Chile, and the plantation supplies their house, plots of land for gardens, and firewood. They can buy vegetables very reasonably from the farm; and their three- to six-room houses are better built than the Chilean average and boast of wooden floors. The missionaries were assured by experienced Chileans that no *inquilino* family could appreciate such a luxury, that they would tear up the flooring for firewood. But

97

that has not occurred. In fact, the employees show increasing pride in their houses with windows as well as floors. Water is piped near if not quite into the houses; many have electric lights and there is a plan to supply them all. A sewage system — a rarity in rural Chile — is being extended rapidly. This has led to the making of four-inch cement tiles and added a training project to the school. Householders are encouraged to make their own furniture in the practical way of offering them designs, assistance, and the use of the farm shop and tools. Women are given instruction in the care and feeding of a family, in making work easier. And children attend schools provided by the farm, as the law requires.

There is, of course, a Methodist church on the place, and two other "preaching places." Evangelization also reaches out to the nearest village of Hue.quén, where many of the El Vergel workmen live. The mission bulletin states: "High rents, poor housing conditions, and general disregard for the enforcement of liquor laws characterize the town. . . . Very early in the development of the farm, a religious center was opened in the village where, under the supervision of one of the missionaries, the people from the farm testified to the new life which was theirs in Jesus Christ.

" If you can imagine an attentive audience of 120 people crowded into a room which seats 45 people comfortably, you have a picture of a typical Sunday-night service in Huequén when there is an illustrated lecture. The people of Huequén are humble, sincere, and destitute, and are desperately in need of strong religious leadership." The bulletin describes the church's organizations and a new department of social service which " is entirely new in Chile."

Few would cavil at this social work. Some might wonder why North American Catholics are not offering such aid to

Chile. Before I left that country I was to hear a distinguished
Catholic divine discuss that possibility. " North American
Catholics," he said, " have failed; they have left the field to
Protestants, who, along with much fine social work, are combating our people's faith, disrupting our families, sowing
dissension everywhere." He smiled. " Dissension, I notice,
even among themselves."

The agricultural school is directed by Mr. Dilman S. Bullock, whose qualifications are extraordinarily varied. As an
Episcopalian missionary he spent ten years among the Araucanians. A graduate of the Michigan Agricultural College,
with an advanced degree in science from the University of
Wisconsin, he also served on an agricultural mission from the
United States to South America. His hobbies are boys, bugs,
and a small museum he and the boys are making.

Mrs. Bullock, a Canadian, gave me tea by the Franklin
stove. A quilted cozy kept the pot warm, a Toby jug held the
milk, and there was strawberry jam for the home-made bread
and butter. We were interrupted several times by boys who
came for the red sashes Mrs. Bullock had made for their costumes or to bring the glad news that there would be a dance
after all.

There were forty-four pupils in the school, all living in.
They came from every class; rich hacendados like their boys
to have the scientific training El Vergel gives; clever Araucanians recognize its advantages, as do the Germans; and a
certain number of boys are carried even if their fathers cannot pay for them. To enter, a boy must be between sixteen
and eighteen, of good character and health, and must have
completed five years of schooling or its equivalent. In addition to regular secondary-school courses, he will study religion, zoology and botany, accounting, and various forms of

agri-, avi-, horti-, and aboriculture. There are also classes in reforestation, cattle-raising, dairying, crafts, farm mechanics, rural administration, and physical training. It is a three-year course. Along with all this each student works fifteen hours a week on the plantation, gaining practical experience in every phase of its operation.

El Vergel's announcement states that the requirements are very similar to those of " the practical School of Agriculture in Chile. There are, however, two very important differences. First, the practical work is all carried on under good commercial conditions; and second, the whole atmosphere of the school is Christian, which is essentially different from Government Institutions."

In its seventeen years El Vergel's school has graduated eighty-seven students. Fifty-six of them are in agricultural work, mostly in positions of responsibility. Six are on one big fundo, which is asking for six more. Several, including some Araucanians, are working their own farms. Two or three have government posts in agriculture. One is in the American Museum of Natural History. Three work at El Vergel. No failures are reported, and many graduates are now sending their own sons back to El Vergel.

After tea Mr. Bullock conducted me across the tennis court to his museum. His collections are known not only in Chile but in museums in the United States. Six hundred Chilean birds have been skinned and flattened out on cards — an array of lovely color, which represents 140 species. The collection of insects runs into the thousands, including fifty new species. Mr. Bullock and the boys, ranging the countryside, have inevitably happened upon old Indian pottery, unique burial urns, and stones worked into weapons, tools, or images for worship. Everything is of interest to this man whose eyes glow with the joy of the trained observer. It would be hard to imagine a better companion for boys.

My visit ended in the very early morning when I sneaked downstairs as quietly as I could, trying not to wake the family. But Mr. Reed was up, and before I had finished my oatmeal, eggs, coffee, and toast, he was there, dressed for Sunday, and insisting upon seeing me to the station. It was a misty morning, offering a gentle hope of sunshine; and the air was scented with all the fragrances of spring. As we stood in the station, surrounded by Sunday travelers bound for the shore, I sensed in my host something suggestive of a good apple's soundness. Invited or not into this country, welcome or not, he and the other Iowa farmers at El Vergel were showing in their lives qualities finely representative of our country: willingness to work hard with the hands; unbowed heads; conviction and idealism. One need not agree with a man's faith to admire him and his way.

So I had seen Chile of the Germans, the Indians, and the Iowans. Now for Chile of the Chileans. For soon we should have followed the Rio Vergara to its confluence with the Bío-Bío and crossed that deep dividing flood into central Chile — the Chile about which all articulate Chileans have written and talked in prose and poetry, the Chile all visitors have loved. Central warm, friendly Chile which the Spaniards took and made their own, where they left their impress most deeply.

IX

THE CENTER

[CONCEPCIÓN]

AS ONE TRAVELS NORTH, SOUTHERN CHILE YIELDS almost imperceptibly to central Chile. Instead of trim cottages with fresh paint and tidied gardens, we noted sprawling houses on laxer farms — weathered woodwork, patches of woods uncleared, or pastures abandoned to red erosion. The Nazi Gauleiter who infests every Chilean train still met his subordinates and gave them directions in hard clipped phrases. But at the station now were men of another breed. With slim legs in long fine boots, they swung their long black ponchos as no German ever could; often they wore dull red or orange Mapuche ponchos, short enough to show a red sash. These men met one another courteously with ready smiles under flat black hats. Easy people to live with: easy perhaps, to lull into disregard of Bund meetings, of armed and marching men or clever Nazi propaganda. But once aroused, they would show all the vigor and courage of Spain and of Araucania too.

The Bío-Bío, largest of southern Chile's rivers, is a wonderful limpid stream, rushing gladly down from the cordillera with water for man's use. It gurgles into rapids, spreads out into pools shaded by low branches, saunters under bridges where towns have made parks, pours smoothly into irrigation canals, turns millwheels. The countryside that Sunday morning was a spring scene misted over by distant rain on the mountains and by daisies in the meadows and pale blossoms in the hedges. Whenever the train stopped, damp flower scents rushed in as women came aboard with armfuls of lilacs, laburnum, and iris. Then a salty scent cut across the sweetness, and we knew we were nearing the sea.

Concepción is Chile. German names still appear on business houses vying with English ones, but this metropolis of the south (it has a population of 90,000) is Chile of the future as of the past. It antedates the Spaniards, for when Valdivia built his first palisade on the Bío-Bío he chose the site of a settlement where he had defeated 20,000 Araucanians (so he wrote the King). The name was due to a miracle. For in the heat of battle the Holy Virgin was seen emerging from a falling meteorite to admonish the Indians to cease fighting. They chose to follow the devil, who also entered the scene. So Valdivia explained the occurrence to the King, attributing his victory to divine intercession.

Since then Concepción has moved across the peninsula to a more sheltered location, but it carried its tradition along. From the beginning whoever lived in Concepción was in for a turbulent life. When Lautaro took it, the Spaniards fled to Santiago, but returned to rebuild. When gold washings proved profitable, old settlers were dispossessed for political favorites, but the city grew. During the colonial era Concepción was the refuge of settlers fleeing from Araucanian raids; soldiers clanked through on their way to the wars or returned combat-weary or wounded.

During the wars of independence Concepción, like so much of Spain's colonial empire, was alternately royalist and revolutionary, changing hands in fierce, close battles. But in 1817 Bernardo O'Higgins, son of an Irish adventurer and a Chilean mother, met the Argentine José de San Martín at Chacabuco and defeated the Spaniards thoroughly. Two years later the Scotsman, Admiral Lord Thomas Cochrane, brought up aid by sea, and Chile finally rid herself of Spanish forces.

O'Higgins, declared Supreme Director, then set himself to put his country in order. He built roads and cobbled streets; instituted night watchmen and street lamps; cleaned the garbage out of the plazas; and forbade night processions. This was an annoyance to Concepción, which gladly tolerated a bit of crime and license as cover-up for certain old Indian fetishistic rites. Concepción also resented the effort to abolish bullfights and cockfights. But the director was supreme and Concepción had to submit to modernization.

Among all these disturbances were the recurrent earthquakes, which never left the little city too shaken to rebuild her fallen walls. The last earthquake, of 1937, is still clearly marked by the cracked stone walls of churches and piles of tumbled bricks behind fences. But also by evidences of thorough cleaning up, by new buildings constructed to withstand seismic shocks, and by rows of quickly erected tenements as pristine and probably as temporary as a California "tourist court."

Agustín Edwards wrote: "In Concepción the most courageous, audacious, and stoical of the conquerors gathered. They gave it character; the Indian wars strengthened its will, and the assaults of the elements tempered its soul."

Modern Concepción palpably vibrates with the combative spirit of its warlike past, now turned toward the future. It has every material advantage. Vast coal mines at Lota extend for three miles out under the sea. They provide fuel for railroads and shipping and they run factories which produce every little thing. This is literally true. Things to eat and wear, household needs, even furniture are made in Chile; but heavy industries are still lacking though the country has ample iron deposits and unequaled opportunities for electrification in its water power. The stumbling-blocks are three: (1) lack of Chilean capital; (2) a patriotic effort to protect Chilean industry by restricting foreign capital; (3) low wages. *Buy Chilean* is the national slogan, and often Chilean manufactures are not too good. Above all, Chile's workers — not only farm laborers, but factory workers and white-collar people — are paid so little that many of them must work a month for the price of a pair of shoes and a hat. But as these conditions are bettered Concepción will be ready to go ahead.

Aside from coal, she controls the agricultural output of the fertile Bío-Bío basin. And her port of Talcahuano is second only to Valparaiso as a commercial harbor and naval base. A huge breakwater makes it capable of harboring Chile's entire fleet; on shore are bases for repairs, arsenals, oil tanks, a naval hospital, and a submarine base.

Chile has a proud naval history. Since Admiral Cochrane cleared her coastal waters of Spaniards and helped Chile achieve her independence, her Navy has never been defeated. It has also been very British, partly, perhaps, owing to Lord Cochrane's tradition, but also because British naval officers have been detailed to train her officers. In 1940 Chile owned one battleship, bought from Britain, four cruisers, eight destroyers, nine submarines, besides training and auxiliary vessels, including a sub-depot ship and two oil tankers. There was a complement of 8,000 men, commanded by well-trained officers educated in the national naval academy at Valparaiso. Hardly a force adequate to protect that lengthy and squirming shore, but vigilant and jealously determined that no foreign enemy shall land. Chile has about two hundred airplanes, too, and the aid of various sea and aircraft from the United States. In case of war striking at Magellan, the port of Talcahuano would be a vital spot in the defense of the hemisphere, and not a helpless one.

Concepción is building Chile's future in a university as well as through business and trade. The Universidad de Concepción, founded in 1924, looks new and feels young. It is set against old hills and dark eucalyptus groves, but its many-windowed buildings are white or pale, and baby trees grow around fresh new lawns. The young professor who conducted me about remarked that most of the professors are young too.

" But," he smiled to say, " you would not expect a young mother to have old sons."

Starting with schools of medicine, industrial chemistry, pharmacy, dentistry, and pedagogy, the University of Concepción now also includes colleges of law and philosophy. It was founded by public-spirited citizens. Perhaps they were animated by the southern metropolis's dislike of being second to Santiago, as well as by its indomitable spirit. Their university also exemplifies a Latin trait which contrasts curiously with the puritanical Nordic tendency to deny certain natural impulses. For it is supported by a national lottery.

The realistic Chilean, like all Latin Americans and many Europeans, accepts gambling as something that everybody does, and garners its fruits for the public benefit instead of leaving them to society's enemies. Racetrack gambling, as well as lotteries, are government-controlled and pay a large percentage into the public till.

By a law of 1933, when the general crisis had created dire want in Chile, the Congress passed a law to establish *La Polla Chilena de Beneficencia* (The Chilean Lottery for Charity). It was to combine the features of the Irish Sweepstakes and the older Chilean scheme of ticket-selling. It is administered by a manager with a small consultative committee, all gentlemen of unquestioned and unquestionable probity. Assisted by only nine employees for the clerical work, they announce the dates for the drawings and determine the amounts of the prizes, which sometimes run as high as a million pesos. The tickets may be split so many ways that a few cents will give one a chance at a small premium. The law stipulates that no less than 60 per cent of the take must go to prizes and no more than 10 per cent for commissions and expenses. The remaining 30 per cent is then divided between the *Casas de Socorro* (Charitable Institutions), government hospitals, and the University of Concepción. Tickets go to agents, who resell them to subagents for sale on the streets, in tobacco booths or small shops. The general agents get a commission of 8 per cent, out of which they pay the subagents. Many of these, who solicit on the streets are old, poor, or crippled people who may be the first beneficiaries of the scheme.

Concepción, then, has real character tempered by hardships and hard luck and quick to see and use its advantages. It has everything needed for a rich and brilliant future, plus the enterprise and vigor to make good use of these things. The first Spaniards were the hardy ones, mostly Basque and Catalan, who dared to venture so far. They have intermarried now for a century and more with similar stock from northern Europe, especially England and Germany. Consequently they have the sturdy virtues, the push and go of pioneer peoples anywhere, including the typical frontier city's envy and scorn of the

softer, more powerful capital and metropolis. Everything indicates that as Chile becomes industrialized, Concepción will
lead.

[CLASSICAL CHILE]

Gabriela Mistral describes the central zone as the classical aspect of her country. Ten provinces, about 800 miles in length,
still know the sort of life that George Washington and Plato
lived, and that has changed little in Chile to this day.

The railroad trip from Concepción to Santiago reveals the
country's unique configuration and its most typical beauties.
The great central valley forms a long trough between the
Andes' true spine and the coastal range, which greater age has
softened into gentler outlines. The many bright clear rivers,
fed by tempestuous streams from the cordillera, muster
strength enough to force their way through the lower hills to
the Pacific. Meanwhile they water the loveliest countryside imaginable. This is the land that forces every writer, native or
foreign, to his most lyrical pitch. Only Biblical phrases seem
adequate: land of milk and honey; green pastures where fat
kine stand in pools of shade; still waters floating lilies and
water hyacinths; long poplar-lined lanes where sleepy oxen
haul slow carts with men snoozing on loads of fragrant hay.
And always the hills to which to raise one's eyes. I remember
it still under a soft-toned haze like a dream, too perfect to
be true.

A North American finds it almost inevitable to compare
Chile with our western coast, turned upside down. Physically
central Chile is like the California we know, except that instead of wheeling citrus groves, grapevines maneuver in long
lines. On the personal side, it is still the old California we like

108

to read about — California before the Yankee hit it hard with his cement roads, his terrifying trucks, his forests of oil derricks, his mammoth industries. And, too, before a democratic invasion had broken up the old Spanish haciendas into thousands of small one-family farms. Central Chile keeps on dreaming the life of great ranches with uncalculating hospitality and the careless way of accepting from land what it will yield without effort, as a gift of God, never to be forced.

Instead of lumber towns redolent of fresh-cut wood, we stopped at stations named for the fundos or the vineyards from which fruits and wines would later go north to Santiago or to the ports.

At intervals never too short for aristocratic exclusiveness, we glimpsed the plantation houses through iron gates in high garden walls. Never pretentious, they are comfortable old homes which have spread, as the family grew, around patio after patio; generally they are one-storied and with tiled roofs. In November gardens were masses of spring flowers, and beyond great barns and stables orchards were in full rosy bloom. Vines were still bare, but at the station women and children offered pale pink or rich black cherries cleverly braided into garlands, and flat baskets of Chile's strawberries, the sweetest ever tasted. There is a large pale one called frutilla (*Fragaria chiloensis*), which is said to be a native of the Bío-Bío Valley, from where one Frézier took it to France in 1714. Edwards says he described his find as larger than a walnut, sometimes as big as a hen's egg. The enthusiastic Frenchman enhanced the size a bit, but the flavor could never be too glowingly described.

Life on Chile's great fundos, even as glimpsed from a passing train, appears so idyllic that one must envy people who can see only the comfortable mansion and never the rows of battered hovels in which the inquilinos live. One is assured that " in the good old days," and even now if " Communism " has not ruined the good old ways, masters were always kind, dependants always humble and willing, and ladies most charitable and condescending. That is, they were so between long seasons in Santiago or abroad.

Mariano Picón-Salas, ever trenchant, has summed up the gentleman owner very neatly. " What do these northerners know of the cultivation and the value of these lands? For many of these families the fundo in the south, although oaks crown it and araucarias ennoble it, is the place they rent or vacation; where one summer day the *mayordomo* with the carriages awaits the señoritas' arrival."

The fundo is the descendant of the Spanish *encomienda* system, which gave each worthy conqueror a certain number of Indians to civilize and Christianize while they worked for him. Valdivia began it in Chile; several central valley fundos are still owned by the families to whom he awarded them. McBride quotes the words in which the conqueror bestowed on Inez Suárez, his mistress, " the chief called Apoquindo, with all his sub-chiefs and Indians and subjects who have their seat in this valley of Mapocho, and to you is given his lands and Indians that you may make use of all of them." All together this lady-love got 500 Indians; Valdivia himself 1,500; some encomiendas were as few as 50. In the south they ran up to 40,000, but the Araucanians proved so intractable that most southern haciendas did not materialize.

Because there were many more Spaniards than available lands a sharp social cleavage developed between landowners and landless citizens. It became everyone's prime ambition to be a landowner served by willing serfs. Many achieved this by marriage with Indian girls, which gave them a share in communal lands; many, as older families decayed, purchased their estates. As Alberto Edwards shows clearly in *La Fronda Aristocrática* (*The Aristocratic Branch*), that group was a constantly changing one.

Many Chilean writers explain their national and class characteristics as hereditary; economic causes seem to interest them little. Alberto Cabero in *Chile y los Chilenos* says that the conquerors, soldiers from southern Spain with the daring and courage but also the laziness of the southerner, married Indian women and produced progeny who sank readily into a lower class. Later comers, " old Castilians " and Basques, with their northern blood and hardier virtues, took over commerce, agriculture, and mining. " The colonizing immigration preserved its blood pure or lightly mixed . . . its children, born in Chile, provoked and accomplished the revolution, seconded by the mestizos, and proudly governed the country, forming an oligarchy set at an enormous height above the governed mestizos, who, badly paid, performed the heavy work."

Chile's upper class has been steadily modified by newcomers from Europe, especially the northern countries. Among such Basque names as Larraín, Yrarrazával, Errazuriz, and Ochagavia, the social register lists many German, English, and Italian patronymics. But among the richest five families, as listed by *Fortune* in 1938, none have Spanish names. They are Couseño (Italian), Claude (French), Ross and Edwards (English), and Braun (German).

Cabero characterizes his people as " the least Latin of Spanish Americans. . . . Because we are less imaginative, less abulic, less passionate, and more practical and active than tropical Spanish Americans, we have been called the English of South America. There is a basis of truth in this.

. . . We are hospitable and active; we have push, physical and intellectual vigor; manly frankness; a wide-awake spirit, practical, assimilative, adventurous, and individual charm; we have domestic virtues and warlike qualities; and above all a patriotism not limited to boldness and self-sacrifice in war but which extends also in peace to that honesty in public men, seriousness of government, and international honor, which constitutes our racial pride."

Cabero is describing the nineteenth-century character, which, he laments, is being lost. The good old virtues have a way of disappearing, but happily they often turn up again in another guise in a younger generation.

In colonial days these dominant gentlemen were called *pelucones*, wigged ones, in contrast with the *pipiolos*, low-caste fellows. The power of the pelucones was enhanced by the institution of entailed estates; this assured the strengthening of the old families, who gathered unto themselves all threatening newcomers by marrying them in. The law of primogeniture was not abolished until 1857; the custom still persists. Though all children share in the heritage, the fundo is generally managed by the elder brother, who owns the big plantation house.

The actual work of the fundo is done by the descendant of the Spanish-Indian who worked the encomienda. Through the years many laws have been promulgated for his betterment, but as the illiterate laborer has seldom heard the news the effect on his actual situation has been slight. Spain, aware of its abuses, abolished the encomienda system in 1720. But the Indian still found that in order to eat he had to work for a master, that if he ran away he was hauled back, that no other master would employ him. At the end of the eighteenth century Ambrosio O'Higgins, that Irish Viceroy of Peru whose ideas were so far ahead of his time, abolished all encomiendas still existing. By that time the *Indio* had disappeared in the Chilean, who was known euphemistically as *inquilino*, tenant. As he had always been allowed to cultivate his own patch of ground in his off hours, this made no practical difference. Even the establishment of the Republic of Chile left him still a serf; his rulers were freedom-loving aristocrats.

Even with such suppressed and ambitionless labor, the vast, rich fundos produced plenty not only to support the family well at home, but to let them flourish splendidly abroad. Consequently there was no incentive to better their farming methods. They could disdain the example of the only considerable number of foreigners, the Germans in the southern swamps and forests, which the pelucones had never wanted anyway. They accumulated little capital. Foreign capitalists were building their railroads and later developing their mines. These activities, well taxed, even relieved the governing aristocracy of the need to tax themselves. It was, and to a certain extent still is, the most perfect imaginable system for the landowner. His desire for perfection could come out in the beauty of his gardens, the appointments of his stables, the fine-blooded racehorses he shipped all over the world. This is the Chile of song and story, whose lower classes appeared as the picturesque guaso squatting in the shade or moving leisurely across the fields with his oxen, driving fluffy flocks of sheep down shaded lanes, singing at night in front of his low-roofed house, or dancing and drunken at the harvest fiesta.

The classic scene appears to be doomed by world conditions. Chile felt the pinch when synthetic nitrates cut off the sale of natural nitrates as a rich source of taxes twenty years ago. The pressure of the modern world and the rising middle class is spreading literacy; people who read develop needs and wants; manufacturing is increasing; if the people will eat more than the typical fundo allowance of wheat and beans, Chile must raise more or distribute more evenly. For the beautiful fundo, so lush and lovely to look at, becomes — in the harsh light of statistics — a very unsatisfactory farm. Hubert Herring, who sees the truth through statistics, has worked it out in *Good Neighbors*. What with northern deserts, southern forested islands, and the steep Andes, Chile has only about 75,000 square miles of arable land out of her total of 285,000. That arable center is in holdings which vary from fundos of 500,000 acres down to tiny farms. But most of it — 52.4 per cent, to be exact — is owned in large estates by 626 people. What with unirrigated lands which are used for stock-raising and their lazy way of farming, only 8 per cent of this arable land is productively farmed. Intensive farming is almost unknown in Chile. Intensity is a trait incompatible with the character of the gentlemen of leisure who own the fundos. Old methods, of hand plows, ox-drawn carts, and inquilinos who will work for a few cents a day, produce all they need. Why push beyond that point? Only a vulgarian or a Yanqui — terms almost synonymous in Chile — would do that.

A confirmed democrat, believing that a country may reach its full stature, or even attain decency or safety, only by developing the full potentialities of all its citizens, has difficulty everywhere in understanding why the privileged few are so persistently shut-eye against realities. They know that no one class has a monopoly of either virtue or brains. They see their own aristocracy constantly recruited from " below." They admit that the " lower orders " (from which their forebears doubtless rose) are going to take their share of opportunity, power, and wealth. By yielding sensibly to the inevitable they could so easily avert the revolution they dread. Yet they persist in trying to make their dream come true by staying asleep. This is true in every country. No town in democratic United States is too small to illustrate the design. But in Chile the picture is exceptionally sharp and clear because Chile's lands and wealth still belong to such a small group. Advantaged by superior education, protected by wealth and reassured by the Church, they can blind themselves to what is actively going on around them.

Thinking thus, I traveled along that classic valley toward the capital. Just before dark we ran into Santiago. Fortunately it was a clear evening and we got the full force of the cordillera which dwarfs every puny human effort to build tall. Against a pale blue sky were peaks which looked not like solid mountain tops but like etchings in silver on blue: the blue of sky and the blue of mountain were the same. Then we were hustled across the station and into waiting coaches, which swung into a wide avenue with shade trees down the center. This is the Avenida Bernardo O'Higgins, formerly the Alameda, where colonial and early republican Santiago took the air. We passed the Civic Center, where the President lives in the Moneda Palace, turned into narrow Agustinas, and were landed at the Hotel Crillon. Santiago, noisy, bright, and gay. And a hotel filled with tourists and Chileans in the midst of the vermouth hour at eight o'clock.

X

SANTIAGO

SANTIAGO PRESENTS ITSELF TO THE TOURIST AS HOTELS, clubs, museums, drives through parks, hospitable people, and (especially from May to November) cold. Pedro de Valdivia wrote the Emperor Charles V that the city had only four months of winter, with infrequent rains and " such pretty suns that one need never go near the fire." Maybe. One can only conclude that that hot Spanish blood is warming in itself. The steam-heated Yankee more readily agrees with Don Pedro that the " sun is never importunate." But the cold is. It sweeps across the city from the overpowering Andes, pursues you into people's houses, sneaks up your back at dinner, invades your bedroom, your bath, even your bed. Chilean women wear sweaters at their own firesides (euphemism meaning home but not connoting fire) and fur coats at formal dinners. Northern visitors should provide themselves with well-lined garments, preferably fur, for indoor formal wear.

The hotels are good, and smartly thronged at the vermouth

hour. The men resemble North Americans, well groomed and well dressed, but with the Yanqui look of casualness rather than the high polish of the Latin. The women, except for a few in English tweeds, are distinctly Latin, but French. *Soignée*, with sleek hair, and the restrained elegance of shining black. Physically Chileans vary in type as much as any group in the United States, from short to tall, from fair to dark, from thin to fat.

Between vermouth and the dinner hour, which seldom begins before nine o'clock, the streets are at their giddiest. Shops may be closed behind iron shutters, but neon lights run along their fronts and signs flash on and off over the sidewalks. Magazine stalls display dozens of Chilean, South and North American publications gaudy in color and lurid in appeal, and venders offer Panama hats, Araucanian blankets, fat squirming puppies, and paper flowers. Motor horns, streetcar gongs, flat wheels screeching, and radios blaring make a deafening racket. Even hotels, restaurants, and clubs reverberate with mechanical din impossible to shriek through. Night-club singers hide their faces behind microphones which magnify their croonings into Gargantuan waterfalls of sound roaring around, above, and below the natural voice, which could quite adequately fill the hall without mechanical aid.

Dinner is a joy, for Chile dines on the best of everything. Crustaceans from Robinson Crusoe's isle, tender oysters and small lobsters of a delicacy unequaled, crabs and shrimps; Chile's special conger eel, congrio, and dozens of other fish. Even opulent Buenos Aires advertises Chile's seafood as the rarest treat. Fowl and meat are good, but fish and shellfish are superlative. And served with just the right white wine — dry and smooth and nutty — followed by Chile's savory vegetables dressed with cheese or excellent sauce, meat with salad and red wine, sugary dessert or fresh and juicy fruit — every Chilean dinner is a banquet.

Dozens of movie houses offer North American pictures, in English but with Spanish captions which convey the sense with none of the flavor. As many more specialize in Argentine and Mexican films in Spanish with favorite stars. Houses of exclusive news reels are always crowded. German propaganda in both news and dramatic form attracts German audiences, with a scattering of Chileans. Often, especially after Pearl Harbor, audiences would enthusiastically applaud the Stars and Stripes, President Roosevelt, or the United States Army or Navy in action. In one popular house a feeble patter of hands when Hitler appeared was hissed right down. When I mentioned that to a Chilean gentleman of the aristocratic and conservative branch, he made sure that I had actually attended a theater on the wrong side of the tracks where his compatriots did not smell nice. Then he said: " But clearly. An audience like that! " How could one say more plainly that Uncle Sam's friends are of the people, not the patricians?

The popular vaudeville house is the huge Balmaceda, which is so crowded that one can get a seat only by going with plenty of " *anticipación*." But the late arrival may have more fun, packed in among the pipiolos, who laugh and shout without restraint. The skits are always funny, generally very vulgar and quite comprehensible enough even if one has not Chile's racy Spanish of the streets. After such an hour it is fun to dine in a small spotty restaurant which specializes in native Chilean dishes and cheap wine, and where the waiter will readily discuss politics.

Santiago has no sparkling night clubs comparable with those of any other city of its size — a million inhabitants —

anywhere else. And the few it has advertise Argentine, Mexican, Brazilian, or even Russian performers. Only Chile's lower classes dare to be Chilean.

Always seeking native flavor, I visited La Plaza del Corregidor, almost the only spot in Santiago which retains any colonial character. Under the moon it was still and empty enough to suggest the sixteenth century, especially if one slanted one's glance to leave out an apartment house on one corner and to include an old iron gate and carved wooden balcony on the other. La Posada, said to be Santiago's oldest house, looks it, with its ancient pockmarked pink plaster, dark, overhanging eaves, and a sagging wooden door with an iron latch. Indoors, in the murky smoky light, tables were pushed close together and a solid mass of men and women sat entwined or rose to dance, close-gripped and scarcely moving their feet. The music was a thin stringed orchestra and the singers were the guests who joined in with humming and occasionally with shouts and table-poundings. It was most effective, at first. Only after we had been there awhile did its phoniness emerge. All those people were, like us, visitors from another sphere, come to see a low-life dive from which low life, averse to being looked at, had slipped away, leaving the curious to gaze at one another.

" Do you know anyone here? "

Our Chilean friend, not looking around, answered: " No. Nobody knows anyone here. This is a place where men bring their companions precisely because they do not wish to be recognized." So La Posada del Corregidor has that element of romance or mystery to offer. " Nice Chilean wives, of course, never come."

Outside the night was sweet and fresh with a snowy breeze from the cordillera, and a new moon clearer than a street light, though not as sharp as Orion above it. We strolled along then, as far as the Museo de Bellas Artes, where a few old houses are reminiscent of the early nineteenth century. There we were in the Parque Forestal, planted on land reclaimed when they pushed back and channeled the Rio Mapocho. Agustín Edwards says that the Quechua word Mapocho means " river that suppresses itself." It hides in the dry summer, but threatens in the rainy winter. That spring night it was pouring along a dark flood of snow waters, smelling of rich mud from many fundos it had watered.

Santiago is an easy city to know because it centers in the hill of Santa Lucía which rises between the Mapocho and the Alameda. Its history began there because Valdivia chose it for his first fortified camp and there his lady, Inez de Suárez, displayed that courage and originality which characterize the Chilean woman still. Left in command while Valdivia was away, she scotched treachery among his followers and disheartened the Indians by beheading seven chiefs held as hostages. This episode was most gorily portrayed in a modern opera of the lady's name. The heroine, sung by a stately Argentine in sweeping velvet robes, stood on the hill commanding. In impassioned song she overbore the less resolute males and with outstretched arm ordered off the savages' heads.

" Bang! " went the orchestra, and to shrieking voices a dripping head on a pike rose over the outer wall.

"Bang!" again, and another head, until seven bloody heads had risen and fallen with the music, and Valdivia's fortified hill had been saved for Spain.

Later Santa Lucía became identified with the softer side of the Chilean nature. In the 1870's a generous gentleman, rich in human understanding as well as cash, gave it to the city for a park. He was Benjamín Vicuña Mackenna, whose career swung him from youthful exile as a dangerous radical to most respectable posts as Congressman at home and diplomat abroad. Luis Galdames, a Chilean historian who died in 1941, evaluates Vicuña Mackenna as a diplomat who was a good collector of historical material and a historian having "ample imagination and ability to link documents together and thus to fill innumerable volumes — more than one hundred — but little else." But nobody need leave a better monument than Santa Lucía, which Vicuña Mackenna beggared himself and his wife to purchase and landscape.

One is stopped for a coin at the monumental, pillared entrance, as French as Versailles; but the rest of the hill is less formal, with lawns and flower beds between walks of orange-colored sand and the original rocky cliffs, now softened with hanging vines. Above are woods of dark, light, and gray green — heavy verdure interspersed with the flickering foliage of lacy pepper trees. The walks rise between stone walls and marble balustrades, to a chapel on the apex. Statues of Chile's opposed but equally venerated heroes stand at entrance and top: Caupolicán and Valdivia. All along the climb are views of the cordillera and of the hill of San Cristóbal, topped with a white statue of the Virgin, which is flood-lighted at night and to which the faithful make prayerful ascent, often on their knees. Subercaseaux describes San Cristóbal as " that hand which the Andes extends to warn that it [Santiago] may approach no nearer."

One evening I made the climb. Old gentlemen with newspapers sat near the bottom. On the first flat spot a young father was teaching his tiny daughter to ride her bicycle while the mother jiggled a baby in its pram. Above that, where I sat to puff, a group of well-dressed children with a nurse were playing a game; and a widow in deep weeds stood gazing at the view and wiping her eyes with a black-edged handkerchief. I bought a bottled drink to watch the coarsely pretty woman who sold it and a tattered roto whom she treated to a beer. His shoes were split, but polished, a well-knotted tie covered a dirty shirt, his hat was gallantly set, and his posings were straight out of Chile's national dance, the *cueca*. His affair was progressing though by no means accomplished when I set out for the top. Students paced the lanes studying aloud for the exacting examinations, which can be passed, it seems, only by learning a mass of matter by rote. Now and then a boy and girl studied together. But most couples had more pressing interests as they walked or sat embraced, always entranced and with their backs to the view or to the passers-by.

Every opening in the trees offered another view of the busy city's tall buildings and moving traffic, all of it dwarfed and minimized by the Andes' majestic peace. I know no city of like size which is so dominated by mountains. The cordillera forever lures the eyes to infinite heights outlined in snow against the monotone pale blue of mountain and sky. Below Santa Lucía is the National Library, entered from Avenida O'Higgins. It is a double avenue and its center near the old red brick Church of San Francisco is the fresh and fragrant flower market. The National University and the Catholic University face O'Higgins and dozens of streetcars, buses, and automobiles zoom along it toward the newer, smarter residence districts.

The National University is the hub of the city and of the country as ours never are. Students, instead of being absorbed in sports, are strongly partisan and often play a decisive role in politics. And professors are not cool observers of affairs from a cautious cloister, but are practicing professional men and women active and influential in medicine, the law, newspaper work, or government service. I found them the most illuminating commentators on Chilean life and manner of thought and notable for the keen wit and breadth of vision typical of the best Chilean minds.

One day I asked one of them at tea to explain Chile's political parties. He took out paper and pencil, reviewed his country's history for a century, delicately differentiated between Liberal, Radical, and Conservative, each with its own Right, Left, and Center; he explained how the Communists, swinging easily from anti- to pro- and back again to anti-Nazi, could claim credit for the Frente Popular; he showed how parties had swung around each other; how the Church had managed never to lose influence without ever gaining control; how labor was gaining both.

" Perhaps," he suggested, " the only way to attain stability is with a dictator."

" And then how does one get rid of the dictator? "

" Oh, that's easy in Chile. A *golpe de estado* (a *coup d'état*).

But seriously he averred: " Socialism is bound to come. Only the state can prevent that private exploitation whose results are always bad. And our dominant parties, like yours, are inevitably swinging that way."

The more he talked, and the better I seemed to grasp each point he made, the more confused I found myself. Only his summing up gave me hope that a mere foreigner might understand how Chilean politics come about if not what they actually are. Laughing at my bewilderment, he handed me his diagrams, outlines, and lists.

" I'll tell you how to get this straight. Just remember that we Chileans are as true to our one Church as you Yanquis are to your two political parties. And that we start a new political party as readily as you start a new religion." So that's the way it is; anybody could understand that.

The business section lies between O'Higgins and the Plaza de Armas, which Valdivia laid out after Inez de Suárez had the Indians under control. The Cathedral is there on the site of the first church; the post office; several old-fashioned hotels; and on two sides those covered arcades typical of Latin America, which has not gone too far in aping the United States. Between the inside stores and booths along the street is a continuous moving mass of people. At noon they stand to munch sandwiches, or sit enthroned for a shine while they read the midday editions. For those who would lunch more elegantly there is the remarkable Chez Henri, where everything is of the best, exquisitely served, and as immaculate as few of Santiago's eating-places are.

The Plaza de Armas is the city's heart; all its emotions pulsate there. Even the bootblack eagerly discusses presidential candidates, *"imperialismo Yanqui,"* Communists, and war. Often a roto orator mounts a soapbox and gathers a considerable audience to hear his diatribes against northern capitalism, local landlordism, and low wages. Such an orator one evening pounded his chest and with alcoholic hoarseness insisted, over and over: *" Soy roto, yo! Soy roto Chileno!"*

This roto is not a new figure in the Chilean scene. He is the vigorous misfit who kicked loose from the meeker inquilino class as early as colonial days and began to form gangs of independent and drifting laborers. Often denied farm work by hacendados who stood together, the drifting rotos worked the mines, hacked or blasted out the Andean cliffs

La Moneda, the Presidential Palace

Santa Lucia Rises in
the Center of Santiago

for railroads and motor roads, herded on the Argentine pampas, stole when they had to, fought when anybody dropped a hat, were proud as their Spanish sires and fierce as their Araucanian grandmothers. Everybody agrees that the roto is a man: strong, tough, hard, courageous, adaptable, and unconquerable. He has fought and won all Chile's wars, and all Chileans are proud of him. A few are beginning to write knowingly about him: notably Manuel Rojas in short stories of migratory workers in the Andean valleys of the northern mines. And José Gonzales Vera, whose *Vidas Minimas* (*Little Lives*) is an unforgettable picture of how the poor live in the *conventillos*, the sprawling lightless apartment houses in Santiago and Valparaiso. These authors, who have lived with the poor, write of them with knowledge and the sympathy which does not preclude seeing wickedness as well as mistreatment. Their books, translated into English, would help us to understand Chile.

For the roto carries the germ of the future. As long as Chile's aristocratic branch held control, the roto was an outlaw who responded naturally by becoming a dangerous one. Denied any responsible share in government, even honest work, he responded, as strong men do, by becoming violently revolutionary. Now, however, with the growth of liberalism and the opportunity to express himself at the polls, this broken one is picking himself up and putting himself together in political parties and labor unions. As his powers grow so do his responsibilities. It begins to appear that even Chile's rotos will obey laws they help to make. As many of those laws provide for better health, better schools, better living and working conditions, and as the roto always has been an enterprising and intelligent fellow, there is every reason to believe that he will produce the men Chile needs.

Two streets connect the Plaza de Armas with the Alameda, which Avenida O'Higgins is still popularly called. They are Bandera, the man's street with banks and big business houses; and Ahumada, the woman's street of clothes shops and tearooms. *Ahumada 75*, by a young Bolivian, Luis Toro Ramallo, is less a novel than quick sketches of a boarding-house on that street. The boarders include a student who courts the landlady's daughter on Santa Lucía; a social climber; a rundown gentlewoman; and a family of Jewish refugees. The theme, aside from days and nights along the street, is the gradual rise of the Jews who lend money to the ambitious landlady and in time own the house and put her out. I understood then why the book had been recommended to me by a German-Chilean. For Germany is making clever anti-Semitic propaganda, and it is true that Jewish refugees, brought in to work the land, tend to drift to the towns, where their industry, thrift, and enterprise often outdo and dispossess the more easy-going Chileans. But it is not only a Jewish problem.

Santiago, like every city in the Americas, faces a growing stream of refugees. Beginning with Loyalists from Spain, it has been augmented by a polyglot swarm of people from every European country. The richest are welcomed into the highest society; as splendid spendthrifts they dominate the smart hotels and casinos. Those who have a little money to invest do well, but often fail to make friends because they offer a brisker competition than Chileans relish.

Both these groups suggest that the real threat for us in the influx of refugees is that they bring Europe's sick mentality. A curious compound of fear of what they have left, scorn of what they have found, and a determined hope that the United States will save them yet.

An older woman, who had fled her home just ahead of the Nazi entry, shuddered at every item of war news. " Hitler will come here! " she would cry, pointing dramatically at the floor. " Nothing can stop him. You will see. You do not know. *You cannot know!* " At the same time she had only scorn for the country which had given her family sanctuary and a chance to make a good living. " This country has nothing! These people know nothing! " To her, not only Chile but all the Americas lacked everything of value. That the Europe she knew was forever gone only made her more intolerant of new and different standards.

Trust in the United States, and doubt too, were best expressed by a rich, strong, and handsome Frenchman of military age. He drove an expensive car, was popular with the smartest society, and much annoyed that the United States was tardy about sending a rescuing force to his country.

Such people have not come like the immigrants of former days, infused with courage and eagerness. They are already defeated, shattered in spirit. They are sure to modify the American scene. Will they affect the character which has conquered the whole hemisphere? Can we save the American spirit of youth from this hopelessness of age? The most encouraging signs are found in the largest group — the poorer refugees who often need immediate aid, who are always seeking jobs, but who have no tradition of ease and who expect a struggle.

On the downtown streets they stand humbly proffering trinkets for sale or offering to buy in a voice so low as to suggest crime. " Men's clothes, I buy." " Hats, I buy." " Ladies' shoes, I buy."

They dispose of them in the Vega Market. There along the river Santiago's poor buy Santiago's discards. In hundreds of stalls are the old hats, shoes, dresses, and suits. Others show old metal goods, from broken sieves and handless knives to fine old brass candelabra, " hand of Fatima " knockers, and braziers on tripods. Nothing is too battered or too dirty for somebody's use; often real treasures reward the diligent searcher. There is not much native handicraft, but some horse-hair work is amusing; there are reed baskets, quite sturdy enough, I found, for shipping books; some leather and wood-work that is attractive. But the greatest fun there, as in any market, is watching the people. They bargain violently and with the bitterness of folk to whom a copper coin represents hours of toil. They laugh gustily, poke one another, spit side-ways, and buy drinks of fruit juice with heavy allowances of sugar. Venders splash glasses and spoons in and out of cold water, and then pour water from the same jar into the next purchaser's drink. Back from the river, under cover, are food stalls of indescribable filthiness, black with flies.

Santiago is a sports-conscious city. There are private clubs and public playgrounds for all tastes. At one country club British and Yanquis swing clubs and rackets or dine and dance; a French club is notable for excellent tennis and smart spectator costumes; and a German one boasts a cinder track, rifle range, gymnastic apparatus, and an open-air beer pa-vilion. International meets are forever going on with con-testants from both Western continents. Racing is the national pastime, vice, or charitable money-raiser as one sees it. All are worth a look. All are like the same thing in other coun-tries. But the most typically Santiagueño sport is bus-riding and its variant, streetcar travel.

There are two types of buses. *Gondolas,* so called, presum-ably because they have a stately motion, are upper-class; nobody is allowed to stand in the aisles. At important points like the corner of the *Congreso* a starter passes out tokens which entitle one to a seat — though one may have to wait hours to get it. Patient queues of legislators, students, shoppers, office and shop workers, stand reading or chatting until a gondola with an empty seat appears and then board it in order and courteous form. The impatient may grab a *micro* — so called perhaps because of their lesser size. Grab is the only word for the manner of boarding a micro, especially in a busy hour. These are smaller, dirtier buses, jam-packed with fleas and people. They seem to have no off hours; all hours are hectic. Seats are forever occupied and one must stand lurching, held upright only by one's lurching neighbors. Or one may chance a streetcar, which is also class-conscious in that the front car costs twenty centavos while in the open trailer one may ride exposed to the weather for ten. The mortification of streetcar-riding is that one must see all the buses pass — gondolas and micros whizzing grandly on while the streetcar stops on every corner — and note that they, so full downtown, offer plenty of empty seats. Besides, traveling on a track lacks the sporting element of swaying with a wildly careening bus as the driver makes it leap for every hole in traffic, scraping fenders, cutting in ahead of rival buses and even chauffeured limousines, honking indignantly, failing to see would-be passengers hailing hopefully on corners, and pouring plumes of smoke and smell in the faces of defeated rivals. Naturally such a driver has no time for dilatory or cautious passengers. He will stop, yes. But to board a bus one must be ready to leap on the second; to leave it one must be standing with poised foot or one will be carried on to the next stop. Bus-riding has all the sporting elements of taking chances and getting exercise.

Santiago has whatever one asks of a city of a million inhabitants. The wealthy visitor, or the one who is wealthy only by grace of the exchange between dollars and pesos, can indulge his plutocratic tastes at hotels, clubs, the Club Hipodrome, Chile's famous racecourse, or country clubs, ski lodges, and beach resorts as elegant and exclusive as he may like. For those who like small-town ways Santiago offers the most engaging. For strolling around the Plaza de Armas or along the Alameda is as productive of entertainment as any village center. Early Sunday Mass followed by breakfast in the smart hotels and the later parade along Ahumada, where middle-class ladies go to show off their shining permanently waved hair under preposterously inadequate hats, their " Chilean-made " shoes, which have far more heel than either top or toe, and their bright clothes. In Chile the lower one goes in the social scale, the gayer the women's colors. And Santiago has many miles of homes where, after all, most of the life goes on. Big house or small, apartment or conventillo, the real life of Chile is found at home.

What the tourist sees is Santiago, certainly. But is it Chile? Does the Yanqui living in Chile see Chile? And what does Chile make of the Yanqui?

XI

YOU YANQUIS

N OUR BUSTLING EAGERNESS TO MAKE FRIENDS WITH LATIN
America perhaps we are overlooking one very important
party to the transaction. Do we know who is seeking friendship to the south? Can we even imagine how the North American looks to the people who receive his protestations, his
emissaries, his literature, and his loans? Doubtless the people
who have formulated and are carrying out the Good Neighbor
policy have a very definite North American in mind — a
sturdy, friendly fellow with democratic principles, honesty
of purpose, and nothing remotely resembling an ulterior
motive. We also know, in our several ways, the "American
South" with whom this Yankee wishes to deal. We have, in
fact, written for ourselves quite a literature on that subject.
But the *Yanqui* whom the American South sees remains to
us an unknown, even an unsuspected character. Even his name,
Yanqui, has connotations so different from our conception
of Yankee that not even the most unreconstructed Southerner
need cavil at the title.

Because United States does not form a euphonious ad-

131

jective — even in Spanish *Estado-unidense* is awkward — and the world-wide application of American to us offends Latin America, a substitute was inevitable. Mexico uses *gringo*. Hubert Herring, in his excellent *Good Neighbors*, has given us " Americans North" as opposed to "Americans South "; and that is good because it is relative. Canadians are north, Mexicans are south of us, though not in South America. But in Chile Yanqui is the common designation for a citizen of the United States. And in Chile it first dawned on me that the Yanqui was a well-defined personality with surprising virtues and vices, some of them so exaggerated as to obstruct any clear and adult understanding between us. Unfortunately for us, Americans South have not make quick trips across the United States and written superficial impressions of our quaint and curious ways, nor how we seem to be adapting ourselves to their superior civilization. They should by all means do this. We, Americans North, greatly need to know what our neighbors think of us. But until those books are available in English, I offer a few notes on the Yanqui which were jotted down during several months in Chile.

This did not come about through design; with true Yanqui complacency I was not concerned with what Chileans thought of us; I was thinking about them. But it soon became apparent that Chileans are sensitively, even painfully aware of us. Many conversations in that country sooner or later get round to polite questions about " you Yanquis," to categorical statements, or even to half-humorous " the trouble with you Yanquis — " From such talks a character begins to take shape, even a whole family of characters with whom Chile is dealing while we plunge blindly ahead in the smug assurance that Chile knows us as we think we are. It is easy to say that Chileans are often mistaken, to cite instances in disproof of every trait the Chilean considers typically Yanqui. But the truth or falsity of the picture is of little consequence; this fictitious character is, for better or worse, the Yanqui against whom Chile judges what we do or say.

The Chilean knows, first, the Yanqui in Chile. A youth of the port of Valparaiso was offered a scholarship in the United States. He wanted to go, but . . .

" All I knew of Yanquis," he said, " was what I had seen at Valpo: drunken sailors who insulted our women and smashed everything. They always offered to pay for what they smashed, but that to us was only added insult, for it made so clear how little our pesos were worth against their dollars. We didn't want their dirty dollars (that's the way it seemed to us) ; we wanted them to treat us and our things with respect. So I went to the States with real trepidation. I was very young, you see. I had never traveled. I thought all Yanquis were ill-bred savages and when I got to New York and found how well mannered the people were and how kind, I couldn't believe it."

Sailors ashore are rowdy the world over. But men doing business in a foreign country might be expected to put themselves out to make friends, to respect the customs of the land where they live. Yet this summation is typical:

" Your men are interested only in business, they can talk nothing but business. They pay no attention to our politics unless their precious dollars are threatened. They do not read our books. And one of them making a serious study of our history, even of our relations with his own country, is unthinkable. They are smugly, blindly unaware that we have a culture, that a life might be founded on anything besides business."

A sterner indictment of the business man is related of so

many men in so many situations that there must be truth back of it somewhere. This version was told by a professor in one of Chile's universities:

"One of our professors took his students to visit a great Yanqui plant. It is a splendid enterprise and well worth study. The group was conducted about by a young Yanqui who was very casual, almost rude. But our professor, who happens to be half English and a graduate of an English university, knows you Yanquis well. So he put on his Oxford accent and his most insufferable British manner. At once the Yanqui changed his tone to one of complete courtesy. He even asked the group to spend the night, offering the professor a room in the company guest house where ' you won't have to associate with the natives.' Remember that the professor was a ' native ' on the other side."

The professor who told the story will never forget it; whether he was Nazi or not I cannot say. But this is the sort of thing that the Nazis gleefully use against us.

Impossible to explain in Chile, where only gentlemen are educated, the ill-bred Yanqui was probably the graduate of some hinterland college where he might have had excellent technical training without acquiring either culture or manners. We need not be ashamed of him because he is a product of our universal education; he has done well in the line he chose; his children will do better; they may even attain a culture capable of appreciating a foreign country. But we must deplore the fact that he has for so long been almost the only Yanqui Chile knew. The cultivated, considerate gentlemen we have also sent to Chile are always so unobtrusive (according to their kind) that they are looked upon as exceptions. "You would never take him for a Yanqui," is high praise in Chile.

The wives of these business men — with some notable exceptions — Chileans brush aside with light scorn.

" The Yanqui woman never interests herself in Chile, seldom bothers to speak a decent Spanish, knows nothing of our literature or history. She stays apart from our life, gets her clothes from the States, plays bridge with her friends, goes home as soon as she can."

Yanqui women, on their part, complain that Chilean women do not welcome them. This is true for different reasons involving different classes. The small-town Chilean woman, who would be the natural friend of the Podunk woman living in Chile, does not speak English. And the Chilean woman who does speak English belongs to an aristocratic and very exclusive society. Until the war she lived in Europe more than in her own country, she moved among people of great names if not great titles. Chilean society is as inaccessible to many business men and their wives as the society of — say — Philadelphia or Boston, if not more so. When Yanqui women complain of Chilean women, or vice versa, it is interesting to learn what class of woman in each case is speaking and what class she is talking about.

So much for the Yanqui living in Chile. Though many are liked, even loved, the casual visitor with an ear cocked for both good and bad hears more bad than good. The Yanqui in Chile must mend his manners if he (including she) is going to make a vital contribution to international understanding and goodwill.

The impermanent Yanqui, traveling expensively through the country or staying a short time for study, as a government representative, or (most suspect of all) to write a book, has much to answer for. Now and then one hears heartfelt praise, and the terms of approbation are suggestive.

A professor of Chile's national university spoke of a member of our Embassy, recently transferred. " Eddie Trueblood alone could solve all the problems of cultural relations between us. He dominated Castilian (as the Spanish phrase it), and he could use Chilean slang; he knew our history, had read our classics, and kept up with modern books; his best friends were Chileans." Of a student of Chilean literature: " He became one of us. His printed studies of Chilean literature show deep understanding of the idiom and the mode of thought." Of another: " He and his wife became so much a part of Santiago that their going leaves a gap in our social and cultural life. They both spoke Spanish, they worked with the Instituto Chileno Norte Americano de Cultura; they sang in the Ambassador's choir; they were Chileans to us."

Another and a sadder story was told of a group of students from a small college in the United States. Off on a junket, they appeared more frequently in the night clubs than in the lecture halls; they put their feet on the plush seats of special railroad coaches supplied them as a courtesy; they failed to attend cultural or even social events planned for them. On one occasion, when they had been invited to a handsome home, so few of the honor guests showed up that Chilean friends of the United States hastily substituted other Yanquis so that the exquisite buffet supper should not go untasted, that the rude disregard of hospitality should not be too apparent. But it was apparent. That group of students has confirmed Chile's impression that all Yanquis are uncultured and ill-mannered. Many generations of decenter students will have difficulty in changing that opinion.

Writers are looked upon with suspicion. As why should they not be? There is something impudent about bouncing into a country, uninvited, to write about it. A citizen might reasonably inquire: " Who are you, anyway? How dare you assume that you are fitted to write about us? Why should we who live here suffer being presented to your countrymen as we happen to strike you? Is your judgment any good? Is your heart in the right place? Can you speak our language, appreciate our point of view? Do you know our history, our literature? Are you going to stay long enough, study hard enough, to qualify on any of these points? "

Chileans do not formulate these questions, but they were implicit in many remarks.

A woman professor, looking at me with a calculating eye, said: " The most charming and clever Yanqui woman I ever knew lived at a mine. She studied Spanish, published a little paper in English which she filled up with news and items of interest about Chile. She studied at our university and read our books. She stayed five years. When we asked her why she did not write a book about Chile, she said she did not know enough."

A male colleague of hers said: " The trouble with you Yanquis is that you don't stay long enough. . . . You are staying longer? Good! But not long enough. . . . And these Yanqui newspapermen who stay four days, talking in bars with young exchange students who have some figures but who understand nothing, and then write a book *explaining* Chile — well! " Spanish is rich in explosive expressions of scorn.

So Chile judges us by the examples we send. But the Yanqui Chile knows from the movies and rounds out by hearsay is an even more fantastic character. Gangsters, cowboys, divorcees, rich décors, flip youngsters, colleges dedicated to sports, government riddled with graft, homes rife with dissension have produced a composite conception that marks even mature judgments. Impossible to explain that movies select the striking and unusual; that the every day dullness of the law-abiding citizen, the modest home, the student who studies, the honest and efficient public servant lack dramatic appeal. To an extent truly alarming, Chile judges the American home as something fairly represented by *The Philadelphia Story*, *The Women*, or *Susan and God*. And Yanqui women are more misunderstood than men because the contrast is so sharp between the Chilean girl who is educated in a convent and guarded at home and the Yanqui girl who goes to school with boys, plays and works with them and grows up to have a vote and a job.

The mildest judgment of the North American mother comes out in such comments as this:

" Of course your mothers feel no responsibility for their families as we do. We always have to be with the grandmother, with the children, or the husband. You believe in individual rights; you let the old folks and the children look out for themselves. If your women tire of a husband or fall in love with another man, they divorce and remarry; they insist upon their right to be happy. We Chileans are all married to the wrong men because we never know our husbands before marriage. Of course we are unhappy, but we stay with the wrong man for the sake of the children. Our children are our greatest concern, much greater than our own happiness."

Thinking of our intense young mothers with their books, magazines, and lectures on infant care and child psychology, their constant concern that pre-school children shall not be left to servants, I asked: " Where did you get the notion that our mothers feel no concern for their children? "

" From the movies," she laughed, but went on to propound a truly disturbing question. " Please answer me frankly, I have heard it said so often that all your girls begin life at thirteen or fourteen. Is that really true? "

" You mean mature? "

" No, begin to live, to know men. We hear that your way of educating boys and girls together leads naturally to babies; that all your girls — well, maybe not all — but it is the custom for girls to have babies very young, that there are great institutions to care for them; that the girls then enter a life of freedom and adventure and marry late. A friend of mine who was there said one seldom sees young mothers in the United States; that only mature women have legitimate babies."

This speech so overwhelmed my amazed brain that I could only muster up a few denials. I had recently read that the average girl in the United States marries at twenty or twenty-two. I said, but doubt that I was believed, that young people can study and play together without the need of maternity homes. But how can one combat such misinformation? My questioner, who was more than half convinced by what she had heard, was a woman of good family, with a sixteen-year-old daughter, well read, widely traveled (in Europe, not in the United States), a writer, a person of much more than average intelligence.

Later I quoted this conversation to a sensible social worker, a Chilean woman who had studied and worked in the United States and knew our failures as well as our successes. She was grave.

" Yes, such tales are widely believed. The movies partly. Propaganda too. We are not free of magazines which feature the worst Yanqui pictures and lurid news stories as generally true. . . .

139

"But it is more serious that we find you on the whole simple and gullible. I know from my social work that trust is the best way to bring out the good in a person. Chileans do not believe that. They see pictures of your boys and girls together in sports, in swimming suits, unchaperoned; they think you are fooled in your belief that no evil comes of it.

"Yet your American homes, filled with confidence, are wonderful, the happiest homes I have ever seen. And happiness is what you want most, isn't it? With us it is not so. Our mothers tell us to expect unhappiness with our husbands, with our children. . . . We are a lot of neurotics compared with you. A Chilean woman believes that if she loves her husband she must hang on him, if she loves her children she must hang over them and spoil them. Your methods, in comparison, are " — she sought a word — " so professional. In a family everyone is an individual, everyone's rights are respected. I think your confidence sometimes amounts to simplicity. But I think too that you avoid more evils with your methods than we ever do with ours."

Another Chilean woman, who knew only New York, found there a special and curious simplicity. Our guilelessness is a theme dear to Chileans.

"Your young people take themselves so seriously, they have none of the Chilean's deprecating humor. A young Yanqui will say: 'I have a very interesting and unusal job. I'm head of my section in the corset department' (or in the drug-store lunch counter or the hot-dog factory). They push it to the utterly ridiculous. A sober youngster will say: 'I am a writer . . . three plays, a short story. . . . Well, I haven't published anything yet, but I have such and such contacts, hopes. . . .'"

"A Chilean would die before he called himself a writer

unless he had a long list of notable books to his credit — but *notable!* He'd be laughed at until he couldn't stand it. The great difference is that you Yanquis have a self-respect we lack. Each Yanqui feels himself a person of consequence. He has pride in himself, in his job. He is not afraid. We are afraid of ridicule, of failure, we are afraid to try. A Yanqui of ordinary talent can develop and train himself, get ahead, make a success. Here he would be lost."

This brings us to the Chileans who have been in the United States. As a rule they admire our country and like us. Many of them battle for us against their own. Even when their critical observation pierces our pretentiousness and their humor our bumptiousness, their mature judgment sees the virtues inherent in the vices, respects the fine principles on which our government is founded, and has confidence in our goal if not always in our ability to keep steering toward it.

Thus:

The young student who feared that our entire population acted like drunken sailors in Valparaiso finished his story.

"I called up my courage and went. I am a scientist; I wanted to see what was being done in my line. New York was not so good for a South American. But when I got beyond that — I went as far as California — I found the real Americans — kind, friendly, hospitable, generous.

"Your people are generous as Europeans have never been. In Paris I called on the Director of the Pasteur Institute. He received foreigners, they told me, only on Thursday. So I stayed over almost a week to see him. The day I called he made me wait over an hour. And when he did receive me he would give me nothing; his knowledge was a secret to guard against foreigners. In Washington, in contrast, when I went to the bureau which interested me, I was received at once by the chief; in two minutes I was sitting at his desk. And he gave me every aid he could, let me see everything. I did not feel like a stranger in the United States, but like a colleague."

A Chilean girl who spent four years in United States colleges said:

"At first I found the girls too naïve and simple for any use. We, in our *liceos,* had deep philosophical talk, discussions of music or art. Those Yanqui girls seemed to have no intellectual interests at all. But afterward I found they could talk well if they were asked. Their frivolity was a front; back of it they worked hard, and they played hard too — at sports or at week-end dates. And they were marvelously friendly to me. I was taken to the loveliest houses and made to feel so at home.

"I liked the girls' college better. I was in a coeducational one too; but there the competition was as fierce as in a jungle. Sororities make treaties, but their real ethic is a tooth-and-claw one. And the get-your-man struggle is a fight to the death with no rules respected. In comparison the girls college was filled with a wonderful spirit of mutual helpfulness and co-operation.

"I'd like to live in the States, yes. The Yanqui is probably the best husband in the world. But as long as I teach, I'd rather live in Chile. Here there is more chance to use your ideas; we are just starting. There you have to fit into a rigid system; your ideas are no good until you have taken many degrees and are too old to have a new idea."

It is only fair to state that this young woman teaches in the only progressive school in Chile.

Older travelers, perhaps more guarded in what they say, dwell on other qualities which are, after all, not incompatible with gullibility and lack of subtlety.

One, a Chilean newspaper man who spent months working and traveling in the United States, said:

"To me the most impressive quality of the United States was its spirituality — yes, spirituality. I expected commercialism, materialism, preoccupation with money. I found people everywhere concerned with the general welfare, generous in giving money and support to every effort for good.

"And hospitable! Surely there never was such hospitality! Not labored like ours, but casual and completely sincere. They seem to say: 'So here you are! Well, make yourself at home!' And they mean just that. With none of our protestations they make you feel really at home and free to do as you like.

"And kind! Even in your hectic great cities a Yanqui will stop in full flight to understand a South American's halting question, to give directions, even to walk along and show the way."

A woman, who knew only New York, had another impression.

"Any other city," she said, "could be known from reading about it. New York, never, because its most notable quality is its rhythm. Without having felt that, one can never know New York. Everybody is caught in its pace. Let one fall fainting or injured and who can stop to help? Nobody! If one pauses a second on a subway stair he loses his train, misses his connection, arrives late, loses his job. For no human consideration prevails against the rate and pace of the machine."

This Doña Julia had never beheld the throngs that gather round an accident, free to stand gaping until the police push them aside for stretcher-bearers, doctor, and nurse. The importance of her observation seems to be in her impression of a life so geared to the machine that all human values are lost.

An old scholar and gentleman just back from his first visit to the United States had also noted a human lack. He rose to greet me in his library, with busts of the philosophers on the tall bookcases and books piled everywhere, but sank promptly back into the armchair which he had long ago shaped to fit his every curve.

" I should have gone when I was younger," he smiled. " At almost eighty one is too old to stand the excitement, to accustom oneself to strange ways. Meal hours were new to me, and the quantity of food seemed very little. As you know, we Chileans eat too much. And glasses of water with ice in them to take with meals? No, no, I could never do that after a lifetime of Chilean wines.

" And in the United States there are no servants. All my life I have had four or five people to answer my bell, to attend me, to lay out my clothes, to hand me things. In your country there are no servants, only employees. . . . It's democracy, I know. I admire it, I believe in it, I've been a democrat all my life. But I couldn't live it."

A Chilean woman who has lived in our country and really studied it summed us up as she found us at home. This may offer some solace for what Chileans think of us in Chile.

" After three visits to the United States," she said, " I began to gets its essence. Especially after a three-cornered trip I made to the U. S., to Europe, and back to your country again. We are so much closer to Europe than you are. I saw that. I felt your freshness, your youth, your simple directness. Compare Charles Boyer in *El Puerto de Oro* (*Hold Back the Dawn* in English) with the innocent school teacher played by Olivia de Haviland and you will see what I mean. We are closer to the complicated European with his mixed motives, his indirections, his distrust of everyone. You have faith as we have not. In spite of our reputed Catholicism you are much more religious. People talk about their religion. Curious! They always asked me what my religion was. It gave me such a shock the first time. One would never do that in Chile. Never!

" But you Yanquis are completely frank. You say what you think; you are direct and honest. That is why, often, we find you crude. We cannot bear the full clear light you shed. We are afraid to see too much. We do not trust one another as you do. You really have no classes. There are rich and poor and social cliques, but there is constant movement among groups. You have no rigid class lines as we have. The United States, compared with any other country I have known, is a true democracy. Men meet on a level, deal honestly. There is complete unity among you."

This was leaving me even more breathless than some of the critical remarks I had heard. " Unity? " I recalled our politics, our isolationists, our professional howlers. " Unity of what? "

" In your fundamental belief in liberty, in the value and dignity of the individual, in your tolerance. . . ."

" Ojala! " I said using the expressive Spanish ejaculation which comes from the Arabic and means: " Oh, Allah! May it be so! "

XII

LIFE IN PROVIDENCIA

[RESIDENCIAL]

WHEN I SETTLED IN A *residencial*, WHICH SOUNDS more elegant than a boarding-house, my address brought forth a query. " What does Providencia mean? Delightful living? Special delivery? Or just *In God we trust*? "

It means pleasant living in a good residential district, not too exclusive for a few places which welcome the temporary sojourner. It also includes private schools — Northern Methodist, German, and Catholic — to which nice little girls are escorted every morning. Only adult relatives in good standing are acceptable as escorts; no servants and no light-headed brothers who might presumably serve other than fraternal interests. All day the pupils are guarded behind high walls and locked iron gates until the properly certified representative comes to conduct them home at evening. Only the oldest students are permitted to walk the streets unchaperoned, and they only in groups.

Homes as well as schools are barricaded. Doorbells are outside the gate, and the visitor is scrutinized by a servant with a key who opens only when she is assured that no evil is

146

intended. One misses moats and drawbridges, which would enhance the effect of vigilance and offer a challenge to architects' imaginations. But there are no moats in Providencia; only a quiet little stream purling along in the gutter. Gardens, as seen through the barred gates, are lovely: fragrant with lilacs, iris, and pinks, and ready for outdoor living, with garden furniture around lily pools. Architecture is of the varied and mixed styles common to such suburbs. As in Chile it is customary for an architect to sign and date each house, one easily follows changing fads. Many of the architects' names are German as are street names and names on those heavy, locked gates. Locked gates are an old Spanish custom, but neighborhood gossip hinted that there might be more danger from within those comfortable villas than from without. Several were pointed out as arsenals against a possible *Tag* for Chile.

My landlady kept her gate locked always, and at night all the lower windows were shuttered and barred. She was very disciplinary with me. Yanquis, she said, were criminally careless, with no understanding of the dangers of Chile. So I carried a gate key and a house key, tried to remember to lock everything, and waited with interest for the attack to begin. Unfortunately — for writing a thriller — nothing untoward ever happened. Even Ana the maid, who was introduced as a probable thief as well as a sloven and an impudent " type," kept the house immaculate, was most respectful, and never took so much as a bobby pin off the floor. But life is exciting in a houseful of women who expect danger at every turn.

Chile lives from hand to mouth as unrefrigerated countries must. Early every morning the bread man loudly pealed the bell and handed the rolls in to Ana, running out with the key. Meanwhile the landlady had gone round the corner to the milk station, which she endorsed as handling milk " with as much cleanliness as any North American establishment." One could smell its cow smells long before reaching the blue and white archway which a counter had transformed into a shop. In response to a hand bell a woman would slide back a panel and expose a tin milk pail covered with a white cloth. Shooing off the flies, she dipped and poured the milk into the purchaser's pitcher and hung up the dipper ready for the next.

Flies in Chile are an accepted part of life. Screens, in that country which produces more copper than any other in the world, are too expensive for any but the richest. And even the richest are not annoyed by flies.

A doctor said: " Our medical men find the North American phobia against flies rather amusing than anything else. We don't see them, you know; I mean we literally *do not see* flies."

My landlady said: " But if you have no flies in your houses, where do they go? "

After the rolls-and-coffee breakfast I worked at an open window above the garden, freshened by a spraying hose. It was a quiet street, but something passed every few minutes. Two-wheeled carts with three horses hitched abreast: heavy ones carrying grain or rubbish, and smart little ones as gaily painted as in Sicily, carrying bread. Nursemaids in uniform trying to make lively children walk decorously. Ladies and their maids going to market. Maids alone scooting along or lingering for gossip. Men with fruit in baskets, chanting: " Strawberries, fresh and ripe. Cherries, cheap and good. Apricots. See the apricots." At every gate there would be long haggling before a sale was made. A fat woman with a balloon twice her size poised on her head: a sheetful of clothes to wash. Boys pedaling slowly on tricycles fitted up to carry ices, trilling their bells and calling their wares. They came in the afternoon when it was getting hot, and then too came the singers — ragged fellows with guitars or accordions and one with a monkey, who knew our favorites and sang the right one in front of each gate, through which a coin was sure to come.

Almost as musical was the " ol' clo' man," whose chant in Spanish would have been no offense in a cathedral.

> " I buy bottles,
> I buy old papers,
> I buy clothes — mens' and ladies'
> I buy hats and old shoes.
> I buy, I buy. . . ."

My favorite place for lunch was El Capulín, the Cherry Tree, arranged inside like a Mexican patio and serving a few well-cooked dishes. No less than an hour would suffice for a two-course meal. Two waiters, in spotless aprons, moved pontifically from tiled table to well-stocked bar (but no beer, only cocktails and wines) or to the kitchen door, where Mexican gourds dangled from red-tiled eaves. But it was a pleasant place to linger over lunch or cocktails and late dinner.

For tea there was the smaller shop which advertised "kuchen, tea, and beer." There two thin worried women hastened eagerly to serve, pouring in too much milk, ladling in too much sugar. Chileans take so much sugar that waiters generally dump in four spoonfuls before they ask: " How much? " Between their scurryings to the cellule where the stove was and the window where large kuchen oozed with surgary fruit they spoke German to each other and to a heavy-set man who seemed to have nothing to do. Their Spanish was

" improving," but still halting and thickly Teutonic in the consonants. My landlady had told me they were " anti-Nazi." The thinner, older woman with deeply haunted eyes in dark sockets put it otherwise.

" We are German," she explained, " but Jewish. So we have a large English and Yanqui clientele." What atrocities have brought about! Now it is advantageous to state that one is Jewish; it brings the best clientele. " We had a big store in Stuttgart, as big as *Garth y Chavez* here. They took that away. My husband went to a concentration camp. . . . They sent word he had died there." These items came out in a few hard, slow words. " We got away, but with nothing. . . . Now, though, we are doing well. My son studied photography. My daughter will be a nurse."

[ANA]

Ana was the general maid who worked in house and garden, ran — or rather dawdled on — errands, washed and ironed, scrubbed and polished. Never a quick worker, she was steady and uncomplaining. Only now and then she said: " The señora gets cross, but one has to rest from time to time." She seldom missed a day; only the more important saints' days kept her from work.

We laid Ana's dependability to her young husband. Though we had not seen him she admitted to twenty years' difference in their ages.

" It's not bad," she said, " a young husband. He treats one with tenderness, almost like a mother. Not quite, perhaps, but almost, almost."

She must work so steadily to give him things, we told each other. How else could she hold him? For Ana was all of forty, far from fair, and much less than fat. Besides she supported an aged mother and helped a younger sister. It would only be a matter of time, we agreed, until the young husband disappeared for good. But we were wrong; it was Ana who disappeared.

It happened when she went off on her regular monthly visit to the *Caja de Seguridad* (Insurance Office) to have her passbook stamped. Chile's excellent and well-administered social-security laws require regular payments from every employed person, from the employer, and from the state. A domestic servant pays 2 per cent of her wage, her employer 5 per cent, and the state enough to bring it up to 8.5 per cent. Ana may have earned ten dollars a month. If so, she made more than the average domestic in a country which pays housemaids as little as two dollars a month. Her insurance would give her sickness and accident benefits, an old-age pension, assistance in buying a home, and even aid in burial costs. It also gave her a fine sense of importance, perhaps a consciousness of citizenship.

The day Ana went to the " Seguridad," she always worked faster, less thoroughly, and in gingerly discomfort because of her high-heeled, toeless, red kid shoes. Such shoes would cost about 180 pesos. Her hair was tightly frizzled, and before leaving she arrayed herself in a new blue dress she had made of " Chilean fabricated " cotton. She would spend the evening with her sister, she said: the one whose baby was about to die.

" And it might as well," Ana added fatalistically, " because it had never cared to eat, not even when a neighbor offered it her breast."

The next morning Ana did not come.

" She's a worthless slut," decided the landlady. " These

people are never trustworthy, no matter how much you do for them. She just got drunk with that worthless sister of hers, who is a bootlegger and no good at all. No wonder her baby is dying. She's just filled it up with chicha." In the absence of Ana she was too busy for more of her usual indictment of the lower orders.

That afternoon Ana's husband came as soon as he could leave his work. He was a handsome youth and plainly worried. Ana, he reported, had not returned to their room all night.

So our ugly Ana, with all her years and bunions, was the night roamer and the handsome young husband the worrier. Later he came again, even more concerned. Ana, he had learned, was in jail, detained by the police when she presented her passbook. They had kept her overnight and only notified her next of kin the following day. And, as we learned by long questioning, the fault was not Ana's, but her sisters's.

The bootlegging sister had been selling liquor without a license; and the police, bringing family pressure to the aid of law-enforcement, had arrested not the malefactor but the most responsible member of the clan.

Naturally I expected an outburst of fury at such high-handed and unmerited treatment of the hard-working Ana. But not at all. The landlady only thought it was funny. Ana and her boy husband were glad to be out of it so easily, never questioning the right of the police to use them as they would. Ana had promised to see to it that her sister obeyed the law. And she settled back into her comfortable sandals and old dress, less worn, if also more distraught, than after the more important saints' days.

[TEA WITH LA SOCIEDAD DE SANTIAGO]

A letter from Gabriela Mistral had presented me to a friend saying: " I wish her to know a Chilean home, and yours is my choice, for a home and for *Chilenismo*."

Often I dropped in there for quiet tea and talk. My hostess, who had lived much abroad, wore colored dresses and peasant shoes: both considered very odd by her friends, who clung to black or dark blue. She made and served tea in the European manner, and her house swarmed happily with visitors of several generations. Her baby granddaughter queened it for certain guests, her young sons and their friends lolled on the terrace beside the swimming pool, and courtly old gentlemen dropped in as a regular part of the afternoon stroll.

One day she asked friends to meet me and I heard all the proud old names of Chile and met their modern representatives in elegant and charming women who, for my sake, spoke their cultivated British English. They would have been just as at home in French. I heard no German names that day, and no Yanquis were present.

It was almost time for the schools to close and they talked of going out to the fundos for the vacation, complaining of the summer heat in Santiago. They talked also of the recent Eucharistic Congress, which had brought thousands of South Americans to Santiago for the most splendid and impressive gathering ever known on the continent.

I heard one lady say: " It was so moving, so beautiful; and it proved so unexpectedly that Chile is still Catholic."

Remembering what Gabriela Mistral had said: " You will not understand us unless you remember always that Chile is Catholic," I asked:

" But are not Chileans altogether Catholic? "

"They *were*. But with all this underground unrest, all this Communist agitation, all these new laws, we feared that the faith was dead. But the Congress proved that the people still have faith."

In the dining-room we were served tea. Chile's teas seem most typical of the old-time hospitality: lavish, unreckoning, and opulent. Spread on a lace-covered, flower-decked table were Chile's most delectable dainties and those of many other lands and climes. Tender shellfish with *aji* (for in Chile, chile never means a condiment), avocado paste, pastries oozing with sugared fruits, ices, candied fruits and nuts, and an elaborate and crisp concoction of eggs and sugar. Swedish smörgåsbord, French hors d'œuvres, English paper-thin sandwiches, German kuchen, and American layer cakes. Only people who would not dine until ten o'clock could face such a tea; only those with many servants, inured to long hours, could spread such a feast or dine so late.

The ladies were so fashionable and beautiful; the talk so sparkling, so informed about books and paintings, international gossip and affairs; the atmosphere of the affair was so suave and courtly that I was hypnotized into complete forgetfulness of the other Chile outside the enchanted walls. No wonder they believe in fairyland. I did, myself.

Another day a Sunday afternoon call made fairyland seem even truer — and more far-away.

Out on the old royal highway in an hacienda that Bernardo O'Higgins used to occupy, a lovely lady received me for tea. The house was of the type the Spaniards built from Chile to New Mexico. Walled gardens, tangled rather than formal, where generations of children have found a whole world to play in. A chapel. And several houses, not just one. A home, perhaps, for a widowed sister, a left-over aunt, or a couple of old servitors, kept comfortable until they die.

From the outer gate we passed through long cloisters where a talented member of the family, a monk, had painted a fresco of Saint Francis, and into the wide entrance hall. Hung with brocaded satin, set with stately furniture, and aglow with masses of flowers reflected in long mirrors, it could have been a queen's anteroom.

But our hostess, who came from the drawing-room to greet us, was simply dressed, easily matter-of-fact, chattily gay. She led us down wide steps. What grace old houses are given by the irregularities of remodeling! There, in a perfectly proportioned room, arranged for many comfortable conversations, were gathered twenty-five or thirty people. I had been told that our hostess was in delicate health, very religious, and devoted to reading and writing. Consequently she almost never went out and seldom entertained. This, however, was not entertaining. This was the children, grandchildren, and collateral relatives dropping in for Sunday afternoon tea. Students struggling through the difficult examinations chatted with uncles who were on the examining board. Young mothers had their babies brought in by nurses for a moment's show-off. Older children were learning to pass cakes. Debutantes, very *jeunes filles de la maison,* were giggling and gay, but with the thoroughly good manners convents instill. From convent training, too, and from aristocratic tradition these tender young things have a strong sense of obligation. Some hours every week go to church work and charity and to quiet calls on old or helpless people. A few girls of their class have taken training in social service, but generally they stick to old-fashioned charity.

155

It was a family conclave and representative of the best of Chile's aristocracy. What a contrast with the typical grandmother's home in our country! There the old lady probably lives in an apartment alone. Children have scattered from coast to coast. She may not see her grandchildren once in five years. Cousins and nieces have been lost track of altogether; their children's married names are not even known. Inconceivable among Chile's aristocrats not to know your family to all its outermost ramifications. Social life is largely family life. But surely there is nothing stodgy about it. The scene I was privileged to see was one of animated conversation among people of varied interests who stimulated each other. And it all centered in the gracious woman who was mother, grandmother, aunt. They had all come to pay their respects to her.

Another day, another Chile. A busy government man, unable to give me as much time as he wished in his office, took me home for lunch. He and his young wife lived in an apartment. They enjoyed the trickiness of a disappearing bar in the hallway, and adored the plump two-year-old baby daughter brought in by her nurse. My hostess worked, too, I learned, helping at political headquarters. With a few minor differences — a chauffeur to drive the young man to his office, the meal of several courses, the wines — it was like lunching with keen and well-informed young people in any city in the States.

This was a family unit, centered in a charming home; one could not imagine a better-cared-for baby. But what a contrast with the centralized family of tradition! This one would never, for better or worse, shut its members off from a consciousness of their country and their people as a whole.

This young matron did not see poor people as objects of Christian charity, but as compatriots needing better laws and more opportunities. This chuckling pink baby would be trained for some professional service, as well as womanhood. The movement of a changing country was felt in that home. New ideas could blow freely through a modern city apartment as never through a high-walled garden.

These were Chile's advance guard. Patently of excellent birth, of the best education, and of charm and graciousness equal to any, they were not of *la alta sociedad*. Probably they had little time for high society. They saw their country and their people not in layers of classes, but as one. The talk flashed fast from Chile's Popular Front to our New Deal; from a recent exhibition of United States paintings to an Argentine singer; from classical Spanish to clever and wicked *Chilinismos*. There I often got lost, but was put right again in quick asides, helped to understand the folksy richness of Chilean speech.

" Our talk," said my host, " is enriched from our rotos as our life is in every department. Chile has everything. But her greatest riches are in her folk. We must go ahead, steadily and unfalteringly ahead, to give all our people every advantage — health, decent homes, adequate pay." He broke off suddenly. " Wouldn't it be wonderful if your wealthy and generous country would help us with these fundamentals? Money for roads and ships and factories, yes! They are important. But most important are our people. Perhaps when we have peace again we may actually get loans for health and education."

In Providencia, thanks to good luck and good letters, I had touched many phases of Chilean life. On every level I found

Chileans to like and to respect, interesting and challenging. But always baffling, difficult for a foreigner to assess.

One day a Chilean woman, fixing me with stern dark eyes, said: "I have a criticism of how you Yanquis write about Chile. Your books give facts of economics and of politics, yes! But the real Chile, the soul of Chile, they never express."

About that there could be no argument. Surely no outsider but only a Chilean could hope to capture in words anything so elusive and so complex as the soul of this country. The foreigner sees only the surface, catches only reflected impressions; and even those are bound to be distorted by his own limitations and prejudices.

XIII

EDUCATING THE ELITE

U NDERSTANDING THE LATIN AMERICAN, THAT PER-
sistent preoccupation of the Nordic American, may prove to
be impossible. Perhaps it should be impossible. Perhaps international relations can be more interesting and quite as
valuable, as personal relations often are, if there is exciting
uncertainty along with appreciation of the other's worth. But
appreciation there must be, and that is often helped by knowledge of the influences which have formed the exciting stranger.
In our dealings with Latin America nothing is of more immediate aid than a study of his educational system, because
it is so different from our own. A Chilean professor, who
knows them both well, summed it up aptly.

" Your aim," she said, " is to educate as many people as
possible, to attain one hundred per cent literacy. Ours has
been to select the best minds in order to turn out a thoroughly
finished product. Perhaps we may say, too, that your education aims to produce better living; ours to develop a cultural
and educational elite."

Aside from Chile's aristocratic conception of education her

159

system differs from ours as certain basic conceptions, rooted in our history, differ.

Chile's rigid centralization and uniformity are direct descendants of the Spanish colonial empire; our heterogeneous, diffuse, uncoordinated system the heir of government based on the town meeting and states' rights. Chile's stiff examinations, designed to eliminate all but the very best, come from the old Spanish concept of *hidalguía* (nobility) while our tendency to lower standards so the child from an uncultivated home may do as well as the professor's son is perhaps the excess of democracy. In Chile hidalguía must be reckoned with in every phase of life. Anybody will admit it privately; nobody is willing to be quoted to that effect. Sharp distinctions exist between upper- and lower-class education, in spite of the fact that Chile, with her law of 1813, was the first country in the Americas to establish national public education. Her hidalgos had fine democratic principles.

Only recently was a lower-class child expected to arrive at secondary schools. That they do now, in increasing numbers and with much success, is due to the rapid democratization of Chile. Most Chileans, however, must be content with primary schooling, or less. Elementary teachers study six years in normal schools after six years of elementary training and attend courses in professional training as long as they are in service.

"Chile," said my *Profesora* friend, "had the first normal school in Latin America. I think we have the best-trained teachers in Latin America, and practically a hundred per cent of them are normal graduates." An elementary teacher can seldom hope to become a secondary teacher. This is because all secondary teachers must be specially trained in the subjects they teach.

Forgetting her democratic principles, the Profesora elabo-

rated: " There is a sharp social, economic, even moral cleavage between primary and secondary teachers. Our classes differ much more than people of different countries. . . . But
don't quote me! "

The elementary course takes six years. The curriculum includes Spanish, history, geography, science, mathematics,
physical education, music, manual training, and art, with
sewing and home economics for girls. Always there are separate schools for boys and girls. Only in the universities do men
and women attend classes together. Chile is as shocked at our
mixed education as we are at Russia's mixed bathing.

The secondary school requires six years more, making a
total of twelve as our lower and high schools do. Chileans
maintain that their secondary education is so much wider and
more thorough than ours that their students, when ready for
the university, stand on a par with our junior-college students.
The methods are so different that perhaps a really fair comparison is impossible. The Chilean student, for instance, has
much less practical experimentation and application than the
United States student. He learns more by rote, is given less opportunity to develop individually, extra-curricularly. And he
has no electives, except that he may choose between English
and German and French and Italian. Uniformity and centralization are so complete that it is said a teacher in Punta Arenas,
a thousand miles from the capital, could not close her school
under threat of an iceberg without authority from Santiago.

In the *liceo,* secondary school, the student faces six years
of hard work with no organized sports, no campus life, a little
physical education (the authorities agree that all study and no
exercise leads to illness and neuroses, but fear also that sports
carried to the extreme of fatigue may cause harm). Whether
the aim is the university or a technical school or marriage (in

the case of a girl), the course is the same. And this is it:

Two years of philosophy, which includes logic, a history of philosophy, psychology, methods of science and ethics. One Profesora said: " It seems strange to us that you offer no philosophy to your young people at the age when they are seeking answers to all their problems. . . . Maybe ours are more mature at fifteen and sixteen, but we find them deeply interested in pure thought and eager for speculation."

Six years of two foreign languages. No Latin and less Greek. But Greek and Latin roots of Spanish are studied, as well as Arabic. The liceo graduate knows his Spanish. In Chile an educated person who does not speak his own language correctly is inconceivable. The college professor, even dean, sometimes encountered in our universities who fumbles his gerunds if not his simpler forms would probably be shot at sunrise in Chile. As his like has never been known, the idea is pure speculation.

One year each of political economy and civics. Three years each of chemistry, physics, biology, algebra, arithmetic, and geometry. History and geography are taught together for six years. Spanish, music, art, and physical education run all through the course. And manual work in boys' schools and domestic science in girls' are taught for four years. As every student takes everything, this results in thirty to thirty-six hours of classes weekly, from half past eight to twelve, from half past two to five. Wednesday and Saturday afternoons are free and there are two vacations — two months at Christmas, three weeks in mid-winter.

I gasped. " And is your adolescent mortality high? "

" Quite," laughed my Profesora. " It is really a survival of the fittest. Those who graduate are those who survive. And you must remember that our professors are concerned to eliminate as many as possible, not to get them through. It is not at all unusual to fail as many as eighty per cent; the best professor, . in fact, is he who fails most. It has been estimated that only students with an I.Q. of 110 have a chance of graduation."

At the end of the secondary-school course the student takes exhaustive examinations, both written and oral, under boards appointed by the Department of Education and the university. One of his two languages is chosen by lot — which is certainly no help in cramming — and other variations are permitted according to the profession the student will study for in the university. Those who fail are given a second chance three months later. But only one chance. This examination is called the *bachillerato*, and those who pass it are *bachilleres*. Herein is a source of misunderstanding of our system by Chileans who assume that our bachelor's degree, taken after four years of college training, is only the equivalent of their high-school diploma. Many Chileans rest content, well educated in the humanities and distinctly of the chosen few, with this degree. Those who go on to the universities may — as in medicine, law, or engineering — have to stand another examination.

Chile's university is not a unified institution with a campus, athletic fields, a central library, dormitories, and fraternity houses. It is housed in various buildings throughout Santiago and even in Valparaiso, where it maintains schools of law and business. Each faculty (professional school) is governed by its professors; the rector elected by them holds a post of much honor but little real authority. Chile has three universities: the National University of Chile, founded in 1738; the Catholic University of Chile, founded in 1888; and the University of Concepción, founded in 1915. Besides this there is the private and endowed University of Santa María in Valparaiso.

Only the national university has all the faculties of medicine, law, engineering, dentistry, pharmacy, pedagogy, architecture, agriculture, veterinary science, commerce and industry. Courses vary from three to six years and medicine has recently added a required internship which brings that up to eight. In actual time, therefore, the Chilean professional graduate has put in the same number of years, with more hours per year, as the graduate in the United States. Perhaps the man in the United States has had more laboratory work.

Adherents of each system claim that theirs is the best. Chileans maintain that their bachilleres are better grounded in the humanities, more aware of the world's culture, better able to enoy it as adults. North Americans counter that the Chilean, who has learned by rote, has not developed individuality, self-reliance, or originality. In actual practice students transferring from one system to the other do well.

The young Chilean bachiller is not sure of admission by his chosen faculty because each faculty sets up a quota. In Chile the doctors and lawyers in actual practice are also the professors. As practitioners they do not wish to see the profession overrun; as professors they see to it that only the best qualify.

From the point of view of education the most important faculty to consider is that of pedagogy, which produces all secondary-school teachers. Chile is proud of being the first country in Latin America (probably the first in Pan-America) to require professional training for all teachers. Her first normal school was founded in 1854, and the university school to prepare secondary teachers in 1889. The course in pedagogy now requires five years, making the degree, *Profesor del Estado*, equal to our master's degree.

The student pursues his specialty for three years and has besides two years of professional subjects and six months of supervised practice teaching. He then prepares a thesis in his

specialty or in education, and stands examinations in both —
oral and written. Then, and only then, may he teach in a secondary school; and he may teach only his subject. For this
reason and because salaries are low, many teachers give
courses in private as well as public schools.

The *Profesor del Estado* may have difficulty in eking out his
inadequate salary, but he is highly respected as an accomplished and distinguished person. One of them said: " We
cannot understand the attitude toward educators in the United
States. One of the principal arguments against President
Roosevelt seemed to be that he turned to professors for advice.
Imagine! To us it seems quite natural that a president faced
with economic and social problems should consult experts.
We cannot reconcile your attitude in that case with your general respect for the expert."

Chile's many private schools are obliged to conform to the
system if their students wish to enter the university or take the
bachillerato. All examinations are conducted by the state, and
only the state can give degrees. Private schools are based on
the teachings of a foreign language (with who knows how much
alien ideology!) or on religious instruction. It is curious that
Catholics of the United States, the greatest Catholic country
in the world, maintain no school in Chile, though Spanish,
French, and German orders conduct schools for boys and
girls.

Catholic influence in public education is said to be non-
existent. " Chilean education," I was told, " has always been
in the hands of Liberals or Radicals, and both parties started
as anti-clerical if not anti-Church. Religion is simply no issue.
And most professors are thoroughly liberal in thought."

Perhaps the most interesting development in private education, because it so clearly shows the influence of the modern

industrial world, is the University of Santa María, at Valparaiso. It was founded in 1926 by Federico Santa María, who had attained wealth by cornering the sugar market and who uttered, if he did not quite originate, the aphorism: " Great riches confer great responsibilities," which is carved in bronze on his statue. The idea for the school occurred to Señor Don Agustín Edwards, who, being Chile's Ambassador at the Court of St. James's, spent his vacations in Germany and came to admire the German technical schools. Through his influence Señor Santa María's will stipulated that the school's professors for twenty-five years should all be Europeans. As the first faculty were all German, their successors have naturally been so.

Boys enter Santa María from the secondary schools, but need not have taken their bachillerato. They are given one or two years of technical training, according to their preparation, work one year at a genuine job outside, and return for a final year in school. Many leave after that as trained technicians. They are much in demand in industry, which could absorb many more than the school provides.

The student who enters the superior school has a choice — or rather is carefully selected for fitness for training — as a technician in mechanical, electrical, or chemical engineering, or as a graduate engineer in one of those lines. The engineer takes as many years of theoretical training as the university graduate, besides the years of practical work and experimentation that Santa María requires of all students.

The boys come from all classes and show no difference in aptitude or intelligence. Of about four hundred applicants a year, seventy-five are selected. After the first three months' term, another twenty-five are eliminated. The remaining fifty are then in line for the lower courses, but many, of course, never become graduate engineers.

" After the actual engineering courses begin," said the professor who was my guide, " we have several more chances to get rid of the unfit." Here, too, Chilean education is a selective process, designed to train an elite. By curious contrast a Chilean engineer told me in another connection that Chile has not yet produced engineers as altogether competent for exacting posts as are the graduates of European or North American technical schools.

At Santa María the boys work in fine stone buildings set above the sea between Valparaiso and Viña del Mar; they wear uniforms; and pay no tuition. Living quarters are provided for a hundred and fifty; others live out. There are thirty-five or forty professors and teachers; the professors are Germans. " After 1933 many good Germans were available," my informant said. Many of the teachers of technical processes are Chileans and are often expert workmen without degrees.

Santa María marks a first step toward a new education for Chile — an education which shall train men to work in an industrialized world, to make a living. As such it is a sharp break with the old education founded on the hidalgo tradition. It is significant also that this pioneer school, which is being copied by the government, is German- and not Yanqui-inspired.

That fact probably indicates that the country's changing educational methods are the result of world-wide changes, and not of Yanqui influence. And it is important because many Chileans fear the influence of Yanquis, who, as is well known (in Chile), have no feeling for the finer things of the spirit. We Yanquis cannot hope to understand Chile until we know and admit this fact. It will lessen the North American's naïve assumption that Chile wants nothing better than to imitate us. Quite the contrary. Many Chileans cite the United States and United States education as horrible examples of what not to do.

I quote from *El Hogar Chileno,* a novel by Senén Palacios. Young Rodolfo, employed in a Yanqui mine is conversing with his Saxon-hating uncle.

"We have not sufficient preparation to meet their competition because of the erroneous direction of our education. . . . A young gringo, almost a boy, an ignoramus, in an examination in our schools would certainly get a *3 black* in all branches; he knows only one thing, but he knows that thing well, and it is something practical and useful."

"But in our schools also they teach useful and practical things."

"Purely theories, Uncle . . . encyclopædic for the variety of knowledge . . . but taken from books and learned by memory with the sole object of passing examinations."

I also quote from a book by an educator, *Crisis y Reconstrucción de la Segunda Enseñanza* (*Crisis and Reconstruction of Secondary Education*), by Arturo Piga.

". . . We should find intolerable . . . the educational system . . . in the United States, where the influence exercised by money and by utilitarian preparation, quick and specialized to the point of being one-sided, has succeeded . . . in suppressing all consideration of historical evolution as a prerequisite of a systematic and organic development of a culture. . . .

" The prevalence of economic and utilitarian factors . . . has gone so far as to result in that country in complete ignorance of the enormous practical value of general branches of knowledge or fundamental elements of education in the professional or technical training of youth.

" One could say much also of the moral damage resulting from such an anomaly, which produces grave deficiencies and incalculable consequences in the psychological formation of youth; so much so that, instead of obtaining a youth of high spiritual quality, there rise up, in that atmosphere of unoriented and mean culture, individuals haughty, superficial, vain, ignorant, lacking all historical sense, and above all without knowledge of and respect for the culture and way of life of which, nevertheless they take advantage as parasites and adventurers."

One might reply to these strictures in various ways. A low rate of illiteracy — 4.3 per cent in the United States as against 25.2 per cent in Chile in 1930 — inevitably produces many people who are educated or trained without being cultured. Even Chile may soon find such people an asset, as her middle class develops and her industries demand trained technicians. And a survey of the United States might reveal as many cultivated folk as Chile can boast — either in proportion to the general population or in actual numbers. But Señor Piga's pronouncement is most significant because it is published as the considered opinion of an educator in an important government post. We must recognize that this is what some Chileans may have in mind as they deal with us. And we must

eliminate the bad feeling which lies behind it by our appreciation of Chile's fine education, its purpose, and its value.

Señor Piga's determination to hold onto what is best in
Chile's culture while avoiding the mistakes we have made
arouses only admiration. The ideal would probably be a com-
bination of Chile's hidalguía — the high standard imposed
by and for an aristocracy — and our almost hundred-per-
cent literacy with a highly trained and technically efficient
populace. This, it appears, is the aim of Chile's evolving educational program.

Much of it is already in operation. Not only at the University of Santa María but in other institutions the revered humanities are set aside for an earlier and quicker training in
industrial arts and crafts. There are schools of mines, agriculture, and commerce, besides the national Army and Navy
training schools, which do not demand the bachillerato as a
prerequisite. For women there are schools of social service and
nursing. The famous Summer School of the University of Chile
tries to widen the horizon and increase the culture of the here-
tofore little-considered primary teacher of both sexes. A deeply
considered and brilliantly written program for rural education is part of Amanda Labarca's *Betterment of Rural Life;*
she therein shows the influence of Mexico's rural schools, with
their emphasis on agriculture and animal husbandry for boys,
domestic science and baby care for girls, practical assistance
for adults. Similar plans look toward the preparation of city
children for lucrative crafts at an early age. Much of this work
is well begun. Adult night schools were one of the projects
of President Pedro Aguirre Cerda, whose noble dictum: " To
govern is to educate," has left a deep mark on Chilean consciousness.

In education, as in her political life, Chile is taking notice, perforce, of her rising and demanding middle class. No longer dominated politically by her hidalgos, the government is educating the people to meet the demands of industry, modern life, and Chile's great need to develop all her vast reserves of power and wealth, human as well as mineral.

XIV

RODEO AT CURACAVÍ

THE REAL CHILE IS TO BE FOUND IN THE RODEO AND THE cueca; its typical figure is the guaso. Like all America, Chile is cattle country. Fine animals are handled by men who are more at ease on a horse than afoot; men whose strength and agility, picturesque garb, and outdoor life make them folk heroes of a similar type. Our cowboys, Mexico's vaqueros, Venezuela's llaneros, Argentina's gauchos, and Hawaii's paniolos are of the same breed. Their jobs differ only in so far as Venezuela's llanos are wet, our plains and Argentina's pampas dry; their characters have been formed by the need to dominate animals, to disregard danger, and to act with speed and judgment. And they all relax drinking, dancing, and making love. In Chile their dance is the cueca. To know the real Chile one must see a rodeo and a cueca. Both are staged, nowadays, at fairs and for visiting delegations. The one most redolent of old Chile would, of course, be in the country, arranged by natives for their own diversion and with no outsiders expected.

One Sunday morning I found the newspaper announcement I hoped for. " Rodeo at Curacaví." It named prizes, promised

172

a " Great Social Dance," from midnight on, and stated that
" *gondolas* " would leave every hour from the corner of San
Pablo and Matucana. A bus ride, I decided, would be the best
way to start a day among the folk, besides being the cheapest.

Arrived at San Pablo and Matucana, I found the gondola's
windows soaped with enticing items about the rodeo. A round-
faced boy sat at the wheel, two others lay flattened in sleep on
the back seat.

" You leave at twelve? " I queried with assurance. Curious
that some years of experience in Latin America had not cor-
roded that assurance quite away.

" At twelve," agreed the driver. " Or at five."

" Twelve five? "

" No, señorita, five of the afternoon."

" But the advertisement said . . ."

" *Claro!* " In Chile nothing is too obscure to be called clear.

He disappeared to return soon with the news that we should
indeed go, and immediately. An older man took the wheel,
the reclining boys with a shout " *Al rodeo!* " sat erect, we spun
round, and rattled off — for half a block. At that point the
driver and all three boys disappeared completely, leaving me
alone with flies, who divided their attention between me and
an uncovered garbage cart up ahead. It was one of Santiago's
poorer districts. Everybody who passed looked poor — women
with huge bundles and tagging children, men with pushcarts
or trays of things to sell, two-wheeled carts hitched with two
horses in place of three, a battered old surrey pulled by a
bony nag. Finally one of the boys came laggingly back to
smear more soap on the windows. He had been sent with the
bad news. We could not go until they had a load. " *Claro!* "

I advanced again that silly Yanqui notion that one who advertises to send a bus at a certain hour is under some obliga-

tion to do so. It met, of course, the equally fixed South American conviction that all cases are alterable without notice if circumstances change. We were both polite, both firm, and altogether incapable of mutual understanding. Again that rock on which hemispheric solidarity so often runs aground if it does not split. Only tolerance will serve. I tried to recognize that if his bus was not filled up he could not go. And he, on his part, showed the unfailing kindness of Chile on which I was learning to count.

"Perhaps a taxi. He will charge a mountain of pesos, but it costs nothing to ask."

"*Claro!*"

Meanwhile I read my noon paper. All Chile, and even some very important North Americans, seemed overwrought because a Yanqui weekly had described Chile's President in such saucy phrases as it habitually used for all notables everywhere. I had seen no indignation from either North or South America about far more scurrilous attacks on President Roosevelt in the Chilean press. Good neighborliness sometimes seems to be a one-sided gesture.

The boy came back, bowed under the weight of the mountain of pesos he must mention "Two hundred and fifty pesos to take you. No return."

"And the bus returns?" I understood that its return must depend upon whether or not it ever went. But as a truly promising Chilean the young man suggested no doubt. "At eleven at night."

The prospect was not too good, but I hated to admit failure. So I collected my fare back again and descended to speak to the taximan in person. Did he, I asked, really propose to abandon me in Curacaví and return with an empty car? He was a short broad-shouldered chap and he grinned at the vision of me walking home while he drove grandly past alone. Three hundred pesos, he suggested, to take me there, to stay with me all day, to return me to my domicile wherever that might be. That great careless gesture, combined with the fact that three hundred pesos was less than ten dollars, decided me. It was a wise decision, for Don Boleslo turned out to be widely informed and sure of everything. As we rode he talked.

" I used to be chauffeur for a private family. Rich people, fine and kind, but they paid me only three hundred pesos a month — ten pesos a day — and for that can a man support a family with any decency? He can buy no more, after all, than the merest food. But such people do not know, do not think. They go off to Europe, they spend enough uselessly to support many families well. But they are ignorant of the conditions of the workmen. That's the trouble with Chile, señorita, the ignorance of those people."

He spoke of President Aguirre Cerda. " He understands," he said with conviction. " You see, señorita, in Chile we have no home market because the people have no money. We must have factories and pay such wages that we can buy home-made goods. Don Pedro knows that. He will see that the good laws we have are enforced, make new ones, help the Chileans."

He drove at the moderate uniform pace of a good driver. The midday sun was hot, but a breeze from the retreating snow on the cordillera freshened the air. Summer days in Santiago, in spite of rainlessness and sun heat, are neither clear nor bright. The sky is generally palely misted, for the sea reaches inland and waters the sky if not the land. But its reach is soft; no wind is strong enough to bring rain. Chile's June in December is static without exciting promise of either better or worse. The road was paved, but so narrow that many an insistent middle-of-the-roader forced us off onto the graveled shoulders.

" Let them drive like that," said Don Boleslo calmly. " I'll be alive long after they are dead."

Once really in the country we met few cars. The direct sun had forced all shadows into retreat under willows, which in Chile seem to weep so copiously, and against dark rows of poplars. Tall thistles with periwinkle-blue puffs as large as dahlias grew in unirrigated fields, but most of the country was " under ditch ": wide slow ditches rich with brown mud. Along every fundo's fence red ramblers had bloomed, faded, and were about to fall. Big iron gates between stone pillars were open, but everything seemed to sleep. Even an ox cart in a shaded lane moved with the somnolence of a dream. Before and after passing each plantation house we passed dozens of inquilinos' huts. I wondered why the owners did not set such forlorn dwellings out of sight. They seemed as desolate and unkempt as tenant cabins on our Southern platations. In Chile, though, no home is too poor to have flowers. Tall regimented larkspurs and snapdragons, purplish and pink begonias, and scarlet geraniums managed to be gay without inharmony.

Asking about such houses and the people who lived there, I soon established such confidence that Don Boleslo said:

" If the Señorita wishes, we might visit an inquilino home after the rodeo."

" Claro, and enchanted! "

Suddenly we were climbing a hill and looking out on sweeping meadows, vineyards, and orchards marked off by poplars and flowing ditches, and beyond at hills already beginning to brown toward summer. Near the crest we passed a girl walking. As we flashed past I saw that she was sobbing into a wadded handkerchief.

" Shall we stop? "

" No. To stop is only to get into trouble. She had probably

left a car. Who knows who would be in it? Many men have no respect for a woman . . . and not always workmen. We might find a carful of *elegantes cursis* (vulgar dudes). They have ways with the police. No, here we never stop. Chile is not like your country."

Over the hill we did come upon a car parked beside the road. But instead of elegantes cursis it was filled with a comfortable-looking family — plump mamma and youngsters in the back seat, shirt-sleeved papa driving.

We dropped into another valley, quietly verdant, sunnily calm. No towns, no traffic, just our car progressing smoothly along its narrow cement lane.

" This road," he said, " should have gone over the other pass, as the old road did. It made the road from Valparaiso to Santiago ten miles shorter. But the family that owns all these fundos had the power to make them put the road here. That was in the Ibáñez regime. He did whatever the hacendados wanted."

Then we were driving into a town which gradually revealed itself among trees and fields as one long street. Curacaví. We passed the hotel of that name, which is probably the most elegant one, and drew up before the Hotel Inglés. A pink-cheeked boy took our order and came back soon with a well-appointed tray: chicken sandwiches and a bottle of beer; later peaches and coffee. The driver would not eat with me, but retreated to a seemly distance and talked with the barman.

The rodeo was in a valley surrounded by low hills. We paid a fee at the gate and came to rest in a line of cars facing a row of arbors covered with cut boughs drying rapidly in the sun. In each one liquor was being sold, guitars and accordions played, and dancing was going on. But lazily in the day's heat. I decided to take a siesta too and watch the men trotting horses

177

past the cars. They went down dry but came back soon with dripping flanks, looking refreshed from a bath and a drink. The thump and whine of the music withdrew into an insect hum; the sunshine was sifted through dust, which smelled of horse and eucalyptus. A truck drew up beside our car and several young women suckled their babies, changed, diapers, chatted and laughed with men who stopped to greet them.

They were good-looking fellows with the sharp features I had come to know as Chilean, sun-colored but not dark, often with light eyes. Mounted, they rode with the horseman's easy seat, relaxed shoulders, and flat back. Afoot they had the grace of legs lengthened by sharp high heels and slimmed by black leather leggings buckled above the knees, fringed below. And every one sported dreadful spurs with rowels three or four inches in circumference. Some wore short jackets, but the poncho is the noble garment which broadens the shoulders and falls gracefully thrown back. The sombrero is flat-topped and often held by a string under the chin. Like the cowboy everywhere, Chile's guaso makes every other man look dully conventional or a plodding clod.

" *Buena' tarde' !* " Chile habitually elides the final *s*.

" *A Usted!* "

Their manners were formal, with none of the casualness upper classes have acquired. Their attitude toward the curious Yanqui watching them and trying not to be rude was that of perfect poise and courteous disregard. But when I tentatively smiled and spoke, they were easily friendly. One young man, who had been amusing his baby by spinning his silver-mounted spur, agreed to show me the intricacies of the Chilean saddle, on which the rider sits a foot or so above his horse.

Amused at my interest, he brought up his horse and saddled him. First he laid on evenly four square mats of natural wool,

Waiting to Enter the Arena

A Guaso and His Horse

The Arena is Padded like a
Basket

five or six inches in height. Then the saddle, low of pommel
and cantle, rather like our McClellan and with equally long
stirrups. He fastened it with one cinch, a wide woven band.
Then protection for the man: a series of soft woollen mats,
bringing the cushioning up to a foot or so. These are strapped
to the saddle. Surely no hardy horseman in all time or any
place ever rode so softly seated as Chile's guaso, who is the
peer of the best of them.

Benjamin Subercaseaux describes the Chilean guaso as
" cruel and superstitious. His loves are mute and enjoy great
promiscuity. He rides little horses, shaggy and enduring, and
as a horseman he has no equal. He speaks seldom and when he
does he does not answer questions directly. His acts may seem
guileless, but generally they hide great shrewdness and profound distrust. He loves and defends his patron as he would
defend himself. The Communists have given proof of intelligence in attacking just this redoubt of reaction. The guaso
is, in reality, the bourgeois of the popular class."

Though the guaso is so talked and sung about, he is not,
like the cowboy or the vaquero, a man of horses and cattle
who would scorn the bucolic pursuits of a tiller of the soil.
The guaso, when he is not dressed up and on a horse, is a
humble inquilino like any other, subject to his master's orders
to plow or harvest, to weed, water, or milk. And any inquilino
who shows himself adept with horses, saving enough to buy
leggings and spurs, may hope to ride in a rodeo some day.

It was almost five o'clock before people began to enter the
fenced enclosure where the grandstand loomed up as a shelter
of cut branches. At the gate I was charged ten pesos by a red-
faced man with hazel eyes afloat with alcoholic tears, but
erect and formal withal.

In the stand women in summer dresses and men *de guaso*

greeted one another and called out to the master of ceremonies, who was adjusting an amplifier in his box. They
looked like small-town people or ranch employees. Certainly
no elegantes, unless some of the heavy-set and hearty men of
middle age were hacendados come to enjoy themselves with
their dependants, to take pride in their skill, and to praise
them for taking prizes. Later I learned that was surely true,
and that many of the performers were hacendados too, proud
to prove themselves guasos " of the first."

Horsemen were gathering in the ring, which was strange
to a North American. Oval, it was cut across the long way by
a stout log fence which made two half-moons of it; it is called
media luna. The outer fence was made of upright poles, slant-
ing outward and woven together with withes like nothing so
much as an old-fashioned laundry basket.

"The brothers Martínez. . . . Hernández and Aguirre!
. . . García and Armenta! " The master of ceremonies was
intoning through his amplifier.

At each call a pair turned their horses into a forming line
or came trotting through the gate. Later I learned that often
these pairs were composed of master and man. A señorita of
the upper class told me that even she could not tell which a
man might be until he spoke. "The commonest men," she
assured me with surprise, " often have as highbred features
as the hidalgo." So even aristocratic Chile has noticed that
biological fact!

Forty-four men were soon in the line which filed past the
stand, saluting friends who called out to them. As handsome
a lot of men as one would wish to see, completely at ease
with their mounts, comfortable with each other and the on-
lookers.

Then a bunch of two-year-olds was let in, one of them cut

out and driven along the outer fence while two men followed. Compared with our more violent northern cowboy sports it seemed tame. The young steer was forced to trot along the basket's side while the men followed, keeping close enough to touch and finally causing the victim to turn and run back. If he turned, the men scored. If not, they lost. It took skill certainly, on the part not only of those men, but of the horses, who must spin in their tracks, respond to the lightest touch. It is a game of fine points, but without dash, daring, or danger. A surprisingly gentle show for descendants of the fiery Spaniards and fierce Araucanians.

I was curious to know if this rodeo is a company performance and how cattle were handled on the range. But this is the manner of subduing cattle for branding, altering, or shipping to market. On the range just such media lunas are set up and loose cattle driven into them for handling.

Though Chile is not one of the great cattle-shipping countries, she supplies her own needs. Every fundo runs cattle on its unirrigated lands — a total of two million, besides half a million horses and mules — and moves them up, during the dry summers, into the Andean valleys. Guasos then live the typical life of the range, sleeping on the ground in temporary shelters, living on meat, cheese, and hard bread brought up from below. Cattle show little tendency to stray out of a well-watered valley with plenty of grass, so it is not an exacting life, though it may offer the occasional excitement of a puma or a condor voracious enough to attack a lamb or small calf. The working rodeo takes place when the cattle are driven down from the mountain range in the autumn.

I did not wait to see the end of the rodeo, but went out to stroll along the booths where dancing was growing ever noisier and more general. Every arbor was dedicated to wine,

women, and song. Slatternly girls and slovenly older women
were trying to lure men in to buy chicha. The caterwauling
of female voices forced to loudness was accompanied by
guitar and accordion and by the thumping of bare hands on
upturned boxes. Men sang much better, even when steady
libations of chicha had hoarsened their throats. All afternoon
I had heard them from a distance and seen the bobbing and
weaving figures of couples dancing the cueca, Chile's famous
national dance. Now I set out for a tour of the arbors to see
the cueca at close hand.

XV

LA CUECA

CHILEAN WRITERS WAX MOST LYRICAL ABOUT THEIR cueca. " This is the cueca . . . in which the soul of the people surges up from the depths of its ancestral boredom and apathy to prove that there is still in every breast a strong tincture of sane and robust optimism, a spiritual energy." So Luis Durand in *Interpretación de la Cueca* as quoted in *Panorama y Color de Chile.*

Joaquín Edwards Bello, in the same collection, expresses what it means to the Chilean:

" The cueca is music's intoxication, and no Creole can hear it without feeling drunk with the indefinable. . . . It is a dance of history or of allegory, of conquest or of submission. . . . In other dances the woman may at times take the man's part; in the cueca never. . . . The sexes in the cueca remain barbarously defined. . . . A dance characteristic of a race formed by two elements which united fighting; in the cueca resound the tambourine of Castile and the Araucanian rattle, always dominated by the fatalistic solemnity of the Araucanian festival."

For the Chilean this music and dance most poignantly recall the happiest times of youth and home. It is not the actual cueca, its steps or gestures, that fills him with sad nostalgic joy, but every dear memory that it evokes. So all people, especially those who yearn backward to country folk and fun, are reduced to tearful and uncritical rapture by their native reel or jig.

No foreigner could possibly emulate these Chileans, or even see the cueca that they see. One can only report, objectively, what may be read or seen through eyes quite unmisted by tears.

Historically the cueca has been traced back to Guinea in Africa. Few Negroes were imported into Chile, as the long journey down the coast would have killed them off, slave ships being what they were. But the few who reached the Chilean ports — perhaps with conquerors from Peru or with slave-traders on their way to Peru — have left an unmistakable imprint in the loose-legged clogging, the general easy laxness of the cueca. The very word comes from *zamba*, an African dance, through *zamba clueca* and *zamacueca*, to *cueca*, as it was known in Chile. Curiously a similar " scarf dance " reached Argentina, where it is still danced as the *zamba*.

The music of the cueca, like Chilean folk music generally, is light, fluid, and very Spanish in feeling. Students attribute its gaiety to lack of Indian influence, which gave Mexican music, for instance, its undercurrent of sadness. Here is no *tristeza*.

The dance, having evolved in Peru, is thought to have returned to Chile with a famous Negro battalion which naturally presented it in the lowest cantinas and dives. In the 1820's, when a French traveler described it, the prudish middle class was shuddering away from the vulgar cueca. But

certain daring señoritas were so bold as to perform its flirta-
tious flouncings in the most exclusive drawing-rooms. In time,
then, the conservative bourgeoisie accepted it with the cachet
of the salon upon it, and the cueca became a part of every
Chilean feast.

Eugenio Pereira Salas, in *Danzas y Cantos Populares de
la Patria Vieja*, says that the cueca is the expression not only
of popular lyricism, eroticism, and satyrism, but of Chile's
whole history. Every important happening, that is, produced
an anonymous singer who chanted his ballad as the accom-
paniment to the cueca; travelers in every decade of the nineteenth century reported on the typical cueca of the period,
generally a dance and song inspired by the latest revolution
or foreign war.

The cueca has little form; its theme is a meeting which
leads to flirtation and moves quickly through courtship to
as suggestive a conquest and surrender as the dancers care
or dare to give it. It is always a duet, though several couples
may be on the floor together. Being of the poorest, there is
no special costume, though when it is staged the man appears
" de guaso," the girl in long full calico skirt. The one requi-
site is a handkerchief for each. In the beginning the girl lures
the man, lifting her skirt to show her foot, advancing and
whirling away. His game is indifference. One song makes
him say: " When I lose interest, I quit! " She taunts him:
" Don't be a coward! Come closer, man! Here you're offered
this world and the next! "

He responds, teasingly, buys her a drink, shares her glass,
putting his lips where hers have been, maliciously leading
her on, but becoming himself more and more ardent. On-
lookers incite them with remarks and by joining in the music
with singing, stamping, thumping on anything at hand. Finally

she has him completely aroused; he pursues her openly and finally catches her in an embrace.

José Gonzáles Vera, in his brilliant series of pictures of low life *Vidas Minimas,* describes a cueca thus:

" The movements imitate pursuit and flight. The woman appears and the man, stirred, follows her. Suddenly she, feeling herself sought, begins to flee.

" The man hesitates, but aroused again by desire, follows her with his glance and step. The woman accelerates her step, and her face shows a certain mute disdain.

" A growing ardor possesses the man. His gestures, ever more unrestrained, are an impatient solicitation. His eyes burn with overmastering gleam.

" The woman no longer flees so fast. Her circlings are slower. Masculine insistence is entering her heart like a command. Her face softens and flushes.

" The man, aware of the woman's new submissiveness, is filled with savage joy and his dancing becomes tumultuous. He dances around her, adoring her and controlling himself; he could take her, he could caress her, he could carry her off, but something restrains him.

" The woman no longer fears; the man's desire has entered her and she waits . . . until suddenly in the last whirl, pushed by equal desire, they rush together with trembling and open arms."

This was going on in a dozen arbors, each with its wine cask and plank bar; its two or three musicians and women trying to attract the men strolling uninterestedly by or reining in their horses to give the offering a cool once-over. One couple, seen from a distance, seemed promising. He was quick and graceful, she lithe and expert; their timing perfect. I went nearer, and that was a mistake. For the faces they turned to

The Cueca Is a Courting Dance

As Benito Román Sees the Cueca

*Benito Román Painting His
Ceramic Figures*

each other and revealed to me were ugly, old, snaggle-toothed. Their clothes were poor and dirty, their shoes ill-fitting. It was a mean travesty of love-play. Yet they danced with vigor and fine rhythm. They delighted their audience, who bought them drinks and egged them on with cries: " Catch her, she's a star! " " Go to him! " " Arr-rr-rro! "

As people left the grandstand the crowds grew in size, in noisiness, and drunkenness. When a man said to a woman: " A turn with me? " they turned first to the bar and downed a glass or two of chicha or fragrant *mistela*. Between turns he offered more, or their admiring friends did. Now and then a seated drinker toppled over and was hauled out, but the dancers only waxed more vigorous and suggestive in their gestures as they drank. All along that line of arbors, however, the dancers were middle-aged or more. It was not that no young people were there. Girls, many of them pretty and dressed in modern print frocks, sat at tables, beating out the rhythm, tapping their toes, looking hopefully at the guasos But those caballeros, handsome and young, kept their horse bridles in hand, or entered only to drink. It was as thoug only the aging knew that the way out of life's misery was assume a gaiety if they had it not. Youngsters may be gro ing self-conscious about the old peasant dance if not asham of it.

But the oldsters were artful and inventive. They var the endless circling, dodging, and overtaking until they m every dance seem individual. The men made loops of t waving handkerchiefs, the women postured provocativ Men forced their bodies against their partners, making t spread their skirts like a fan to evade the kiss which have been very alcoholic against the face. They ended al with a fast and furious clicking of heels on the board

the mounting tempo of instruments and voices, the whoops of excited observers. The woman was shyly overcome at last and the man, leering and strutting, was the conquering male. And all, mind you, with misshapen bodies and feet, ugly old faces, poor and often dirty clothes. If the stranger cannot see the happy carefree Chileno, but only sad-seeming people drinking and letting off the fumes of drink as they sweated in the dance, one sees the invincible spirit of the Chilean.

Once, as we stood at a booth's entrance, I was roughly pushed aside by a man running. Another followed, reeling with drink. Then we heard cries; men pushed out to look and in again, telling each other that one had stabbed the other. Immediately carabineros were on the spot and in command.

" It's time to go," advised Boleslo at my back. " The drinking will get worse. More shootings, knifings too. The police are here, and it is never well to be around when men are killed and the police ask questions."

I was ready to go too, but I made it a lingering stroll along the arbors in vain search for the young and pretty dancers that appear on all the postal cards and in the tourist guides. I could only hope, as we drove off into the reddened dust cloud of sunset, that the pretty girls would show up at the *baile social* that night. Lush enticing young things with flashing eyes, rounded figures, and dainty feet under full skirts. They would be the partners for those handsome guasos who had all afternoon been too assiduously attending their horses.

Later, looking for photographs to illustrate the cueca, I found the very girls I had missed, but looking somehow only palely posed, too stagy in their rippling skirts, shoulder shawls, and heeled slippers. Even the guasos, all correct in leggings, spurs, and ponchos, were characterless in contrast with the real cueca dancers I had seen. In dull clothes, ugly

and old, they yet had danced with verve and style, they were funny and full of character. No pictures gave any hint of the real folk quality of the dance.

Then, when I was sunk in discouragement, I came upon some ceramic figurines in the Bellas Artes. I stood laughing at the very uncouth and comical peasants I had seen at Curacaví. I returned repeatedly to be delighted again. There was the rough joviality, the vulgar voluptuousness, the actual cueca as actually danced. They were the work of José and Benito Román, brothers of Chile's distinguished sculptor, Samuel Román Rojas.

These brothers, all three, are typical and most promising of the new Chile. Of a poor village family, the older brother's genius took him to Santiago, made him a place in its schools, galleries, and museums. Later he brought his younger brothers there, and they amuse themselves, while they teach and study, by modeling the Chileans they have always known. Few Chilean painters have discovered their own country. Though they paint Chilean scenes, they are such scenes as they might have painted in France, as many in fact did paint in France. But Samuel Román Rojas makes Chileans in bronze, and his young brothers, with their impudent humor, make the Chilean guaso, inquilino, and drunken cueca dancer to the very life.

As I could not show my readers the figures in their gay strong colors, I had them photographed and here they are.

XVI

INQUILINO FAMILY

RIVING TOWARD SANTIAGO WE WERE BUCKING THE
Saturday afternoon exodus to the seacoast. Luxurious limousines swam stately past, bearing portly grandees and grandes
dames; pretty girls in headkerchiefs and youths in collarless
shirts darted heedlessly along in open roadsters. Among them
was every make of cheap and broken car. Chile must be the
port of missing automobiles, so many might have been resur-
rected from junk yards to run a few more kilometers. None
is ever too rattling, steaming, or bumping to clatter along at
its fastest rate, dodging in and out of slower traffic. Careful
Boleslo's cautious pace seemed fully justified. But something
besides threatened disaster was on his mind.

"Would you like to visit an inquilino family, friends of
mine? They live just here."

Of course I should be charmed. I was afraid he had forgotten his earlier suggestion. He made a false stop at a bridge
across the roadside ditch where a lace vine festooned the
hedge of red and pink geraniums. The right place was the

next one, where the geraniums were set off by spires of blue
and dark blue larkspur and a heavy grapevine weighed down
a rough pergola. An old woman sat there patching pieces
for a quilt and shooing off the chickens that came pecking
among her pile of rags.

A younger woman ran out to greet us, wiping wet hands
on her apron and pulling forward four children to introduce
them. She urged me cordially to come in, gabbling excitedly
to Boleslo about his family, her husband, the state of the
weather, crops, children, and pigs. The old woman rose rheu-
matically from her low chair to add her welcome and to introduce a half-grown girl who emerged from the house. In no
time we were seated on chairs under the peach tree. From
there I could look into the house.

Its set-in portal opened into a dark room; each wing might
have held another. It appeared that there were no windows;
the floor was mud, the foundationless walls were settling
crookedly into the earth, and the plaster was peeling off. It
was, in fact, the typical inquilino home.

Our hostess offered tea at once and retired into a wall-less
thatched shelter to stir up a fire under the pot. Her manner
was that of any lady in her home as she directed the older girl
to bring out a small table and lay it with a clean cloth, with
cups and spoons and a bowl of rough brown sugar. Meanwhile Grandmother did the honors, inviting me to inspect the
vegetable garden.

"The vegetables, you see, are coming up well." There
were carrots, beans, potatoes, and peas, and off against the
wall several rows of corn. " The weeds," she said, and I could
well see, " are growing fast too. I hoe, but I cannot keep them
down. My old bones move too slowly now and my daughter-

in-law and her niece are too busy in the house. My son, of course, works on the fundo all day." She made no complaint; she stated facts.

The inquilino is allotted a plot of land to cultivate as his own, but as he works six days a week from dawn to dark on the fundo, he must depend on his womenfolk or on hired labor for his own crops.

The orchard of a dozen peach, apple, and apricot trees seemed tidier, but only because the trees rose above the weeds and lack of pruning did not detract from their charm.

" And this tree? " she asked. " Do you know this one? "

Yes, I knew the fig tree, loved to eat its luscious purple fruit.

" Then you must come again when our figs are ripe. You shall have a chair right here and a basketful to take home when you can eat no more."

As she talked she had been gathering flowers, which she apologized for because there were no rare ones. It was a beautiful bouquet all the same — red and salmon geraniums with white and yellow snapdragons and enough blue larkspur to pacify the distrustful colors.

When I asked if they canned or dried vegetables or fruit or sold the surplus, she laughed.

" Oh, no, everybody has plenty of fruit and vegetables. If there is too much we give it away or let it rot."

I remembered the President's dictum: " To govern is to educate."

Then the man of the house came in. It was not yet sunset. He had been excused from work because he was ill. He certainly looked it, yellow and feverish. I could have diagnosed the national complaint — liver — even before he explained his symptoms with accurate particularity.

"I could not even eat my beans," he complained, turning to his wife for help. Part of the inquilino's wage consists of a daily ration of beans, toasted flour, and occasionally sausages and a potato stew.

His wife promised him immediate relief in a cup of strong tea, as one reassures a child, and I strolled back to the grandmother, who had shaken her patch quilt free of a couple of kittens and was working on it again. She refused to join us at the table; poked up instead her own tiny fire where she was boiling water for maté. Her gourd and bombilla stood ready, and when she poured in the water the infusion steamed up a rich and stimulating aroma.

"We old Indians," she laughed, "like our maté better than the white man's tea." I noted that here, as in so many places, people will refer to themselves as Indians, forestalling anybody's calling them so. She settled comfortably to suck, with a baby and a kitten sharing her lap, a dog at her feet.

I should have been glad to share the maté — its sharp fresh flavor is refreshing and good — but the white man's tea could not have been better as our hostess poured it almost boiling from the pot. As usual I barely saved mine from an avalanche of sugar and was allowed to pour my own milk. There were buns of a texture like beaten biscuit, fresh from the outdoor adobe oven; cheese, also home-made and white, creamy, and delicately flavored. A bowl of pink and white cherries stood ready, and when we could not eat them all, they insisted that I must carry the rest home in a catalpa leaf.

My hosts were politely curious about a visitor from so far away, especially a Yanqui from that land of fabled wealth who lived in an adobe house at home and who knew about outdoor ovens. They gradually understood that New Mexico

193

was the other end of the Spanish civilization they knew and we drew nearer under the ancient ægis of Spain and the comfort of a common language. But Boleslo was not satisfied with chitchat. He had brought a writer to see how inquilinos lived and he was bound to make his point clear.

" Wouldn't it be splendid," he said, " if Don Alfredo here owned this place and could farm it properly? See, his vegetables need weeding, his corn hoeing, his trees pruning."

Don Alfredo shrugged, liverishly hopeless, but his brisker spouse took it up.

" And look at my house. The plaster is peeling; it's worse inside. And the roof leaks like a sieve. And will the patron do anything about it? " She threw her arms out dramatically. " Nothing! Absolutely nothing! "

Born on the place, Don Alfredo had begun to work as shepherd at the age of eight. He had never lived anywhere else, had never been as far away as Santiago. Of schooling he had had none; his wife had attended the plantation school for two years and could read and write. The three older children were in school now.

Don Boleslo interposed, bound that I should not miss the full implications of that statement. " But three years! What is three years? These are bright children, they could learn anything, acquire a trade, attend the university. But what chance have they? None, none at all! It is not like your country, where anybody, even the poorest, can work and earn and go to school. These children have no chance at all." I wondered if Boleslo was deliberately stirring up envy and dissatisfaction, remembering that envy and dissatisfaction have improved many a peasant's lot.

This family is typical of Chile's agricultural population, which the United States Bureau of Labor Statistics for 1939 estimated at 2,600,000 people, including dependants. The same authority calculates the laborer's daily wage at 5.50 pesos in cash and perquisites. The perquisites mean the worker's ration, such a house as Don Alfredo's with its couple of acres of garden, a larger parcel of land for cultivation, and grazing rights for two animals. As the man gives, in return, about 240 days a year, from dawn to dark, and as a pair of shoes costs about 150 pesos, the inquilino's chances of bettering himself are slim indeed.

His predicament and what it means to the country as a whole has been brilliantly summed up by Amanda Labarca in *Mejoramiento de la Vida Campesina* (*Betterment of Rural Life*): "Today we are paying for more than a century of lack of foresight on the part of our ruling classes.

"Chaos and political disorientation above. Discontent, undernourishment, and physiological misery below. Poverty in almost all. . . . What are we waiting for? The revolution? . . . It is a mistake to imagine that submission, humble resignation, and fatalism are eternal. . . . Rapid evolution or tragic revolution. . . . I think it is high time to begin to evolute." Chileans always picture their ills with more vigor than any foreigner would dare to employ.

The misery of the lowest class she outlines as due to fatalism, which is "a sign of racial psychic weakness." Laziness and shiftlessness she lays to undernourishment, which also produces a deep sense of the worthlessness of effort. The typical Chilean, she says, expects to gain only by finding a mine, discovering a treasure, inheriting a fortune, winning in a lottery, or — by revolution. The general fecklessness and lack of responsibility she lays to the Spanish conqueror, who went about "sowing sons," for whom he assumed no responsibility, letting the woman take the blame and the onus.

195

All this tragic picture took shape through our casual talk that day. The plantation, under the new law, was supposed to provide medical care, even hospitalization, but this family had never been visited by a doctor. The grandmother had delivered these babies and those of all the neighbors. That law seemed no better enforced than the one requiring " adequate and hygienic housing." The children might get three years of schooling. The whole family went to church when the priest came, once every two months or so; but always on the day of the fundo's patron saint. That day, apparently, was as notable for drunkenness as for religious fervor. It was the great fiesta.

Others were at harvest time: the lovely autumn days when great wains come creaking in under purple mounds of fragrant grapes which men trample for wine. The threshing, when animals are driven round and round while men and women toss the golden grain to winnow it. The rodeo, when guasos test their skill with cattle and race their horses along the straight roads under the poplars. And National Independence Day in September, when the whole country explodes into joyous license.

Drunkenness is the one attribute of Chile's laboring classes which all observers agree upon. Saturday drunk, fiesta drunk, drunks in celebration, in mourning, and to relieve despair. The country drinks more wine than milk: 60 liters of wine per capita a year, according to Labarca, to 28 of milk. (1 liter equals 1.05 liquid quarts.) The new laws require the payment of wages in legal tender; the old plantation chits are outlawed. But each plantation still owns its store and cantina, where much of the cash wage clinks back into the till on Saturday night. So the inquilino, in the hacendados' eyes, is a humble, lovable, improvident, and drunken inferior, loyal and dumb. They state confidently that he is incapable of rising. If he shows any symptoms of rising they are frightened and appalled.

More thoughtful students find that Chile has hampered herself by failing to develop her vast human resources. Indeed, she has allowed that potential source of production to deteriorate. One could quote excellent Leftist or radical writers on this point. I quote Benjamin Subercaseaux, scion of several lofty families and a wealthy young hacendado himself, who has discovered the ugly backside to Chile's beautiful front. He begins with the rivers, which he says " take more from the land than they give it," and which have so washed out the calcium that both chickens' eggs and human bones show its lack.

" The process must be in its later phase, because it is already perceptible in the course of one life. Any man of forty will remember that in his youth chicken's eggs were larger and with heavier shells. Likewise he will remember that year after year the military classes produce men smaller and shorter-legged. It is one symptom of lack of calcium along with bad dental condition. What experiences school dentists relate; and what marvelous teeth the inhabitants of the northern pampas show! Because in the extreme north there are no rivers to carry away the salts . . . the inhabitants are tall, robust, and with enviable teeth.

" What must we do to make the sea return the salts which it takes from us? It is difficult to answer. In any case, a diet of fresh fish — which Chile has in abundance — would be the immediate means of avoiding the degeneration of the race. But this is precisely what the people do not and cannot eat because no business handles fish on a large scale. Everything that is Chile's own, everything which should rightly benefit the men who live in this country, they cannot consume because it is sold at exorbitant prices." (In a note: " Fish, shellfish, lobsters, avocados, chirimoyas, even potatoes, are articles of luxury.") " And this is the best evidence of the improvidence and bad administration of our country. When a people remains dispossessed of the products of its own land it is because it has the soul of a shopkeeper or because its rulers have been inept or ignorant. It remains to be seen if there is another reason which would leave us more credit. I have not found it."

So speaks the wealthy young aristocrat, accepting responsibility for his country's ills, though perhaps he does not see them all. The radicals I do not quote indicate that if the man with poor teeth earned a fair wage or owned a decent farm he could buy the calcium he needs.

The family I visited was bright, hard-working, eager to do its best, actually doing remarkably well with very little: little skill and knowledge as well as little cash.

Its most tragic limitations would disappear with better health, education, and opportunity. I decided, that day, to seek a Chilean hacendado who was trying to better these fundamentals — if not pay. It is too much to hope, in anybody's country, that better pay would be given except under duress. As I bade my inquilino family farewell I knew that they represented the submerged class, the one scarcely touched, as yet, by Chile's social laws or by the democratic ferment.

Even this class, seeming so static, is finding ways out. From it has always come the drifting roto, that fierce potential criminal or radical who is Chile's pride as well as dread. He is *muy hombre*, very man: tough, brave, and cruel. Adrift from the fundo but still an agricultural laborer, he is a migrant and useful to the hacendado, who finds him funny and admirable. The more adventurous, maladjusted, or unstable becomes all that damns the roto in conservative eyes: irresponsible, unsocial, even criminal. With no ties binding him to fundo or patron he drifts off to mines or factories, joins unions, and imbibes notions which are called communistic whatever their real content. Many of these men attain a consciousness of citizenship and manage to educate their children beyond the three primary grades. Out of this ferment is emerging a new citizen to prove that in Chile, as everywhere, neither virtue, wit, nor enterprise belongs to any one class.

Señora Labarca, in *El Mejoramiento de la Vida Campesina*, has compared Chile with Denmark, which is similar in size, in geography, and even in climate in many regions. There, as in most of Europe (she wrote in 1936), the peasant child enters school knowing the uses of soap and water, how to spin, and much lore. The Chilean, in contrast, has inherited no manual skill either from his Auracanian foremothers nor from the Spanish sowers of sons who had no bourgeois pride in handicraft or trade.

"Is our boasted national intelligence," she asks, "a myth as baseless as that of our national wealth?" And: "Is democratic equality only a lying cloak?" Her answer, of course, is a vigorous *no*. And she goes on to outline a plan:

Higher wages and intensified production with better methods so all can eat better. In 1936 sixty per cent of Chile's eighteen-year-olds were found unfit for military service. And twenty per cent illiterate. Colonization of unused lands to develop an independent farmer class, and co-operatives to develop his market and make it possible for him to compete with the hacendado, who is well organized as farmer, winegrower, and stockman. And, always and forever, better education, and education adapted to the countryman's needs.

Even before Amanda Labarca wrote so vigorously in 1936, Chile had inaugurated the excellent social legislation which her Popular Front has carried on. In spite of what she calls " silent but effective resistance," many Chilean leaders in government and in education are trying to bring the inquilino up and out. So far nothing has been done to alter landowner- ship; Chile is proud that her progress is meticulously consti- tutional, though slow. But as education spreads, individuals are making their own way.

Boleslo, my driver, was an excellent case in point. Of the inquilino class, he had gone to town. Doubtless as a younger man, picking up jobs as he could, he would have been classed as a roto. He might have become a roustabout, even a crim- inal. But because he had good health and mechanical ability, he had finally found work in a garage and a chance to learn. Then he was hired by a wealthy family as a chauffeur. Now he was a capitalist with his own car. And he was intelligently aware of what his country needed, ready to use his vote to get it.

The three hundred pesos I had paid to ride for a day with Boleslo had proved a rewarding investment.

XVII

FUNDO AND FREE VILLAGE

[HACIENDA CHACABUCO]

THE HACIENDA OF CHACABUCO LIES NORTH OF SANTI-
ago on a road which skims easily over low hills. In December
they were bare of grass, but studded with the changeless green
of mesquite, chaparral, and acacia and the insistent accents
of tall cactus. The cordillera was banked with hard eternal
snow, which on the lower slopes had yielded to summer and
was brimming the ditches with life-giving water. It was the
pattern most homelike to a Southwesterner. Above the ditches
bare hills cracked open into red gullies or rocky canyons,
and below them lay cultivated fields. We passed a few small
houses, each one with flowers, mostly geraniums. Then the
scarlet plants ran together into a hedge and we stopped before
a tall gate where a pink Martha Washington framed a grassy
court. A pleasant young man came out to welcome us: Señor
Petrinovic, a tall, gray-eyed Yugoslav who was managing the
fundo for his uncle, its owner.

Chacabuco has seen a great deal of Chilean history, even
prehistory. Prehistorically *chaco* (the springs) *buco* (of the
hawthorn) was a place Indians liked. Its ever flowing spring,

at the head of the Aconcagua Valley, was a resting-place for men and llamas on their way south from the Andean plateaus.

Its proudest memory is that of the Battle of Chacabuco, at which Generals José de San Martín and Bernardo O'Higgins decisively defeated the Spanish forces and established the independence of Chile. San Martín had just made his amazing crossing of the Andes, comparable only with Bolívar's similar exploit farther north. At Chacabuco he joined the forces of O'Higgins, who had fought his way through from the south. That was on February 12, 1817. Two days later they entered Santiago in triumph and O'Higgins was proclaimed Supreme Director of Chile.

At the time of the battle Chacabuco was owned by a revolutionary family who put it at the service of the generals as headquarters. It is easy to picture them there, their faces and uniforms are so familiar from pictures and statues in all parts of Chile. The stern, coldly impeccable San Martín, who had spent months over in Argentina preparing his equipment, training his men, foreseeing every contingency; and who had brought them through those passes at 15,000 feet, suffering from mountain sickness and cold, but weathering it and fit to fight. San Martín's steady wisdom then saved the day after O'Higgins, the rollicking impetuous Irishman whose dash and charm warm even the stone monuments, had almost lost it by disobedience and thoughtless impulsiveness.

Afterward they heard Mass and gave thanks for their victory in the hacienda chapel. After their day the historic building was allowed to fall into almost complete ruin; only the walls stood. But the present owner has restored it. Its façade is cream-colored now and adorned with designs like strawberry icing from a confectioner's bag. The effect, set in a garden of greenness spiked with pink and lavender flowers,

is as sweetly pleasing as a Swiss greeting card. The dim interior is what a colonial chapel should be, with soft blue ceil-
ing and brown-stained beams, and pews, altar, and railings
delicately carved by hand. Nothing of what the revolutionary
officers saw remains except a magnificent *Descent from the
Cross,* doubtless painted in Spain. But the vineyard where
they dined and the superb view of mountains are unchanged.
The same arbor drips with fragrant blossoms in spring, which
turn into massed emerald globules and finally into regal
purple clusters. There the generals and their officers drank
their health and that of the new Republic in the good rich
Chacabuco wine.

All through the nineteenth century Chacabuco belonged to
Chilean families who — because of absence or poverty or dis-
interest — let it run down. Those were the years when the
legends grew. Even Señor Petronovic, too busy and skeptical
to be much interested in fables, has been collecting them in
spite of himself because treasure-seekers come to him for permission to dig. Each one has a tale, a chart, and absolute faith
that he will turn up quantities of doubloons, if not caskets of
jewels.

Once a doctor came from Talca with a map given him by
an old man on his deathbed. The site of the treasure was
plainly marked, and there the doctor spent several days with
pick and shovel. Unaccustomed to physical exertion, he then
retired with nothing for his pains — literal pains — but sun-
burn.

One morning a carabinero, serving as night watchman, came
to the patron. He forestalled distrust by his introduction:
"I was not drunk last night." Cold sober, then, he saw something white which sped ahead of him through gardens and
patios, always beckoning, promising treasure, surely, if only

by its presence. But at last it flew to the top of the house where the carabinero, all sober but winded, could not follow. Neither the wraith nor the carabinero made another attempt. Perhaps the watchman never again risked himself out alone at night without a drink.

The most elaborate expedition was that of a Chilean lady who arrived with six laborers, a mysterious gentleman, and five burros to bear away the treasure she meant to find. Given permission to camp on a certain hill, she stayed there for two weeks. The hacendado was curious enough to set a watch on her. That scout reported that every morning, early, the lady hypnotized her gentleman companion and followed him on foot for hours while he moved in a trance from spot to spot. The laborers got little digging, the burros no load, and the city folk only disappointment and worn feet.

Señor Petrinovic gives any seeker permission to dig where it will do no harm, only stipulating that fifty per cent of the treasure must belong to the hacienda. He says that only once was he himself enthusiastic about the prospects. That was when an old man came from Argentina. He knew the location of the spring, his chart showed a tree growing near it, and marked the location of the loot twenty paces away. And it was loot. For his story was that after the Battle of Chacabuco a Spanish soldier found himself in charge of fifteen mules loaded with royalist gold. He ordered the muleteers to bury the money near the spring, then foresightedly killed them all and escaped to Argentina. Never able to return for it himself, he had, just before he died, told the story to his son, who came, twenty years later, to retrieve the fortune. But something had gone wrong. No treasure was discovered.

One naturally asks: " Was nothing ever found? "

Well, yes, a single gold coin was once picked up on a pass

in the cordillera — a Spanish coin dated 1835. It sold for 750 pesos. Another time a huaso reported that he had found old boards under the earth high up in the mountains. When he moved them he found silver coins and a cellarful of armor. But he neglected to keep the coins and could never go back to the armor. So the total treasure trove of Chacabuco was that single gold coin.

As in the fable, the real wealth was in the land. Chacabuco now has 96,000 acres of land under cultivation; some cattle and horses; and 22,000 sheep. Its rams are of the finest; it imports and experiments with foreign breeds, and produces the best wool in Chile.

It was a joy to walk about that farm, so richly fragrant of plowed land, running water, blossoms, and animals. On either side of the famous old grape arbor glistening orange trees bore fruit and flowers at once. Between them were sprigs of nursling olives and the borders were mint. The frame was the high sharp edge of the cordillera against the distant sky, and closer in the round bowl of the hills where cattle and sheep grazed.

On the other side of the spreading house were the stables and dairies. Big airy buildings with every convenience and comfort for fine cows kept contented for milk; and every luxury for delicately bred racehorses. Even the ewes and rams, being readied for a show, were sheltered under a circular roof where clear running water and a scientifically planned ration would bring them to their perfection. Only the houses for the ranch's 1,200 workers were crowded in airless rows, with few windows, no running water, no modern plumbing. It was the old, old object lesson so clear to everybody except to these who house, feed, and care for their animals well that they may breed better, work better, and produce more.

As our host led us back to the house he pointed out a crew of men pouring cement for a swimming pool. It was so big we asked if it was for the hacienda people.

"Oh, no," he laughed. "I'm so big, I'll take up all that water myself — except when I have parties out from Santiago."

[MELIPILLA AND POMAIRE]

We had been told that Pomaire was quaint and remote, a bit of old Chile, untouched by the modern motorized world. It was also a free village where land was owned by the people and not part of some vast fundo's enclave. On the way we could see the Sunday cattle market at Melipilla and have a picnic lunch somewhere beside the road. Friends who had been there said that Pomaire was a hotbed of witchcraft and soothsayers. We might, with luck, find an old lady who would consult the spirits for us and prophesy the future. It seemed perfect.

We set out in a car with a New Mexico license, which my friends Hortensia and Ernesto Maes had driven all the way from a Venezuelan port across the mountains and deserts and thus far on their circle round the continent. Of Spanish blood, perfect and fluent Castilian speech, and Yanqui enterprise, they had had more fun, made more friends, and disseminated more goodwill and international confidence than many a formidable official mission.

True to both Chile and New Mexico, we started late and decided that the soundest policy was to have our picnic first. So we purchased rolls and cheese, fruit, and a bottle of good red wine in a roadside market, and chose our luncheon spot under a willow beside a muddy ditch. As we were finishing on apricots and cherries the roto appeared. Ragged and debonair, he was sauntering along as though going nowhere and in no hurry at all. When he stopped, on invitation, he displayed the utmost courtesy and self-possession. His Spanish heritage was evident in gray eyes in aquiline face; his Indian — if it was Indian — only in a deep reserve and that arrow-straight walk. He accepted with dignity what remained of our bread and cheese and without comment the request that he find some poor person to give it to. The last third of our bottle of wine he thought he could find a place for too. Then he bowed and went his way.

At Melipilla the cattle sale was in full swing. We bought ice-cream cones to top off our lunch and entered the grandstand, where Hortensia and I were the only women among fifty men or more. In the paddocks below, youths and boys were prodding the cattle into the pens. Yearlings and two-year-olds were offered in bunches, oxen in teams, and now and then a valuable animal — a stallion or a bull — alone. Oxen were bringing from 900 to 1,500 pesos each; milch cows from 600 to 800 pesos; steers about 600 pesos; and horses from 1,000 to 1,200 pesos. These figures Ernesto ascertained by questioning his neighbor. For we heard no bidding, though two auctioneers shouted the usual singsong, spelling each other. No bidding was, in fact, made aloud. Only by watching closely could we see men raising a hand, a finger, or even an eyebrow to place a bid. It was a mystery how the auctioneers caught on. One of them at last indicated that he found it difficult.

"Speak up!" he shouted. "Say what you wish. Here we are free men. . . . Yes? Sold to Señor Fulano. . . . Louder, my friend! Here you have no censorship to fear. Make your wants known. This is free Chile. . . . What! No better bid for this fine team? . . . One more? Sold!"

When we tired of the sale we set out again, looking for Pomaire. All Melipilla was *de fiesta,* and everybody we accosted observed that New Mexico license plate and shouted: " *Saludos a México!* " They were delighted to direct us, and a small and scholarly-looking youth drew an excellent map in the dust.

Pomaire has a road now; its remoteness is lessening. But we were warned that it was off the paved highway; we would find rough going. Ernesto won a laugh by insisting that it could not be so bad as the paramos of the Andes. It was not bad at all. We soon turned off the pavement where a tall eucalyptus seemed to be holding up the remains of an adobe wall and drove down a dusty road and up a long easy hill. We paused on its summit to look for the village. We saw fields where black earth had been turned in neat furrows, fresh green meadows with the usual rounded willows and emphatic poplars, shrubs along the ditches and in fence corners, and — yes — those dry hayricks were the thatched roofs of houses. Then we got the pattern of the village, following two roads to a small blue and white chapel against the hill.

Just there our roto overtook us; he must have made a short cut across the fields. There was no sign of our sandwiches, but he had known what to do with the wine, for the bottle hung empty from his belt. He was more genial too, pleased that we were visiting his village. We had no room to offer him a lift, and, in any case, his manner was that of a gentleman walking by preference.

Feeling our way, wondering how to learn how this village lived, we stopped at a small cantina. The proprietor came out, bringing cool bottled drinks. Cool, verging on tepid. But they were wet; and the day was hot. His establishment was one adobe room where men sat inside a long low window drinking;

and an upstairs room reached by a rickety balcony. Our *can-tinero* proved to be loquacious.

" We are all proprietors," he said proudly. " Everyone in Pomaire — we are three hundred families — owns his parcel of land."

Then, urged to a seat on our running board and a bottle of his own sweet nectar, he was gradually led on by Ernesto to expatiate on life and agriculture in Pomaire. Landownership, it appeared, did not connote wealth, though it obviously conferred a sense of worth and dignity. One farm, the largest, amounted to about 2,400 acres. Most of them averaged between five and ten acres. And about a third of the Pomaire citizenry owned no land at all but were farming for the big owner on shares.

" But we eat well in Pomaire," our cantinero insisted, pointing with his empty bottle.

Certainly plenty of good food was in plain sight. We saw growing corn and beans, leaf vegetables, and all the fruits one could ask, from Delicious apples to Chile's special sugar-sweet figs. Pigs lazed in the orchards, chickens pecked around the doorways, every man seemed to have a horse to ride and a cow behind the house. The best animals, our host said, had been sent to the cattle sale at Melipilla. Most of the land, however, was in grapes.

By this time we women had discreetly withdrawn from the conversation, leaving the two men to compare notes on farming methods in Pomaire and a certain New Mexico valley. But I got the figures later. Last year this cantinero had planted all his land to grapes and made his own wine. Having good luck, he sold it all for about 2,400 pesos: say $80. Naturally he spent the pesos. Bills at the store, food, clothes. He did not mention a fiesta or drink more potent than his own red wine.

But why not? At any rate, before he knew what was happening, along came the tax-gatherer and collected about half of his takings. The rest was too tragic for elaboration, though we surmised that Pomaire real estate was not quite debt-free.

Such a village as Pomaire offers little for Chile's growing industrialism. As we drove the length of its two streets we passed fences of rails or brush, not wire. The log and adobe houses were clean and generally well plastered. But mud is cheap, lime not too expensive, and thatched roofs offer little outlet for factories. We saw only one store, with a few dusty cans on the shelves and bolts of cotton cloth. Stopping there brought us sharply up against the village life, for an old dame popped out of her house and engaged us in conversation at once.

Where we had come from and why were interesting enough, but she was shaking with curiosity about a government car parked just ahead of us. Two carabineros, she informed us, had just gone into that house. Now why? A lady who lived there, she admitted, might upon occasion have an experience with strange powers. But she was a lady most correct, never would she do anything irregular. Now, did we think the carabineros could have come to question her about her gift for foretelling? Not, she assured us, drawing back from strangers, that anything wrong went on; but with carabineros one never knew. They question, and who knows? Sometimes they take people away and it may go very ill with them.

So our hopes of seeing a soothsayer in action were dashed. With carabineros in town there could be no hope of getting the lady to use her powers for our entertainment. Sadly we drove away.

Pomaire is on the road now, but still an excellent example of one of Chile's saddest ills. What Amanda Labarca so stir-

ringly set forth in facts and statistics, José Gonzáles Vera
has poignantly pictured in his short novel *Alhué*. Alhué is a
village not far from Pomaire; five years ago it was a two days'
journey by cart from Melipilla. Mail went in by horse, now
and then. There was no school for three hundred children.
Life in such a village — in hundreds of such villages in Chile
— is poverty-stricken not only in material things but in everything. Ignorance and superstition, ill health and undernourishment, hopelessness and apathy, call for quick, strong measures.

The needs are obvious. And not unheeded by Chile's intellectuals both in and out of government. Señora Labarca urges
1,500 additional rural schools with teachers specially trained
for the job. Most teachers, she remarks sadly, deem work in
the country a punishment, village life a form of banishment.
The other great need, beyond education of both children and
adults, is for land and better farming methods. This the government is trying to supply through various agencies.

Through its Caja de Colonización the government has bought
land and settled on it small proprietors, mostly inquilinos of
proved industry and intelligence. Another agency makes loans
for the purchase of equipment and animals. Government
agents offer assistance in management and agriculture. In
some cases the owners of large estates have sold their marginal
lands for such projects. But so far not enough land has been
acquired or is available to remake Chile from a feudal economy to a democratic state.

Such a village as Pomaire — restful and humanly divert-
ing on a Sunday-afternoon drive — is sad in contemplation.
For Chileans are people of great potentialities, and they have
such a long, hard row to hoe.

Driving away again, we paused on our hilltop to look back,
and there again our roto met us. He had found another bottle,

for his reserve had melted quite away and he was tipsily disposed to talk.

"Unfortunately," he said, "I am not a proprietor. My arms are my fortune."

Exhausted, he sat down on a log, begged pardon, and took a pull at the bottle. He waved an arm out over the view and seemed to be settling into sleep, when another idea struck him.

"I dedicate myself at the moment," he assured us gravely, "to wood. To the chopping of wood and hauling it down to the patron." So there was a patron? Well, yes, all the land from here on out to the hills and the other way too; that was all of the patron. The patron, fortunately, always had work to offer and a man who was a good workman — we were allowed to assume that our friend was indeed that — could always get work. But by the day, surely, by the day. Pressed, our friend would not admit that he lived anywhere, really. He worked here at times; then again in the mountains. He personally had never been to the mines. But he had friends who had. By this time he was too sleepy to combat longer the urge to slumber, so we considerately drove away.

XVIII

A PRESIDENT IS BURIED

DON PEDRO WAS ILL, AND THE CITY WAS SAD. PRESIdent Pedro Aguirre Cerda was habitually accorded the intimacy of his first name; often even the affectionate diminutive Don Pedrito. For days the country waited, hoping that his heart could carry the load of a deep bronchial congestion. But in spite of the prayers of thousands in the churches and the efforts of Chile's best physicians in La Moneda Palace, Don Pedro died. The country went into official mourning, but deeper and truer was the unofficial grief of the mass of Chilean people, who felt they had lost a real friend. Thousands of them passed the bier where he lay in state. Sad and simple folk moving humbly through the magnificence of the palace and the funereal pomp of enormous floral pieces where uniformed men stood stiffly at attention.

The girl in the beauty parlor said: "I knew something dreadful would come, some great tragedy for all of Chile. For during the Eucharistic Congress one who carried the San Miguel in the procession stumbled and fell. They caught the

213

blessed image, but it was a portent; something bad was sure to come. And now, you see? Don Pedro died."

Boleslo, the political-minded driver had said: " Don Pedro understands."

When I spoke of such evidences of true mourning and personal affection to a lady of *la alta sociedad*, suggesting that the people had really loved the President, she shrugged. " Well, yes. Chileans of a certain class."

But he was respected and mourned by another class too, the liberal professional people who led the parties which elected him. " The group," one of them said, " typical of moderate change. . . . Aguirre Cerda was a statesman with wide knowlege of men and profound political perspicacity. He was able to unite political parties and to arouse popular fervor. Few men are able to do what he did: to steer a country through a transition period of restless social development without ever endangering legal forms or constitutional rights. Chile has seen revolutionary changes not only without spilling one drop of blood, but without political or economic oppression of any section of the public. It will be difficult to find a man to carry on what Aguirre Cerda has been doing."

A teacher assured me: " Chileans are bright and highly educable people. With one generation of a decent government which would advance schools — even if it advanced only schools — we could take our place alongside the most advanced countries in the world. Don Pedro knew that, for he was a teacher. He said, you know: ' To govern is to educate.' His death is an irreparable loss; we have no equally far-seeing leader to take his place."

Dr. Claude G. Bowers, United States Ambassador to Chile, and a sound old-fashioned Jeffersonian Democrat, said of President Aguirre Cerda: " Fifty years from now he will be

La Señora de Aguirre Cerda

Carreño

President Pedro Aguirre Cerda

revered as he is beloved now by the people. He was always their friend. Long before he was president he had stood out for social reforms, for the education of the masses, for the amelioration of the condition of poor children, and for governmental facilities for the conservation of the health of the people. He was a great humanitarian, and he was intelligent. . . . But he had so little time! "

Pedro Aguirre Cerda was a Chilean who knew his country and his countrymen at first hand. His father was a farmer, and not a wealthy hacendado. Young Pedro, as one of eleven children, attended the village school and qualified as a teacher. Not until he was twenty-four years old was he able to enter the Pedagogical Institute in Santiago, where he studied law and political science. Admitted to the bar in 1904, he taught political economics at the University of Chile and watched both politics and economics as practiced in the capital. His friends say that his eagerness to see his country advance destined him for a political future; his enemies that he played his cards well. In any case, he won a scholarship which took him to Europe to study, to the United States to observe. Young Aguirre Cerda was a coming man, but one who brought with him knowledge of how life looked to the poor man, and the respectful appreciation of education of a man who has worked for it.

He served as deputy in the lower house of Congress, as Minister of Education, of the Interior, and as president of the Chilean Winegrowers Association. For by this time the country school teacher was an hacendado himself. He had married his cousin, a lady of wealth and social position. Clearly, though his parents were poor, they were of good family. So the affable little school teacher, for all his simplicity and unaffected manner, was unabashed in society and quite able to make himself felt among the most astute men in Chile. He became president of the Radical Party, which, in Chile's complicated political scene, is rather to the Right of Center but socially minded. Farther Right are the Liberal and Conservative parties and the Falangistas. The last two are strongly Catholic and all speak for the landowning class. Far to the Left are the Communists and Socialists. The Center is generally considered to be the Democrats and Nacistas (Chilean Nazis who deny any connection with the party in Germany). No party is strong enough to elect a president unaided; fusions are the rule.

By 1938 there was a fast-growing dissatisfaction with President Arturo Alessandri Palma, a powerful and leonine man who, starting as a Leftist, had fathered Chile's social program. But by the time he had been thrown out twice and come back twice, he was a convert to stability. So he came out as the stern suppressor of strikes, the opponent of radicals of every hue.

The Communists, the best organized Leftist group, countered by joining the Socialists in a *Frente Popular*, which won over the Radicals and nominated Pedro Aguirre Cerda for the presidency. His opponents, General Carlos Ibáñez del Campo, supported by the Nacistas, and Gustavo Ross, a Conservative, had between them the backing of the Church, the landowners, and the moneyed classes. One of them was fully expected to win. But Chile's new class was awake; perhaps for the first time rotos, factory workers, and even inquilinos were not going to vote as the patron directed. Then, due to a coup which misfired, the Frente Popular got the support of many intellectuals and old-fashioned Chilean Liberals and Democrats who constitutionally dislike high-handed methods.

On September 5, 1938, two months before election day, somebody started a demonstration against President Alessandri's government. Who planned it and who were involved are still moot points. But a group of Nacistas, under orders of Gonzales von Marées, who commanded by telephone from the country, attacked the Moneda and shot a policeman. President Alessandri, in a rage, sallied out alone and dragged the wounded man indoors. He — or somebody — then ordered the police to take the Nacista headquarters. More than sixty young men were killed. This ruthlessness gave the Frente Popular the election. The Nacistas and Carlos Ibáñez went into that camp as the surest way to defeat Gustavo Ross, who, as Alessandri's Finance Minister, was considered the administration candidate.

Politics never made stranger bedfellows than that election. Naturally President Aguirre Cerda freed Ibáñez and von Marées, whom Alessandri had jailed, and thereby became suspect to his Communist supporters, whose adherence made him a Red radical in conservative eyes. But Chile, having elected the first Popular Front government in the Americas, was committed to a policy which the President phrased as a pledge to " end conditions in which the Chilean masses lack food, culture, clothes, and dwellings." In spite of every handicap he never swerved. And the handicaps were many.

He had first to face dire tragedy, for in January 1939 an earthquake, which Gabriela Mistral described as " a blow in the solar plexus," shook central Chile and demolished twenty cities. The immediate concern was relief, but the President, in spite of an opposition Congress, managed to get authorization also for a rebuilding program which included loans for low-cost housing. It is estimated that Chile should build about 4,000 new homes a year in order to get her people even decently housed. And the funds available will permit of only 1,200, a situation eloquent of Chile's problems and difficulties.

The need for rehabilitation after the earthquake led also

to legislation which permitted the borrowing of funds from the United States to promote the electrification of the south, the construction of heavy industries like iron and cement works and of weaving, wood, glass, and chemical factories. The program includes the development of fisheries, of processing plants, and the importation of agricultural machinery and breeding stock.

As President, Don Pedro's interests did not change. The people and their betterment were always his prime concern. Thanks to the good taste and good sense of Doña Juanita, Señora de Aguirre, life at La Moneda was almost as easy as life in Conchalí, where Don Pedro raised fine grapes for the red wine named for the fundo. She was always able to receive old friends, never too busy to take part in a school affair or to visit a maternity home, an orphanage or hospital. Her interest in the future of Chile was as great as his; her devotion doubtless sustained him through hard and bitter discouragement. Their rest was on the fundo, which, not far from Santiago, offered them the retreat of a quiet house with patio and portal and the renewal a natural farmer gets from touching his own soil with hands and feet.

Much of the social legislation which is Chile's pride dates from President Alessandri's earlier and more liberal period. The Constitution of 1925 provided for health measures and even laid the groundwork for readjustment of landholding. Later legislation established insurance for workers, accident compensation, minimum wages, and price-control. Chile even then wrote in laws creating loan banks and low-cost housing projects. Not much new legislation was passed during Don Pedro's short and tragic term of office. Nor was much needed. His great contribution was in the determined and honest effort to enforce the laws already made and in the establishment or improvement of various institutions to give direct, intelligent, and sound aid to the underprivileged, especially women and children. Pedro Aguirre Cerda was a stubborn protagonist for democracy, and though his efforts were largely nullified by unrepentant Rightists and starry Leftists, he never lost sight of his goal: a country run for the good of all rather than for the privilege of a class.

For popular advance and social betterment, then, first came the policy of " the development of labor unions and the settlement of labor troubles by law and not by force." My informant said: " The government is always the arbiter, but if it failed in anything, it was in being more benevolent toward the oppressed classes." Moreover, labor laws which formerly reached only 3,000 people have been extended to cover an additional million.

The needs of public health were alleviated — though not met by a wide margin — by new and better hospitals and sanatoriums for the care of the needy and especially to combat the country's most menacing diseases: tuberculosis and venereal disease. General hygiene has been somewhat improved by pure drinking water, more adequate sewage disposal, and educational measures.

The heart of these measures is always the protection and improvement of the child. Don Pedro and Doña Juanita, childless themselves, were always concerned for children. They gave lavishly of money and of time. But the program Don Pedro visualized was far wider than private charity could compass. It contemplated the protection of every child, but especially the abandoned, ill, or abnormal child on three fronts: the medical, legal, and educational. A member of the health department said that the government proposed to look after the child from the beginning of his mother's " embarrassment " (as they speak of her pregnancy in poetic Castilian) until he is sixteen years old, at which age the Chilean becomes a producer.

This ideal has been expressed as *Defensa de la Raza,* a phrase which implies betterment as well as defense of the race. It is the title also of a great government social center in Santiago, which was one of Don Pedro's dearest projects and one of the last he dedicated. The ambition of the place is to give working men and women " joy in living, apart from houses of prostitution, gambling, and drink." It is to serve as a model for similar centers on a smaller scale in all parts of the country. It stands now, in its beautiful sunny park, as a great empty shell. Well planned and equipped with class-rooms, rest-rooms, club-rooms and athletic and sports fields, it lacks funds for an adequate staff and operation. Like so much of Chile's social program it is a brave blueprint for a fine future, so far unrealizable in its entirety.

Don Pedro's funeral procession brought together all the people he had worked for, reflected all of Chile. For days special trains had brought Congressional deputies, prelates of the Church, military and naval officers, and hundreds of private citizens. The 29th of November was a fair spring day and thousands who could claim no place in the cortege lined the streets. Sidewalks were crowded from earliest daylight on. Windows rented at high prices. Roofs were fringed with hats and parasols. Boys were perched on bridges and on the scaffolding of a new hospital. Patients had been moved onto terraces and roofs. Those who could do no better swarmed like locusts over the hills around the cemetery, giving the impression that beyond those hills all Chile stood reverently attentive as they carried Don Pedro on his last sad march.

Only the diplomatic corps and high government officials

were admitted to the Cathedral, where the Archbishop of Santiago performed the Requiem High Mass. They then marched afoot through the streets, where half-masted flags drooped and many authorized groups waited to follow the gun carriage with its flag-covered casket. Units of Army and Navy and every Chilean institution of government and learning were represented, as well as many foreign organizations.

Instead of joining the North American women carrying the Stars and Stripes in a Pan-American section we chose to see the whole procession from the cemetery. There we rented chairs and settled down to wait and watch the people. A fat woman, creaking on painful feet, had set up a rickety table for the dispensing of a drink, made of crushed fruit and corn gruel. She impartially used a bucket of water for thinning her concoction and washing her dishes. A small boy aided her — the kind that any country should cherish and train for big things. He showed enterprise, going out to seek customers when the waiting line lagged; assiduity in keeping everything neat; good humor, cracking jokes with all comers; and good business acumen in collecting, making quick change, and assuring himself that any doubtful customer had cash before he served him.

A well-dressed lady with two daughters tried by sheer weight of manner to secure chairs where none were to be had; then organized a group of boys who went away and returned with wooden tubs and a wide plank. The bench they made looked wobbly and when a mass of people surged up onto it, it threatened to spill them all, but miraculously it held, and the lady and her daughters were able to see across the crowd to the central monument.

Students had brought their books, mothers food for frilled babies, little girls their dolls, bootblacks their boxes, country people large bundles on which they sat. Buttons, flags, and other adornments were on sale, as well as a long poem on Don Pedro which the seller chanted lugubriously to prove its suitability to the occasion.

It was long past noon when a thrill finally ran through the crowd and we felt rather than heard that the procession was coming. Carabineros, smartly accoutered and shiningly groomed in mounted and foot detachments. Cadets from military and naval academies in tall shakos and white horse-tails: precise, serious, and touchingly young. Infantrymen with wreaths hung over their shoulders so they formed a linked chain of fresh flowers; other floral tributes massed in carriages, scenting the warm air. Cavalrymen on beautiful horses, beautifully controlled. Officers and men of the Navy: sunburned, crisp, and smooth in their march. A band playing a funeral march. More carriages with flowers drawn by horses plumed and netted in black. Dignitaries of the Church followed a car in which rode His Excellency Archbishop José María Caro. Cabinet officers, members of Congress, and the diplomatic corps.

Then the catafalque under a mound of flowers attended by bareheaded officers, preceded by Chile's flag, and accompanied by a military band. The Archbishop had taken his place at the monument in the center of the plaza. From there he made his funeral address. It was a dignified and simple tribute to a great humanitarian, and it came from a prelate who was well known to be a humanitarian himself, one of those Chilean Catholics who stood too for social betterment. He spoke of Aguirre Cerda's true adherence to the Church and his constant effort to harmonize Church and State. And he said: " The people had reason to love him and to render him the most heartfelt expression of their gratitude."

Chile's Popular Front President was gone. Chile would now have to choose a successor. And before that election date the Western Hemisphere too would be at war. Who would be the next president? What stand would Chile take when America was drawn into the war?

XIX

THE HACIENDA DE SAN VICENTE

AN VICENTE, AGREED GOVERNMENT MEN, INFORMED foreigners, and many Chileans, was *the* fundo for seeing what up-to-date methods and a fine social conscience could do. Señor Hugo Jordán, its manager, was cordial and frank.

"Come any day," he wrote, "and we will show you what we have and answer any questions you care to ask."

We drove out of Santiago on a cool fresh morning along the highway which leads north along the central valley, over the crest of Chacabuco, and into the upper Aconcagua Valley. There, tucked in close against the cordillera, nestles Los Andes, the last considerable town on the Chilean side. Train schedules are so arranged that passengers for Argentina must spend the night in Los Andes. An arrangement said to be in the interest of hotel-keepers, it seems to set apart the high, cold snowy world of the Andes from the humanized valleys below.

From Los Andes skiing parties go on to Portillo on El Lago del Inca, which mirrors infinitely lofty peaks in infinitely deep crystal blue. All winter Santiageños ski there; in summer they fish; in autumn they hunt. Its beauty is overwhelming; the air's electric clarity makes the whole body vibrate; and every year new tales recall the merciless might of the Andes. Planes are lost, trains are stalled, pack animals slip and pitch down beyond sight and sound, and men disappear forever or re-appear with stories of hardship and heroism.

Los Andes is a town of quiet dignity. It would be a good place to stay a long time. Air breathes deep there; the people look unhurriedly busy, the buildings sturdily solid; and in the hotel we found comfort and good coffee with kuchen for second breakfast.

Then we turned aside from the road to Portillo and went off between cultivated fields to the Hacienda de San Vicente. It, like Chacabuco, belongs to foreigners who have settled in Chile; and it will soon be turned into a government project for training agricultural engineers.

As we entered the central compound everything indicated a working farm. Big barns and tall silos. Whooping guasos dashing past on ponies they were breaking. Men in the fields and grazing animals beyond. We crossed a running brook and stopped before a shady portal where the Jordán daughters met us, speaking English easily and full of questions about their school in Santiago.

Their mother, who quietly followed them, was the typical mistress of a large plantation in any age. A commander. But a gentle commander, who shares her husband's responsibilities and upholds his authority; directs her own children; orders and sees to men and maid servants and their families; manages a complicated household and knows what everything costs and where everything is; supervises chicken farms and dairies; keeps an eye on orchards and berry patches against pickling and preserving time; makes a hobby of the plantation

school and day nursery; and entertains a constant flow of
guests. In her spare time — such a woman always has spare
time when the one in a city apartment is too busy to live —
this hacendada was collecting old folk songs and reintroduc-
ing them to the plantation people. She greeted us with leisurely
graciousness and led us through several stately rooms into one
where we left our hats.

The furniture was of an age when things were expected to
serve generations of large families. Ten-foot carved bed and
dresser tops fitted comfortably under beamed ceilings fourteen feet high. Fragrance of early roses and heliotrope blew
in through the long French windows, and a bowl of sweetpeas
stood on a bedside table. The bathroom was vast, with a deep
tub, wide marble basin top, and a full-length mirror. The
amplitude of everything allowed for dignity in living, which
modern life has lost somewhere. In such a house, with thirty
rooms or so, a family of eight children could find space for
every little ego to expand.

There was time before lunch to see the school. Doña Rosa
laughed a little as she said: " My husband will show you things
afterward. I'm only interested in people." What a perfect division of labor and interest that is! For the man, the things;
for the woman, the people.

The law requires every fundo employing a certain number
of people to maintain a school of two grades. San Vicente has
five; and that is typical of the place. We skirted playgrounds
and ball courts where boys were practicing under a young in-
structor's direction and came to the school buildings. A vine-
draped cottage for the teachers, the school proper, a building
for crafts, and an eating hall. We went first into the school:
a wall-less room where little girls in clean pink aprons were
squalling dreadfully. But they were nice children, and nobody

had ever told them that yelling as loud as possible is not the best singing.

Out of the plantation population of 4,000, 210 children between the ages of six and fourteen were in school. There were seven teachers, two with the rank of professor. Extra-curricular activities include semi-weekly visits of the doctor with special care for all who need it, two hot-water baths a week under brisk showers with plenty of soap and brushes, and a good hot noon meal. We visited the kitchen, also open all round and with a huge stove in the center where a stew, beans, and two green vegetables were cooking. Enormous sweet-smelling loaves had recently come out of the oven, and there was milk for all.

In the industrial building teen-age girls were sewing.

" This came about by accident," said Doña Rosa, who probably turns all accidents into assets. " When the children left school we often did not have work for them, so we occupy them a couple of extra years."

Girls were learning to sew, knit, weave, and crochet by making clothes for themselves, curtains, and table and bed covers for their homes or their hope chests. The materials were cheap, but the effects exceedingly good. They were also hearing talks on personal hygiene with the emphasis on morals and chastity. And learning to care for babies with the emphasis on legitimacy. Doña Rosa was proudly clocking off a steady annual decrease in illegitimacy. Perhaps the wedding, with the patrona for sponsor and a present and a sense of correctness and elegance, has something to do with it.

Boys, beyond school's regular classes and still too young for regular employment, were working in shop and vegetable garden. What they make and raise is sold co-operatively and the earnings put aside. Each boy may, after a year, use his cash as approved by the *profesor*. Recent withdrawals had been for further education, for care of teeth, for the purchase of a pig. Boys were weeding the strawberry patch as we walked slowly along the ridges between irrigated beds; one offered us apricots and grinned at our pleasure in their sweet warm juiciness.

Then the *preventorio* and baby clinic, which are Doña Rosa's pride. Especially a preventorium rather than a hospital appeals to her. If she had her way, Chile's greatest ills would be prevented, not ameliorated too late for cure. On the way we stopped for a glance at the bachelors' hall. Among the fundo's population of 4,000 about 300 are *ambulantes* or *afuerinos*, walkers or outsiders. These migrant workers are generally unmarried, often tough, given to radical notions, and apt to get drunk and disorderly.

" We try to prevent as much as we can," said Doña Rosa, " by giving them pleasant places to live." Every minute made me wonder more why Chile doesn't turn over its social problems to a good, experienced mother and hacendada. What a deal of trouble it would save! The migrant bachelors were quartered in a large house whose living-room, with a fireplace, was just then being hosed out by one of them in rubber boots. Beyond were the dormitories and across the way a big shed where meals were served. But this was Don Hugo's province; I should have to ask him about workmen.

The preventorio was a small fresh building presided over by a trained nurse. Twice a week she assisted doctor or dentist with examinations of lungs, blood, and teeth. Between times she attended routine cases or emergencies and directed her assistants in caring for the babies of working mothers. Several infants making longer stays, lay in hospital cribs enjoying special care or feeding up. One two-year-old was all over the place, rubbing against one's legs like a kitten, loving to be picked up. Her mother had died.

"So she'll probably stay here indefinitely," said Doña Rosa, rubbing the little head. "We'd all miss her too much if she left now."

The record of the preventorio is one hundred per cent. No infant mortality at San Vicente. The first year of the experiment thirteen died of the usual complaints and one of an accident. The second year, no loss — a record which they mean to maintain.

Then it was time to wait for the luncheon bell under a pepper tree near the house. A huge cedar stood near, a jacaranda was dropping pale lavender petals on the grass, a tall magnolia's waxy blossoms scented the air, and palms waved their plumes in a breeze too high to touch us. All the zones from deep tropics to subarctic had contributed to San Vicente; never had I had such a sense of Chile's limitless endowment. A clear stream bordered by violets and lilies of the valley purled at our feet. It was really a busy irrigating ditch, hurrying on its way from the swimming pool to the flower garden's patch quilt of marigolds, daisies, and petunias. Roses clambered on trellises along the portal and swung out long branches trying to catch the pepper tree.

Our group grew as youngsters came in with damp hair and that almost transparently clean look after a long swim. A young couple were presented. He, an agricultural student at the university, was to have several months of practical work here before getting his degree. His wife had been inspecting their house. Doña Rosa promised paint and a man for a couple of days. It would do nicely, the young wife said. She would not bring the children down until her preliminary work was done and she had found a maid.

Don Hugo joined us. A tall slender man, it struck me that he moved like a Yanqui. But he bowed like a Latin and, once ensconced in a big wicker chair, he relaxed completely, smoking, smiling, chatting. He explained himself at once.

" I am Yanqui," he said. " Chilean, of course, but Yanqui-trained and *muy aficionado*. I graduated from Ames, you know. My son is there now. . . . Yes, I may send the younger ones. We Chileans need what your farmers know. But even more we need to understand the real democracy of your country. We've got a long way to go, but here we are trying — by education, by improving our people's physical condition, by advice and so on — to bring them along. But," he sighed wearily, " it's slow, slow! So many of them are utterly ambitionless. They will not work even to gain more."

I quoted a man in Venezuela who, speaking of his backward folk, said: " Now in three generations . . ."

" Well, yes," admitted Don Hugo, " there is something in that. They have been held in ignorance so long. But one of our great handicaps is that these people have heard about their rights before they heard about their responsibilities. A responsible citizen is still in Utopia. We are doing what we can, but it will be a long pull before we can develop anything like the sturdy farmer I knew in Iowa."

Don Hugo has managed San Vicente for ten years, during which he has built up a superb dairy herd and established a profitable business of powdered milk. The fundo, which belongs to Pascual Baburezza, a Yugoslav, has 70,000 acres of dry land — that is unirrigated and suitable for cattle in some parts, sheep in others, woodcutting among the hills, and for nothing at all above and beyond that. An additional 4,800 acres are under irrigation and productive of practically anything you could name.

Then lunch was announced and we went into a long narrow dining-room easily able to accommodate twenty people — not an unusual number, I gathered. I sat next Don Hugo and we had fun comparing his country and mine. He laughed at my description of a Chilean rodeo in a padded basket and reminded me that in my country rodeos were savage performances and really dangerous.

" I don't know where the world gets the idea that you Yanquis are soft. Everything you do is hard, demanding not only good physique and courage, but a certain daredeviltry. If Hitler comes up against you, he'll wish he hadn't."

Lunch was the typical Chilean meal. Vast. Our hostess had prepared for me a chicken stew, without which she said no country lunch was complete. It was a hearty meal in itself, but it was followed by *empanadas*, crisp turnovers with a sweetened meat filling, another meat course, salad, and a delicate flaky dessert with strawberries. Its effect was that of an old-fashioned Thanksgiving dinner. One is consciously eating too much, but each course is too good to skip. By the time we had returned to the sun-flecked lawn for coffee, I was in no condition to ask intelligent questions or to understand what I was told. But out of that haze of sleepy repletion I remember a few facts and figures Don Hugo gave me. Providentially he was called away from time to time and I could doze and catch up.

" Later," he promised, " we'll see the dairies. Meanwhile what do you want to know? . . . Our inquilinos are paid twelve pesos a day, six days a week, all year. No layoff, no unemployment. Besides, each one gets his ration, his house, two acres of garden, grazing privileges, wood, and we lend animals to work his land. Many of them raise and sell wheat, potatoes, and hemp. . . . Oh, two acres of wheat will sell for 2,000

231

pesos; potatoes perhaps even more. Many take in that much from what they raise; others do well with animals. We graze about 2,000 animals for the inquilinos.

"No, they're not on the best land. Their steers run about 800 pounds, while the fundo's average 1,400. But they can sell them to advantage." He chuckled. "I said no layoff, but you'd be surprised how many inquilinos, living in our houses, using our land, tools, plows, and animals, can't find time to work on our land, they're so busy on their own."

"So you are developing the new self-supporting farmer?"

"Well, yes, but he's not very self-sustaining yet. He counts on us for a good deal."

I was figuring. "So a man might handle as much as 5,000 pesos a year in cash. What can he buy with that?"

Doña Rosa was quick to answer. This was touching her department — people and how they lived.

"On twenty pesos a day," she said, "a family can eat, but not dress."

Don Hugo laughed. "Well, they raise enough to eat; they get milk from us. They have to buy only their clothes; they should be able to do that on what we pay. Perhaps they buy the clothes; that should be their province. They get eight pesos. But don't forget that we are giving these people physical care, education, and training they would never buy for themselves if they had the money outright. . . . I sometimes wonder if we don't have to educate the backward peoples before we give them rights."

True. But in what country has the dominant group ever really educated the backward people before they had forcibly gained enough power to demand their rights? It is, I thought sleepily, the present-day version of the conundrum of the chicken and the egg. Then Don Hugo finished his coffee and

The Trans-Andean Railway

The Milch Herd Grazes under the Peaks

excused himself to go off with a tall, booted youngster who had summoned him. The Señora showed me her collection of old songs, allowing me to copy what I wished, and we chatted des- ultorily until the growing shadow of the tallest palm warned of late afternoon and time to visit the dairy.

San Vicente manufactures powdered milk which is sold all over Chile for babies and invalids. We saw the whole process. First the imported Holstein bulls in their paddocks, fierce and puissant, with great restless eyes. Young bulls and heifers grazed in the rich pastures fenced in by rows of slender trees and brooded over by snow peaks. Cows with their young had special nursery meadows with shaded brooks and pools, and the newly weaned were indignantly learning to subsist on im- personal feed. All along the way we had passed milking girls. Unfortunately they were not musical-comedy milkmaids, but heavy-set peasant women in distressingly dirty aprons. In the milking sheds they sat on stools expertly squirting milk into tinkling tin pails. Men handled the animals. There were a few mechanical milkers, but not many yet.

Don Hugo smiled, as employers have a way of doing, as he said: " When we have more mechanical aids and employ fewer people we can pay more. Then what will you advise about the ones we throw out of employment? " But Don Hugo's bark is much worse than his bite, and his growing business and the number of young people he is training for mechanical jobs an- swer his facetious question. Not to mention the Chilean babies who need milk they are not getting.

The milk, still warm, goes directly from the cow to the fac- tory. We followed it into a large corrugated iron building, all white inside, served by white-clad men, and smelling of milk. The men looked keen. Don Hugo pointed out one, who spoke rather sullenly, as the labor leader.

" Now and then," he said, " a Communist comes out from town and stirs them up to strike. . . . They always strike for higher wages, they can't think of anything else. . . . Oh, generally we compromise it. The men aren't really class-conscious, you know. They like to work here; they always have; they can't imagine anything else."

He was more interested in the process.

" The milk, you see, is poured in here. It is evaporated at a low temperature: a process which preserves all its food values. There it loses about a third of its volume. Then it is pumped into this dry chamber and literally blown into powder."

Men were tending the machines and, by hand, fitting tops onto cans and pasting on their labels. Whole milk is canned and sold as *Leche Marina*; separated milk as *Milko*. It is chic in Chile to use English names, especially for manufactured articles. I tried Leche Marina from a can Don Hugo gave me and found it better than the milk from that " scientifically clean " but fly-ridden place in Providencia. Butter is a profitable by-product which sells locally; so far there has been no surplus milk for cheese.

As we strolled back toward the house, along a lane striped with poplar shade and sunshine, Don Hugo talked about the new inquilino houses.

" We're trying to build practically indestructible houses in which people can live with perfect cleanliness if they wish. Each one has a good roof of tile or fabricated material, a cement floor, a porch, a shower bath and W.C., water piped into the kitchen and dining-room, two bedrooms, ten by ten, and another room for storage or for the *allegado*. Every family has one, you know."

He laughed at my bewilderment; I thought *allegado* implied transience.

" Yes, it does," he answered. " An arrival. A dropper-in.
But in Chile he — or more often she — stays on and on. Perhaps they do their share, taking care of children while the
mother works, or making a crop for the man of the family
while he works on the fundo. Anyway, it's the Chilean way.
Nobody is ever homeless, no matter how helpless or forlorn."

He suggested our calling on a family — " one of the most
hopeful " — on our way out. For it was nearing time to leave.

As we made our farewells we met a long procession of
schoolchildren, crossing the back patio toward the chapel. It
would be Christmas in a few weeks; they were coming to practice the songs and hymns they would sing for the fundo celebration. Doña Rosa called one of the older girls to guide us
to the inquilino house we were to visit. The child bobbed curt-
sies and made herself as small as she could in the car, answer-
ing questions in a shaky voice.

The house we visited was as Don Hugo had described it. A
good housekeeper could have made it a charming simple
home. But, at five in the afternoon, it was disordered. Beds
were unmade, a broom, exhausted by the very sight of so much
litter, leaned against the wall; cold ashes from the fireplace
had blown across the floor; unwashed dishes waited on the
table. Two women met us, serenely unaware of the mess in
which they lived. One picked a bouquet of bleeding hearts,
geraniums, and daisies from her garden, which she had just
watered. The other was shooing at the chickens, who alone had
any notion of disposing of the dropped crumbs.

That was discouraging. But San Vincente all together was
an exciting portent of Chile's future.

XX

A CHILEAN CHRISTMAS

CHRISTMAS IN CHILE IS LIKE THAT SEASON IN ANY Catholic country, where the emphasis is on the Nativity, and they call it *La Noche Buena,* the Good Night. It is the children's season, as with us, but little Chileans are concerned with the Holy Child, not with presents. Gifts come later, on *Día de los Reyes,* Day of the Kings or Twelfth Night, when the kings brought gifts to the Holy Child.

This is the tradition. But Santiago, thoroughly cosmopolitan, is as crowded as any northern city with shoppers seeking imported luxuries, toys, Christmas trees, and shining ornaments. The Alameda flower market near the lovely red brick Church of San Francisco displays evergreens from the snow fields along with roses and gardenias, sweetpeas and specially grown orchids. For Christmas in Chile is hot. A young German-Chilean laughed about how unsatisfactory he found his first Christmas in the Fatherland with no corn on the cob, no cherries, and no swimming parties. Society in Santiago expands its usual program with more formal balls, debuts, and din-

ners in town, greater races with higher betting, and bigger
house-parties in the country or at the beach.

I was most interested in the folk Christmas, which is naturally most Chilean.

In Los Andes I found a *Nacimiento,* Nativity, as touching
as a primitive painting. It bespoke at once the simple devotion
which brings pretty and valued things to honor the God, and
the tender understanding of a clergy which allows such artless
expression.

In the place of honor, near the high altar, the people of the
parish had made their Bethlehem. The background was cactus-
studded hills, not because Judea was a semi-arid land, but
because the state of Los Andes is. There was a thatched house
and an outdoor adobe oven because if Joseph and Mary were
seeking lodging in Chile, that is what they would find. The
cow and the ass were there, according to the tale. But their absence from Biblical lore had not banished from this hospitable
scene two Teddy bears, one riding a camel, the other in a
wicker rocker, or Mickey Mouse, grinning impishly. Chinese
lanterns and cut-out white rabbits filled up the foreground.
None of this, of course, detracted from the reverence of the central scene. The Babe was almost as large as the Virgin Mother
— they had clearly never been meant to meet — and Joseph
was of a different category altogether. But the spirit was true,
and several women knelt before it in prayer.

The same engaging simplicity appears in the songs these
people sing. Señora Jordán at San Vicente, had permitted me
to copy a few quatrains made for Our Lady of the Rosary at
Andacollo. Andacollo is a mining village in northern Chile.
But it is also a sacred spot which attracts the devout from over
the Andes in Bolivia and Argentina and from up the coast in

Peru, as well as from all Chile. Coming in fulfillment of a vow or to ask for intercession, pilgrims sing their message, addressing the Most Holy Mother of God as simply as one would address a near friend. To them she is also a young mother, needing advice, and the Son of God a tiny, tender baby.

> *Tan pobre niño te miro*
> *Que a saber tu desnudez*
> *Hubiera traido un poncho*
> *Para abrigarte con el.*

> I see you so poor, O Child,
> That knowing your nakedness
> I should have brought you a poncho
> To wrap you warm in it.

There was sound advice, too, for a young mother with her firstborn. The hacendada was delighted with the good effect of the health program indicated in these verses.

> *Y también le traigo peras*
> *Que al azúcar dan envidia.*
> *Que no coma mucho el Niño*
> *Ne le vaya a dar lepidia.*

> Also I bring you pears
> That would make sugar envious.
> Don't let the Child eat much
> Lest it give Him stomach-ache.

> *Señora Doña María,*
> *Le mande decir mi abuela*
> *Que si no vacuna al Niño*
> *Le puede dar la viruela.*

> Señora Doña María,
> My grandmother says to tell you
> That if you don't vaccinate the Baby
> He may get smallpox.

Men's pleas stem from different worries, but express the same intimate confidence.

Señora Doña María,
Yo he venido de mi tierra
Solamente a preguntarle
Que sabe Ud. de la guerra?

Señora Doña María,
I have come from my country
Only to ask you
What do you know of the war?

Men's advice, too, is different, and perhaps less reassuring to Chile's hopes for social betterment.

Y para que se refresque
Después de alcanzar Victoria
Le traigo un calabacito
Lleno de chicha de jora.

And that you may refresh yourself
After victory comes
I bring you a little gourd
Full of *chicha de jora.*

Perhaps Andacollo would be the place to seek the soul of primitive Chile, however remote that might be from the essence of the country's sophisticated aspects. Moreover, a folk festival is excellent protection against nostalgia in a foreign country at Christmas time. I decided to go to Andacollo.

As northern Chile is not considered vacation land, it does not appear in the *Guía de Veraneantes* (*Vacationers' Guide*), and tourist agencies profess complete ignorance of train or ship schedules and will not make hotel reservations. For getting beyond the range of tourists — that constant ambition of the seasoned traveler — in Chile one need only go to its third city.

The early morning train from Santiago was crowded. Were these dressy passengers with smart British luggage the pilgrims? No. At La Calera the parlor cars departed for Viña del Mar bearing " salon society " off to beach, casino, and racetrack. That left the station thronged with poorer and more religious folk and their baskets, bundles, bottles, babies, and bunches of flowers. The northbound train was already packed, with people standing in the aisles. It seemed utterly hopeless to secure a seat, but a porter whispered that another car was being put on ahead and rushed us there and got us seated just as the engine began to puff.

" With two extra cars the engine will never make it," hazarded a man in English. There across the aisle was a Yanqui who explained himself as one who had lived twenty years in Chile and would not live in the States again " if they gave them to me." But he was going home soon to see what he could do about the war. " They'll probably tell me to come back and produce more copper, and that's all right too."

He was not quite right about our never making it, but almost. The train crept along, toiling, straining, steadily losing time. It seemed fitting penitence for a pilgrimage. We passed vineyards and orange groves, then orchards and fields of grain. But soon we had left all that and were laboring up ridge after ridge, puffing through a tunnel and then gathering slight momentum as we went down again. Rugged country which Benjamin Subercaseaux named " the country of the broken trail." For here the Andes have thrown out small ranges which " like immense arms unite the cordillera and the sea. . . . The cordillera, in this region, throws out its chest and raises its head in a gesture of supreme pride. It has no volcanoes nor wishes them. It is enough to possess the highest mountains, the most difficult passes, and to look seaward with the severe frown of its ranges and its valleys free of any volcanic slag. Aconcagua, the highest peak in the Americas — 22,835 feet high — rises here. Chileans think it is in their country, when in reality it is an Argentine peak. But we do not despair; in the same region we see the crest of Salado rise to 22,640 feet, and this time fully in Chilean territory."

Between those bristly strong arms of the cordillera are irrigated valleys. La Serena is in the state of Coquimbo, the northernmost reach of agriculture in Chile; there the crops are as fine as usual where it costs struggle to produce them. Agustín Edwards describes the Coquimbo Valley as a place for all who seek solace, with its tepid atmosphere, intense light, and sweetness in the air and in the fruits. The fruits, which here attain their most luscious perfection, are those whose names suggest poetry and fairytale: figs and chirimoyas, melons and grapes, olives and pomegranates.

To Edwards this country is " a symphony of contrasts. Multicolored aridity on the mountains and slopes; green exuberance cut by rivers which misspend, in impetuous mountain streams, their volume of melted snow and arrive almost exhausted at the lands they could really fertilize."

The contrasts of the land seemed reflected in the people on the train. Every sort of Chilean was there. An exquisite white-haired lady with two daughters with the magnolia skin, deep dark eyes, and shining hair, brows and lashes that seem so completely Spanish. In contrast I noted a woman of pure Indian type with round high cheek bones, coppery skin, and heavy lips. Her stoical brown baby shared the seat with the weak white child of a beautiful young couple who took turns caring for him. Both these babies, like all the many babies aboard, were quiet and quietly handled. One old woman was the typical Spanish peasant. Strong-featured, deep-bosomed, and imperturbable, she sat stoically all day and well into the night. Two girls with her were in curious contrast, with skins lighter and finer, slimmer figures, and much less self-control. A white father, perhaps, or perhaps the older woman was a servant, though she did not seem so.

When lunch was served on trays hooked over the seat in front, the Yanqui moved across to talk. Here was a Yanqui who gave the lie to many of those unflattering Chilean conceptions. He was a mining engineer, operating his own mine. His talk about Chile and Chileans was marked by intelligence and understanding, and I had noticed that he had been reading a well-used volume of Shakespeare. An intellectual Yanqui business man!

With the midday heat there was a general shifting about and letting down. Six men started a bridge game, cutting in. One of them, who had been cherishing a paper sack, finally opened it to display gardenias, waxily fresh in cellophane. They shared a baked chicken, which they dismembered and consumed with beer and gay talk. They laughed uproariously, but circumspectly lowered their voices before the loudest laughter.

During the long afternoon hours a group of young hacendados got aboard. They all wore the symbol of the Chilean Falangistas, that small but significant political group which is the despair of their aristocratic and conservative families. Their mothers devote themselves to charity; their fathers to gathering in the income and holding back any social advance. But these young men, knowing the Encyclicals of Pope Leo XIII, have joined together under the leadership of Eduardo Frei Montalva, who hopes to waken his own class to the misery of the poor and the danger of revolution if only Communists and agitators concern themselves with social welfare. The group on the train were beautiful young men — beautiful with youth, gaiety, intelligence, and with health, good care, and easy carriage. They laughed and talked, drank wine like water. One carried a book and I caught its title: *Adventures in the Catholic Life.*

It was well past midnight when we reached Coquimbo. The morning's prophet of despair had been right. The one-engine train, overloaded with pilgrims, was reaching La Serena at three in the morning instead of seven in the evening. The Yanqui said: " This railroad evidently has no use for pilgrims, or means to make their penitence severe. This happens every year, and I've lived around here for twenty."

Many pilgrims left the train at Coquimbo. It is a better take-off for Andacollo, and a busier town than La Serena. Even at that hour it seemed wide awake. After a long pause the train went on, rounding the bay and bringing us to La Serena: truly serene and beautiful under a star-dusted sky even at that hour.

Serene as the little city is now, La Serena was a misnomer for the palisaded fort built to guard the trail from vice-regal Lima to Santiago. Juan Bohón, a lieutenant of Valdivia, built the first stockade in 1544. Four years later it was destroyed by Indians and Bohón killed. According to legend, his naked body was found marked with the sign of the cross. Another legend tells that the original town was never destroyed, but that it still exists and may be clearly seen on Good Friday by the faithful.

All during colonial days, while England fought Spain, the port of Coquimbo and the productive valley were an unfailing magnet for pirates. All the famous names occur — Drake, Hawkins, Davis, and Bartholomew Sharpe, who reported that the valley produced not only all the fruits known in England, but wheat, wine, oil, and copper. Sharpe was almost out-smarted by an official of La Serena who held him in dicker about a ransom while the town's entire population escaped. The annoyed pirate then burned the city and sailed away.

Charles Darwin, in the *Cruise of the Beagle*, relates how recent were those raids. He was entertained, in 1835, by an ancestor of our author Don Agustín Edwards. "Don Joaquín Edwards is a young man and the son of an Englishman, but till some years old did not learn English. . . . He told me he recollected . . . when a holiday was given all the boys to see the Captain of an English ship. . . . He believes that nothing would have induced anybody in the school, including himself, to have gone close to the Englishman; so fully had they been impressed with all the heresy, contamination and evil to be derived from contact with such a person. To this day they hand down the atrocious actions of the Buccaniers; one of them took the Virgin Mary out of the Church and returned the ensuing year for St. Joseph, saying it was a pity the poor lady would not have a husband."

Don Agustín Edwards, writing of this episode, adds: "Both images were of solid silver. In no other way is explicable such refined veneration for the saints."

La Serena, as the metropolis of the north, played its part in the revolution, and during the nineteenth century opposed, as Concepción did in the south, the dominance of the pelucones of Santiago. Culturally the little city developed. Its eighteen churches were built, one by one, by Franciscans, Dominicans, and Augustinians. In 1821 it had a liceo; in 1840 a bishopric. But in 1825 the discovery of silver gave Coquimbo a new wealth and a new human element.

In that year a muleteer named Pedro Cuellar camped in a stone-walled corral belonging to Don Ramón Varela, a colonel of militia. As the night was chilly, Pedro built a fire against the wall. Then his son, scratching at the blackened stones with a knife, turned up a gleam of unmistakable silver. It was the beginning of a series of discoveries along the hill of Los Arqueros which greatly enriched Don Ramón and many others. Don Agustín Edwards does not state whether the poor muleteer and his son shared the wealth they had found. But La Serena was thereafter a mining town and as far from serene as any town stampeded by rough miners and gold-seekers from a generally poverty-stricken country.

La Serena, under the morning light, revealed nothing of its rougher days and little of modernity. It is an immaculate, well-tended city of colonial houses whose solid façades of worked stone with iron gates and grilles are pointed up by the towers of its eighteen churches. The plaza, surrounded by substantial government buildings, the archiepiscopal palace, and the splendid Cathedral, was a pool of rosy pink. Snapdragons, dahlias, cannas, and geraniums, set off only by green foliage, were as luscious as the season's fruits: split and juicy watermelons, figs bursting over pink centers, warm and fragrant plums, and pomegranates full of ruby seeds.

The gardener, basking in praise, explained that at other seasons he displayed other colors. White for the Virgin's month of May, the national red, white, and blue for Independence Day in September, yellow or purple when they best suited the occasion. " Every saint," he elucidated, " likes his own color best."

I made two calls in La Serena.

Señora Barraza, Gabriela Mistral's beloved sister, was delighted to welcome one who had recently seen her Lucila. She is proud of the famous poet, but she loved most to talk of the child. She showed me a picture of Lucila's first school, now adorned with a bronze plaque to honor her. And she lingered over the plush-backed album, tracing the development of the serious big-eyed child into the noble woman I knew. A copy of Gabriela's first book of poems, autographed for her mother, is now the most treasured volume in my small collection of autographed "firsts."

His Grace Archbishop Juan Subercaseaux Errázuriz, received me in the palace. The patio was filled with color and scent, but the rest of the building was simple to austerity. I waited a few moments in a spacious sitting-room with a few fine pieces of furniture, an exquisite carved crucifix, and two old Italian paintings. Then His Grace entered and I forgot everything else. Tall and slim, he was the perfect type of Church dignitary and of the aristocratic lineages he embodied. But his manner was as friendly and simple as that of a village priest greeting an old friend. Just back from his first visit to the United States, he was eager to compare his impressions of my countrymen at home with those he had known in Chile. He wondered, as so many less learned Chilean Catholics do, why Catholics in the United States have not sent help in education and in the social services.

Since my return to the United States I have received word of the death of Archbishop Subercaseaux. It is a great loss to his country and to mine. He was a Chilean who might have done much to cure the misunderstandings between us.

The city was animated all the long summer evening. Stores stayed open, cinemas were crowded, homes showed lights as though guests were expected. In certain quiet dim spots the guest had arrived: a lad standing under a window's grille to talk with his enamorata inside. The plaza slowly revolved in the old Spanish pattern of boys going one way and girls the other like two highly charged wheels enmeshed. Everybody would stay awake for the *Misa del Gallo* — Cockcrow Mass. After eleven the high colors of youth were shaded and finally dominated by elders in black — gentlemen in formal clothes, women in long black skirts and lace mantillas. Even many young girls went darkly and demurely veiled.

Long before midnight hundreds of worshippers had crowded the Cathedral: a mass as emotionally moving as it was physically still. Above them, softly lighted, huge balls of rose geraniums swung from green garlands. And against every gray stone pillar were pointed spires of cannas and gladiolas making a rosy lane to the high altar's golden splendor, candle-lit and adorned too with rosy red flowers. The color was re-peated in the brocade of the archiepiscopal throne.

The press of humanity indoors was too much, and we re-tired to the plaza, from where the brilliance of the indoor scene was enhanced by the wider vision of the Cathedral spires against the starry sky. Then the clergy emerged from the mas-sive central door, accompanied by acolytes, whose censers scattered incense among the flower scents from the plaza. They entered the palace and returned soon escorting His Grace. His fine ascetic face ennobled even the magnificence of ermine and moire upborne behind him. The procession entered the Cathedral and passed along the nave while the chanting swelled louder. It was the Church at its stateliest.

The plaza had become a part of the temple. As the Mass was sung, people standing there genuflected and crossed them-selves with the worshippers inside. When the high moment ar-rived, they knelt with a sighing rustle, awed by the mystery. Then bells rang out all over the town, distant peals came from the hills and the sea, and near by firecrackers made a merry human din of the tidings that Christ had been born again.

XXI

PILGRIMAGE TO ANDACOLLO

Anda, Collo! Run, Collo! Run through the hills where wealth and happiness await you. Run! "

So the town was named, they say.

Collo was a woodcutter, poor, obscure, and often hungry. Once, between sleeping and waking, he saw a lovely lady, glowing with jewels and with a heavenly light too. It was she who had called: " *Anda, Collo, anda!* "

Collo ran, so the story says, and looked, but found nothing. Then after three days, or three months or some triple repetition common to legends, he pulled up a shrub for firewood, unthinkingly. And there, tightly grown into the roots, he found an image of the Blessed Virgin. And the sands where she lay glowed like the vision of her he had seen. The sands held gold, and from them and the rich vein they led to came such fine gold that for many years " the good gold of Andacollo " was used as a standard.

A priest, writing in *La Estrella de Andacollo* (*the Star of Andacollo*), states that the name is Quechua, as are the In-

248

dians of the region, and means Kingdom of Copper. *Anda* is copper, and *coya* is a form of *cori*, meaning "kingdom." Other theorists connect it with the Incan *Kakan*, a place where the Incas got gold and which the Indians concealed from the conquering Spaniards as long as they could.

But whether Collo existed or not, the image certainly did and does. Augustín Edwards opines that the image might have been carried off when the Spaniards fled from the burning stockade of La Serena in 1549, buried for safekeeping, and forgotten. When Collo — or somebody — found it is unknown. But the cult of *Nuestra Señora del Rosario de Andacollo* reputedly began about the middle of the seventeenth century.

A brochure published by the Church states: "From that time the Image was the object of a singular and enthusiastic cult, especially on the part of natives recently converted to Catholicism. Those men, uncouth and crude, but of ardent faith, used to solemnize the religious festivities in honor of the Holy Virgin of the Rosary with dances accompanied by music and flags according to primitive American custom. These dances . . . were prohibited on various occasions by the Bishops . . . but without success in abolishing them ever."

How long Collo's hill had been a miracle shrine to the Indians is unknown. Possibly, as is often true in the Americas, it had a pagan sanctity that antedated their conversion. In 1658 the first Christian chapel was built there: a log shelter with a straw roof. A century later a stone chapel was erected on Collo's hill and a priest installed. In another hundred years the gifts of the pilgrims had so enriched the Virgin of Andacollo that on Christmas Day 1873 they laid the cornerstone of the magnificent basilica which houses her now. It is characteristic of Indians that they had kept right on worshipping in their way: with dances. And characteristic of a wise priesthood that after several efforts to suppress the dances, they permitted them.

The image is described, also in a leaflet issued by the Church, as " a cedar-wood statue perfectly carved, a yard in height; it is skillfully dressed in the same wood and thus it was for-. merly venerated; its face is small, brunette, and its expression is tender and very sweet. A small crack is noticeable in the left eye, which confirms the tradition that the Indian marred it with the tool he used for cutting wood."

At the beginning of the nineteenth century the mayordomo in charge of the image ordered a carpenter to repair it. The people, outraged, stormed his workshop, shouting: " He is killing our Virgin! He is bringing blood." But the work went on, and as no disaster followed, they accepted the renovated statue in the handsome new garments and found great pleasure in her adornment.

Rome at last took cognizance of the growing cult and " Pope Leo XII conceded plenary indulgences to all the faithful who visited the sanctuary of Andacollo, confessing, communicating, and praying for her intercession. This indulgence is perpetual and may be gained once a month."

Meanwhile the entire region had gained fame for its mineral wealth. Not only gold, but copper and silver were found. The " copper of Coquimbo " was known in Europe for its purity. Gold was so generously scattered that men were said to wash out only what they needed for a day, sure of plenty for tomorrow's panning. The natives believed that the earth was creative, forever making new gold as nuggets were taken out. But mining is tricky. The old diggings that pockmark these barren hillsides mark more disappointed hopes than successful yields, though certain mines are still profitably worked.

Getting to Andacollo was a real problem. Taxis were all engaged; bus seats all reserved. At last we found a bus-driver who agreed to reserve two good front seats in his excellent, large, well-built car. He recommended himself as the most reliable chauffeur in the state of Coquimbo. He would call for us at five; no later hour would do; everybody was going at five.

Five o'clock is early indeed after midnight Mass. But he was right about everybody's going. The bus was jammed with people and honking impatiently as we stumbled through the dark hotel. The town, in the shivery pre-dawn grayness, echoed eerily with other horns near and far away like baying hounds. Our promised seats had been taken; we were crowded onto the long back seat, already occupied by four adults and several children. Children never rated a seat alone. Half-grown ones sat on their elders' laps; lesser ones were packed two or three into a seat.

But as we drove beyond the houses the morning was too fine for rancor. Orchards and vineyards were on both sides, fragrant and full of color in the rising sun. We were traveling the wide floor of that valley, so uniform in loveliness that one must describe its flowers as fruits, fruits as jewels, the sea as a mood, air as a long refreshing drink, and the sunshine as a cuddly blanket of welcome warmth. Welcome, that is, in the early morning; later it was different.

Among our mates on the jouncing back seat was the one never missing in Chile: the friendly helpful Chilean. This one, the owner of a filling station in Andacollo, suggested breakfast at the first stop: a thatched village where the police were lining cars up for the one-way ascent beyond. At the shelter recommended as cleanest we found a plump hostess, prime tamales, and fair coffee. Then on again to climb the mesa.

The road beyond was narrow, rocky, and dusty, between stern slopes whereon grew only cactus and Chile's *Oxalis gigantes,* a leafless plant standing gauntly in carbonized circles of desolation. We were grateful for the one-way rule, as the traffic grew constantly denser. Among the vehicles went many people mounted or afoot. Near the top we passed four men making painful, penitential pilgrimage over the harsh stones in bare feet.

Andacollo is on a circular mesa, ringed with mountains and centered by the massive dome and impressive towers of the sanctuary. Around it spreads the grille of the village, whose thousand inhabitants, miners and their families, live in pitiful shacks spilling over the mesa's edge and down the eroded slopes. We passed through a noisy narrow street packed with vehicles, animals, and pilgrims and hazy with sun-shot dust. The plaza was noiser still and more hotly crowded. Colored finery and once elegant black were graying now with dust; shining black hair was overlaid with it. Surging above the human sea were the feather pennants, paper and tinsel crowns of dancing groups. Eating and drinking booths with tipsy canvas tops and backing automobiles added fumes of frying grease and burning oil to the effluvium of unwashed bodies and acrid dust. Honking and grinding our driver stopped beside a filling station and his passengers plunged overboard into that whirling storm of dust which marked the sky and noise which split the ears and made the head ache.

"This is my place," said our quiet friend. "Call on me if I can serve you. Find a place to stay first. If your friends have written the Señor Cura he will give you a room in the convent." He smiled. "I'll be looking for a car to take you back to La Serena tonight. One day will be sufficient."

It seemed impossible to insinuate one more body into that

mass, but we happily struck the end of a row of dancers, footing it jerkily to the beat of drum and the whine of flute. Clinging to that flying wedge, we came up on a terrace before the priests' house. It too was packed. At our feet sat a singer droning out songs which he sold in badly printed leaflets. A door opened on a busy mart where young priests were exchanging religious publications, statuettes and pictures of the Virgin, candles, and rosaries for coins untied from handkerchiefs or sashes.

Another door had a bell. A pull produced a clanging deep within and, in time, a fresh-faced smiling boy. Inside the hallway several people waited, and two ladies in deep mourning were talking with a priest. Small and stooped, with head outthrust and quick hands in motion, he was like a darting bird.

"Not one room," he was explaining volubly. "The last, the very ultimate room is saved for distinguished foreign ladies, relatives of His Grace himself."

Nothing for us, then, clearly. We should be grateful for our friend's help in getting back to La Serena. Still, we might as well present our introduction. It was embarrassing to learn that we were the expected distinguished foreigners. Far enough from home any foreigner is distinguished. We felt like impostors as the elegant ladies turned away and the Señor Cura conducted us out into the crowd again, skimming like a swallow through lanes opened for him. In the convent two elderly women led us across a wide patio with shaded cloisters. Our room was cool, clean, and sparsely furnished. The clamor of the fiesta came in only as an echo, the dusty glare not at all. If this was being an impostor, I'd be one always.

But the Father, who had not stopped talking for a second, was chirping: "The temple! You must see the temple!" So we reluctantly left our welcome retreat for the turmoil outside.

Still fluting and pecking like a bird, our monitor darted through the throng as through grass taller than himself. We crossed the temple's outer court, entered the great fane, and flew the length of a side aisle smelling of incense, hot wax, and hot people. At a side altar *el Señor Cura* left us and ran off, genuflecting as he passed the altar going and returning with two chairs which he flourished as he made obeisance again. But that was not all. On a second appearance he was dragging two prie-dieux. Then he left us, skimming off among the crowd.

Most of the people were standing, holding dripping candles of every size from the limpest and cheapest penny ones to long thick white tapers, adorned with scrolls and roses and selling for as much as five pesos. Sooner or later they all inched round back of the altar to see the miraculous image close.

Seemingly upheld on stiff gold brocade, it gleamed with jewels, among them a long string of pearls presented by the Infanta Isabel of Spain. The crown flashed green fire from twelve large emeralds set with more than a hundred smaller ones. Fifty-four petals surrounded four roses formed of nine diamonds each. These data were whispered by a woman behind me on the steps.

"And the Holy Child," she gloated, "also has diamonds. See His crown? Twenty-two diamonds, twenty-two emeralds, twenty pearls!" He was a stiff little figure, erect in heavily encrusted brocades.

As we descended, my new acquaintance displayed a wad of wax dirtily pressed into her palm. "*La grasa de la Virgin.*" Everybody wants a candle which has burned on the altar during Mass, or at least a drop of wax. This she had scratched up off the floor. "But the Father blesses enough so all can have some to take home."

By this time our guide had conducted us to the door whereon

is carved the story of the shrine's first well-authenticated miracle. About the middle of the eighteenth century the servant of a noble and devout lady of La Serena was wounded by a knife-thrust. He was, as related in an official publication, " perfectly and instantaneously " cured by a drop of oil from the lamp of the sacrament in the Virgin's shrine.

The church was filled with dancers, jigging solemnly to scraping and wailing instruments. Men and boys, in dresses of cotton or cheap silk, with paper crowns or feather diadems and expressions of utter solemnity. Worshippers slid away from them on their feet or knees, their mumbling uninterrupted, their beads clicking steadily. A few advanced on bare knees, weeping with pain, their faces contorted, their relatives following solicitously. Wax from candles wearily tipped dripped, smoked, and smelled; the air was heavy with human scents. Suddenly the whole thing was too oppressive to stand and we made for the fresh air.

Ricardo Latcham, whose study of these dances is the only one with scholarly pretensions, recognizes three groups organized under their directors. Membership may be hereditary; fathers train their sons. One man, now past seventy, had been to Andacollo every Christmas of his life and had danced since his third year. This form suggests an Indian background, though Spanish *cofradias* are similar. An Inca trace is found in the title *El Pichinga,* given the villager who guards the image as a title preceding his Spanish name. Under the Incas the Pichi-Inca was a petty ruler. A study of these organizations, traditions, and songs might uncover an interesting Indian background. As performed today, these dances may be called Indian only because Indians originally danced them. It seems likely that they have suffered, as so many pagan ceremonies have, from being accepted by the Church. The early

Spanish missionaries throughout America often permitted pre-conquest dances which seemed innocuous, thus smothering the original meaning under the blanket of Christianity and turning the Indian's gift for dance and drama to the uses of the Church. In some places, notably in New Mexico, more pagan than Christian has survived. In Mexico and Guatemala the balance seems about even. At Andacollo the casual observer detects very little Indian indeed.

Of the three groups the smallest is the *Turbantes*, called so because of their turbans of bright silk kerchiefs or conical hats with rosettes and floating fringe. Their dress otherwise was well-washed white shirt and trousers, and their dancing the most monotonous bouncing to the music of little drums and flutes and an accordion. Oldish, discouraged-looking men with worn faces, straining eyes, needing so much the help one prayed they might find. Turbantes are the oldest group; records of 1752 mention them as of Inca origin. They are said to end every verse with: " Hailli! " a word the ancient Incas shouted in triumph. These modern Turbantes use too the word *Mumanchit*, meaning in the old Peruvian tongue " Mother of God." Faint traces, indeed.

The *Danzantes*, Dancers, are most numerous. Often twenty-five or thirty groups come in from as many villages. They were younger men, more gaily dressed and livelier as they frisked through figures like a Virginia reel. The music included a cornet, blown with more vigor than skill, a couple of triangles and cymbals that crashed ad lib.

Newest in point of time, as it dates only from 1817, Los Chinos is the most interesting dance. China is a Quechua word meaning " female of the animals." The Spanish first used it to apply to low-caste women, as our Southerners used

" wench." Later it was applied to men too. By now its original connotation has quite disappeared.

Nowadays the Chino dancers are mostly miners: strong men with sturdy legs and keen faces. They wore the miner's open-necked shirt, and short trousers over blue socks, and blue and purple caps. Ten or twelve groups of them were dancing with vim and as though they liked it. Their instrumentation was limited to long reed flutes, but enough of them sounding at once made a satisfying din. I felt heartened by the Chino miners, especially when I sat to rest on the church steps and fell into conversation with two of them.

" It's a lively fiesta," I remarked as an opener.

" Yes, well enough," replied the younger man, while the older one watched me shrewdly. " Yelling and jumping up and down, when what we need is better wages, better schools, more food for our children."

" You don't come, then, for the fiesta? "

" Oh, yes, we come for the fiesta all right. Chileans always go where there is dancing and drink. We are a drunken lot, you know." Curious how quick Chileans are to cast aspersions on themselves.

" But you have good social laws now. Aren't conditions getting better? "

The older man had decided to take a chance on me.

" Yes," he said, " the laws are all right. But they are not enforced — won't be for a long time. What does our government care for us? Nothing." He spread his hard hands with eloquence. " It's not like your country. There the poor man has an equal chance."

" You know my country? "

" Not to go there. But we know. If Chile had a president

like your President Roosevelt, we could go ahead."

" But your President Aguirre Cerda? "

" Yes, a good man. But he couldn't do it. Wages went up, yes. But so did prices. I can earn only enough for food; a few clothes; none for saving. How can I make a decent life for my children? "

The dancing kept on; the worshippers surged past us in and out. Venders of ices and printed leaflets offered their wares.

On an impulse I asked a resting dancer to pose for one of the itinerant photographers. A woman noticed.

" You see? " she explained to all. " Her *manda* (vow) is that she must have a picture of a danzante! " Everything at Andacollo must be explained as vow or penance. Except the coming Chile sitting on the steps, watching the show with cold hard eyes, untouched, knowing no way to find relief except in drink.

We had been told to lunch at the home of the Señoritas Aguirre. The señoritas were two: a plumpish older one who sat rocking in the *zaguán* (entrance) and a sparish younger one who ran. The plump one was meltingly sweet, even when she knew that we were not relatives of His Grace. The younger was too busy for talk, keeping four maids on the move, and swiping clean an oilcloth-covered table laid for twenty. Her performance was masterly. As people came and went every place was properly laid, the table never lost its look of dainty readiness. The scent of carnations inside vied with roses in the patio, where a hedge of pink cannas against blue plumbago might have been awaiting a bride.

The thin sister, busy as she was, had time to show her joy in the town's great day.

" Last year the alcalde forbade the dances as pagan and unworthy of the Most Holy Virgin. But the miners said: ' She

is our Virgin! ' And they continue to dance. . . . Imagine!
That alcalde! Those dances are two hundred years old. How
can he stop them? He will die, but not those dances." She sped
away to greet new guests.

They were the two ladies whom we had so embarrassingly
deprived of a room. They still had found no place; it was a relief to the conscience to offer them ours. Later, when the
mother had gone to chat with the plump señorita, her daughter
told us why they had come to Andacollo.

" My mother," she began, " is completely devout. I am not.
Perhaps I should be ashamed to say it. But these facts are true:
Two years ago my sister was very ill of a mastoid. As my
brother had died under an operation for the same illness we
were all terrified. Doctors said the only hope was in surgery,
but Mother was afraid to risk it again. She had lost faith in
surgeons, but her faith in God had never wavered. So she
prayed to the Blessed Virgin, vowing that if my sister recovered she would come here to pray and offer candles.

" Well, incredibly, the child got well. I mean the mastoid
cleared up completely. The very doctors who had prescribed
the operation — the best men in Chile — pronounced her
well. So here we are at Andacollo. It is among those things one
can never reasonably explain."

I was reminded that Gabriela Mistral had said: " We are all
Catholic, even those who are not Catholics."

Our hostesses protested our leaving. Even the younger one
added a word to her sister's voluble flow. Unthinkable that anyone should miss the procession.

" It is stupendous! " the plump one cried. " Completely
stupendous! They carry the Blessed Virgin and one can see
her face close. They call it a crude image, but it is not. You
will see her beautiful face with its merry smile looking right

at you. And the Holy Child on her arm! The dancers make a lane and all the people follow. . . . And the noise! All the musicians play their own tunes and there is a band, and all the church bells ring! It is so religious. You will never hear anything like it anywhere."

Doubtless. But pushing our way back to the plaza only sealed our determination to leave. The hard dry hills threw back the hard hot sunlight in waves. The dust-filled air was choking. People milled around eating, drinking from pop bottles, standing at gambling tables. Among them moved the well-dressed carabineros keeping order. Now and then a dance group pushed through. Same dance, same scene, same smells.

We sought out the friend who had promised to find us a bus back to the peace of La Serena. But there was no bus. Everybody was staying on; there would be no down traffic. And we had magnanimously surrendered our cool quiet room! Nothing for it but a search. So we went up and down those pandemoniac streets, asking, following every suggestion. At last we found a rattletrap bus going down; we took a seat and waited.

It was a long wait, but in time several other passengers gathered and we set off. We had been advised to leave the back seats empty, and how wise that was! With a lurch and a rattle the old bag of bolts and bars set off, shaking loose seats, gasoline cans, suitcases, and a choking cloud of dust. Two upper-class young men in berets tried to hold us all down, but it was no use. A little girl in a pink dress landed in my lap in tears, but as her mother was fully occupied holding her baby and her hat, my guest reconciled herself and we made out together. The driver neither stopped not stayed; he had no brakes; our only hope was in his skill and in the horn which his assistant kept forever blowing. When he stopped, with a bone-breaking shatter, it was only that the assistant might retrieve one of the cans and pour water into the steaming radiator. All the way we met ascending traffic and it was, surely, only the Virgin's interest in returning pilgrims that saved us all — unregenerate along with the devout. No police were in sight. Stopping anywhere seemed worse than going on, and on we went. Nobody was killed.

After such a ride who could question the efficacy of a pilgrimage to Andacollo?

XXII

SOME CHILEAN WOMEN

As MY TIME GREW SHORT IN CHILE I REALIZED THAT one should not leave that country without paying special tribute to Chilean women.

In other countries, on ships and planes, I had heard over and over that Chile was a land of women. " They are better than the men, more intelligent, more fearless. Women in Chile understand the revolution that is going on even when the men don't. You will find them well informed as to actual conditions, less afraid of the inevitable coming changes than men are. To understand modern Chile you must know her women."

This advice was offered me by a newspaper man in Buenos Aires, by a writer from New York, by a sociologist in Chile, by casual observers everywhere. But most tellingly it came from a Spanish psychiatrist whom I may not name. Perhaps he will some day make the psychological analysis and comparison of American nations which would help us all so much.

" Chile," he said, " is a woman's country, as Argentina belongs to men. Just look at the stores. In Buenos Aires the best shopping streets are lined with haberdasheries; men's jewelry and men's perfumes and toilet articles are abundant, expensive, and excellent.

" But Chile is a woman's country, and Santiago's best shops and gayest spots are those frequented by women. Chilean women are physically better than men. They win international athletic championships; men seldom do. They are intelligent and they take a dominant position unquestioningly and as of right. They are intent in politics though they have no vote. They hold appointive offices, enter all the professions, and as teachers they exercise an influence almost as wide as that of your women. . . . Perhaps it is not altogether good. Who knows? But it is true.

" Why? Again who knows? You might read up on Inez de Suárez. A historical character, well known and admired, often has great influence. Chilean women have a tradition of courage and resourcefulness. Even the most secluded and modest Chilean lady has always occupied a position of great dignity and authority. I believe the German woman's example has influenced the *Chilena* too — especially in encouraging her to be active outside of the home. The Chilean temperament is closer to the Nordic than to the Moorish-Spanish type.

Chile is surely the only country in Latin America where men are dominated by their women. Here a man might hesitate to make an appointment, for ' What would my wife say? ' They even make a point of reaching home in time for meals. That does not seem strange to a Yanqui, but in these countries it is unique. Chile, I assure you, is a woman's country."

I knew Chilean women of many types. All of them were self-possessed, assured, and busy. They stress leisureliness as a national trait, but have none of it. Santiago is a rushing city. Offices are adorned with bright signs: " *Sea breve*," (" Be brief "), and one may wait days for an appointment or never get it. One woman I hoped to interview gave me two appointments, asked me to telephone to remind her, but was never free to see me. Perhaps women are still so new to business that they feel unduly the pressure of keeping hours. And their busyness is no pose. Many working women are supporting children, parents, and even more distant relatives. It is not at all unusual for a teacher or government employee to hold another job as the only means of making expenses. They are nothing short of phenomenal in their unfailing courtesy, perfect grooming, and the excellent appearance they make on a pittance of a salary.

A newspaper woman, who was practicing that profession in addition to a full-time teaching job, asked me not to mention it to her family. They lived on what she made, but would have disapproved of work so unladylike as interviewing and running a newspaper column. This woman wrote under a pseudonym which is well known, content to get no credit in order not to offend her mother.

The ladylike tradition is as hampering in Chile as it was in our South a generation ago. The heroine of a novel I read summoned a friend to her house with a precipitancy worthy of a fire or an earthquake because a male acquaintance had dropped in unexpectedly at lunch time. This heroine was a widow of thirty or so. I asked a friend if such rigid chaperonage was still required in Chile.

" Well," she said, " I do much as I like because I have lived in the States and people accept me as rather Yanqui. But recently an old friend of my family joined me and my children at lunch in a hotel. When the youngsters went away for tennis after lunch, he refused to stay chatting with me in the hotel lobby. ' It would make talk,' he said, and bowed himself away."

Society girls and even those who work are constantly chaperoned. They attend the vermouth shows with young men, but preferably in groups or with a married friend. Young men do not call on girls alone unless their intentions are definite. Young Yanquis often make mistakes, as when one invited a girl who had charmed him to drive with him to the beach and go swimming. That ended his acceptance in a delightful family.

Even older women, in conventional circles, are hampered by custom. One, a divorcee of the best society, does maintain an apartment alone. But an aunt is often with her; she is often abroad. Her excellent social position, based on wealth and a string of polysyllabic Basque names, permits the fiction that she does not live alone. Divorce, as is natural in a strongly Catholic society, is disapproved of and remarriage generally results in ostracism. A remarried divorcee of good connections and great wealth keeps a precarious position by entertaining many interesting foreigners. As everybody must meet the British novelist, the Spanish philosopher, or the Hollywood star, society attends her functions, though certain ladies of impeccable correctness show their disapproval of the irregular household by refusing to address their hostess. Pure gossip, but suggestive all the same.

Society women are as busy as the workers, forever dashing off to Viña or to the fundo, having just rushed up to town, or pressed with social engagements. They all work in the Red Cross, Allied or Nazi relief societies, Catholic women's organizations, and at many forms of charity.

Asked if society women were interested in politics, an observant Yanqui girl said: " Only in two aspects of it. The Church has filled them with fear of Communism, and they are afraid of losing their fundos. So they oppose any laws looking toward social betterment as a threat of Communism. And they will support any candidate who promises to maintain the *status quo*. . . . Yes, many of their brothers are Falangistas and working as devout Catholics for social legislation. But their sisters seldom share their ideas; they are more apt to apologize for the family radical as an errant sinner."

There are exceptions to this picture of the society woman. Many are in the professions, many are non-Catholic, socially advanced, and awake to politics. Of three women's organizations dedicated to winning the vote, one is composed almost exclusively of society women. Another consists of middle-class women, mostly teachers; and working women have their own association. Chileans still fall unconsciously into a stratified pattern. As the classes fuse, this will pass. If the Spanish psychiatrist is right, women will break down the barriers sooner than men.

[RURAL SOCIAL WORKER]

Hubert Herring had said: " Be sure to meet Graciela Mandujano and believe everything she tells you. She knows exactly what is going on."

When I reached Santiago, Señorita Mandujano was in the United States lecturing under the auspices of the American Association of University Women; and after she got home she was so busy that I caught her only occasionally.

The first time she met me for tea at the Crillon. Arriving early, I watched the gathering of women, with only enough men for background. The Chilean women were of all ages from schoolgirls to grandmothers; all were animated and smart in black. Among them were a scattering of Yanqui tourists in colors. One attracted my attention, she was so brisk and vivid as she swung in and looked around. Chicago, I thought, taking in her brown costume with hunter's green hat and bag, her air of poising in mid-flight. Then she approached me. Graciela Mandujano, just home from the States and attired, even to the North American shoes, " completely Yanqui."

This was the first of several meetings. Once I took a little train out to San Luis for lunch at her country home. It was just like Sunday on a California ranch. The same oranges, oleanders, and dahlias irrigated by small ditches; the same backdrop of blue mountains and foreground of sunburnt grass and dusty roads with scuttling cars.

Señorita Mandujano has acquired a family: a Yanqui mother and her daughter who was born in Bolivia, and a Chilean child, adopted and much beloved. The company included a Scottie bitch with her new puppies. Altogether the household was a perfect example of interracial and international understanding and amity. In my honor they served a delicate pudding of ground fresh corn, and for the baby's sake ice cream and cake. Afterward we had a siesta and walked round to see the fig tree and the papayas, which was more than ever like Sunday on a California ranch.

Later I heard Graciela Mandujano address a feminist group. She, like all liberal Chilean women, was campaigning for Juan Antonio Ríos, whose election they hoped would align Chile with the United Nations, stamp out Nazi propaganda, and assure a continuance of Chile's social program. Ríos was a compromise candidate and altogether satisfactory to no party. His political career had begun with General Ibáñez, whom he now opposed. But as Ibáñez had Nazi support (doubtless quite unbeknown to the Conservatives who also supported him), his defeat was essential in any case.

Graciela Mandujano stood quietly, spoke so fluently and easily, dominated her listeners so completely and so pleasantly that I shall never forget it. Months afterward, at home, I heard a professor speak of her success in the United States.

" She is perfect on the platform," he said. " Charming and at ease, she spoke in perfect English and without a note. She can use humor, intensity, or drama, but mostly she gets her effects by understatement. She gestures little, but when she uses her hands every motion tells. Listening to her is as good as a lesson in public speaking."

It is difficult to get Graciela to speak of the work she inaugurated and is best known for. Her reluctance may be because she is no longer associated with it, though her self-effacement seems rather that of a person who always sees the job, never herself, as important. She willingly related that it began because as a teacher she realized that the schools were missing a large element of the population: adults, especially in the country. She was able to interest the government and, in 1939, a new office was set up: *El Instituto de Información Rural.*

The Institute of Rural Information proposed no radical measures. Its whole function was to inform country people about the excellent laws designed for them, which many of them were too ignorant to make use of. It was a typical woman idea. Men had given Chile the best social laws in all America. It took women to devise a scheme for taking knowledge of those laws to the most illiterate and helpless Chileans.

They began with a little book. Illustrated, it had a bright cover and the title: *El Libro del Huaso Chileno. The Book of the Chilean Huaso* was addressed to him on the title page. " Because the Chilean huaso is honorable and brave, his country sends him this book." Its 1,600 recipients had been recommended by the carabineros as steady, sober, and reliable, but they were not expected to be able to read. Sixty per cent of

A Class of Public Health Nurses

The Public Health Department Tours the Country

Agricultural Economist

Chile's rural population being illiterate, this book was written for children to read to their parents. It gave history, verses and tales, moral precepts, and useful information. Successive issues touched bee culture and weaving, gave hints on gardening and baby-feeding, sanitation and health, and suggestions calculated to offset the old witch beliefs and dangerous superstitions. In time prizes were offered for letters, stories, and pictures of the life of that little reader who was transmitting the exciting new literature to the assembled family.

The response, as might have been foreseen, was quick and plenteous. The Chilean huaso, literate or not, is intelligent, and for intelligent people one need only open the door. Letters came in children's careful scrawl, from teachers or priests, from some proud parents who could write. They addressed themselves generally to *El Muy Estimado Señor Presidente.* The Latin-American peasant holds himself so high that he is disinclined to approach anybody of less esteem than a president. They asked advice about the most personal matters and showed a nation-wide desire to better their condition and improve themselves. The central office, womanlike, decided to answer every letter personally, and did; even when the daily mail mounted into hundreds of letters. Requests for information were referred to the right office, cases of need to the right agency. The new office was a go-between, and its files are a tear-jerking compilation of tragic, comic, unstudied human documents.

Such a lively response had the practical effect of bringing the Institute of Rural Information a bit more money. Their original appropriation of 150,000 pesos (about $5,000) was increased to a million pesos. " Quite enough for Chile," says Miss Mandujano with her quiet smile. It was enough, also, to permit of even more personal contacts with the 200,000 huasos who had asked for books. Trucks were sent out on what, in Mexico, have been called " cultural missions." Gaily painted for illiterate identification and with a staff of seven people to make friends and influence inquilinos, they attracted people from a radius of many miles.

" None of us were technicians or experts," says Miss Mandujano.

But their performance was expert. Traveling in their truck, they made camp under a tree beside a river, slept on the ground, did their own cooking. When callers dropped in, they offered coffee, cigarettes or a share of their *humitas* and beans. Confidence flourishes in that atmosphere. One cagey old man, after watching for a while, seeing books given out, teeth pulled, mothers advised, babies cared for, and receiving, himself, sensible information about his irrigation problem, summed it up: " Now we know the government is our friend." For the first time his government had brought him help, not taxes nor arrest.

The mission found something too. " As soon as they use a cake of soap and a little water," says Señorita Mandujano, " there is no difference between them and us."

Another result was the conversion of a grumpy member of the class that Boleslo, the taximan, had described as the most backward in all Chile. A hacendado, hearing that the mission had arrived in his neighborhood, sent greetings.

" You tell those people that if they come on my land, I'll shoot them like dogs."

The mission proceeded quietly as before. Evidently Old Grumpy was watching, because before they left he met one of the men on the road and growled:

" You tell that señorita to come for lunch. You come too."

Her colleague expressed some doubt; Señorita Mandujano

was very busy. But the señorita herself was too wise to miss her chance. She went to lunch and the result was that Old Grumpy became one of the best friends of the whole movement.

" It was our only opposition," Miss Mandujano said, " and we probably needed that to chasten us."

[CITY SOCIAL WORKER]

This type is most delightfully personified in Luz Tocornal de Romero. Whether it was owing to her marriage to a physician of vigorous and untrammeled mind or merely to a fruitful capacity for being bored with the trivial, she early left conventional society for social work. While Dr. Romero was taking an advanced degree at Harvard, his wife graduated from a school of social service in Boston. On her return to Chile, Señora Romero accepted the post of *Directora de la Escuela de Servicio Social*.

Luz Romero is like a breeze blowing over spicy pinks. In her exquisitely appointed home she is as casual as though she had just dropped in for a moment; and as hostess she has attained the pinnacle of seeming without effort or worry. At her desk she is crisp and definite, keeps level eyes on a speaker until she understands; then she touches the essential point, makes a comment or gives a direction, and dismisses the matter. Too busy for a formal interview in Santiago, she suggested our meeting in Viña del Mar, where she was going on vacation.

There I watched her park her topless roadster and breeze into the smart Hotel O'Higgins. In a rosy sports costume and no hat, she apparently had no thought beyond the casino and the racetrack. Then, talking easily for an hour over tea, she displayed a statesmanlike knowledge of her country's laws and of her people's lacks and potentialities, and unsentimental sound sense. She let drop comments on Yanquis which I have used elsewhere, and revealing glimpses of the " soul of Chile " I was forever seeking. And she turned now and then to stories of her three-year-old son and his amusing hodgepodge of three languages.

" We Chileans cling to the old notion that a woman who takes a job must neglect her children," she laughed. " But I spend more time with mine than many society women do."

Then she told me about the *Escuela de Servicio Social*, which was established in 1925: the first social-service school in Latin America; and as a government institution the first in all the Americas. It operates under the Central Board of Charity and Health.

" The school's purpose," said its *directora*, " is to train young women to discover the causes of misfortune; to show people where to turn for aid; and to indicate gaps in hasty or faulty new measures. It was modeled on Belgian institutions and the first and second directors were Belgian women. But the third was a graduate of the New York School of Social Work. With her we grew more practical. And as I am Yanqui-trained too, I follow her. I believe that we Latins need your practical sense and your impersonality."

The school was a success from the beginning. Girls of the most exalted families found there a better way of carrying on the old tradition of aiding the unfortunate; its professionalism gave it a university stamp; perhaps it was an escape from the hampering home. The enrollment has grown steadily; in 1942, 120 students offered themselves — more than could be accommodated in the pleasant, well-equipped building in Santiago.

All matriculates must have the bachillerato degree, good health and character, and a knowledge of one foreign language. They are finally chosen for previous experience and training, by mental tests, and for seriousness and aptitude.

The three-year course lays a broad base in political economy and labor legislation; in sociology and criminology; in social theories and social welfare. Students also learn what is being done throughout the world in preventive medicine and hygiene, in social medicine, nutrition and diet, and in child-training. They study the social evolution of Chile. Their country has the most honorable record in Latin America; in many ways in all the Americas. Knowledge of the individual comes through elementary biology, anatomy, and psychology; methods of meeting his problems through practical psychology, psychiatry, and mental hygiene. Every student studies the theory of case work and has actual practice under direction. A course in statistics doubtless gives advice as to how to debunk as well as how to collect and use those useful rows of figures.

To attain a diploma the student must pass exhaustive examinations and prepare a thesis. Tuition is free, and all courses are given by university professors. The school, according to Señora Doctora Romero, " has no religious, philosophical, or political bias whatsoever." This platform may have had something to do with the establishment four years later of a similar school in connection with the Catholic University of Chile.

Of the school's first fifteen years' 274 graduates, 10 have died. Of 29 the occupation is unknown, though one might guess they have married. The others are all in public work. The social-welfare office in the school handles 150 to 200 calls a month, which are referred out to such federal agencies as the Cost of Living and Price-Control Board; Juvenile Court; Employment Bureau; Ministries of Public Health and of Labor. That leaves plenty for the social worker, who must show the underprivileged how to take advantage of what his government offers him.

The young case workers run into typical cases. They get casual unions legitimized whenever they can. Often marriage has been too expensive, often a woman prefers unwed freedom. Escaping fathers are traced and returned when possible. Mothers and children are kept together. The school maintains a library of two thousand volumes and professional magazines from everywhere. They also publish *Servicio Social*, outlining not only what they do, but new laws that are needed, especially those to establish a living wage and family allowance. These women, mostly young and of influential families, are inevitably skirmishing on the political borderline, where, though Chilean women have no national vote as yet, they are a potent force.

[DOCTOR AND NURSE]

A woman physician is no novelty in Chile. Since women were first admitted to the university in 1877, many of them have graduated in the professions; perhaps medicine has had a particular appeal for them. But even as late as 1914 when Eleanira Gonzales Donoso took her degree in medicine, women doctors were kept out of sight. Long after she was practicing in full partnership with a male colleague, she was listed as a pharmacist, which for some reason was considered more womanly than doctoring. Doctora Gonzales Donoso is now assistant director of the *Escuela de Enfermeras*, School for Nurses, where I begged to call upon her. She invited me to lunch.

The school is in an old residence on the outskirts of Santiago. After the usual ritual of ringing a bell at a locked gate I crossed a charming garden and entered the original dwelling, where a wisteria festooned a long portal. Inside the patio girls in blue gingham and white aprons were trotting quickly about their work or giggling in corners. In a stiffly furnished waiting-room there was time to observe the portrait of the president of the university who first admitted women, Dr. Amunategui; and of the first woman who graduated in medicine, in 1897.

Then Dr. Gonzales was ready to receive me. A short, dark woman, motherly but brisk, she was cordial and ready to answer questions. Of her own professional life she said that she had always found men ready to help her, and that though some prejudice against women physicians does exist, a competent one can make a good living in Chile. She herself carries on an active practice as consultant and surgeon in addition to her work as acting director of the school.

La Escuela de Enfermeras was founded in 1902, is a part of the University of Chile, and offers its graduates the dignity of a profession " in which a woman can develop the qualities inherent in her feminine personality." It is designed to prepare girls for regular nursing and also for preventive work as public-health nurses. All entrants must be graduates of the secondary schools; those who seek the degree of *Enfermera Hospitalaria* (Public-Health Nurse) must also have the degree of *Bachiller de Humanidades.*

Every effort is being made to give nursing professional dignity and especially a ladylike aura which will attract young women of superior intelligence and background. Unlike social service, nursing is still not quite correct for girls of good family; it smacks of servile position, and the old Spanish disdain of manual work persists. Dr. Gonzales has taken the best means of combating that notion; she laughs at it. She also shows strong and intelligent girls from the villages and the country that nurses' training is an excellent way to attain a degree, to enter a profession, and to be of real service. As all expenses are paid during the three years of training, the school is attracting fine young women who, lacking wealth and social position, perhaps enjoy a greater sense of reality.

The course parallels that given in the United States, and includes both theory and hospital practice; it keeps the girls fit by physical education, and entertained and inspired by a library and a music-room. The degree as a Public-Health Nurse requires an extra year's training in such subjects as child care, anti-tuberculosis work, prophylaxis, psychiatry, social service, administration, and the use of statistics. As in all Chilean education, examinations are frequent and stiff, the professors are " of the state," and the graduates are soundly prepared. All Public-Health Nurses go into government service; most of the others do also, though the demand for private nurses is great too.

We lunched in a big airy room filled with chattering girls; the school accommodates a hundred at a time. As the well-balanced meal came and went — salad, bean soup, meat with vegetables, dessert and fruit — I was assured that it was the regular lunch, not a company meal. I sat between Dr. Gonzales and Señorita Rosalba Flores, a graduate who was dividing her time between certain duties in the school and case work outside. She was as engaging and flowerlike as her name, with dimpled pink cheeks and an air of expectancy as fresh as *alba*, the dawn. The rest of the company was composed of students of public health. The conversation was filled with jokes and laughter, but with plenty of seriousness about the work they faced.

Chile has four schools for nurses, 106 hospitals and sanatoria, and 47 rural health centers; all under the direction of the Ministry of Public Health.

Under the direction of a thousand physicians the country is struggling against much preventable misery, hampered always by lack of funds and by lack of public appreciation of the need. The burden of the Public-Health Nurse's plaint is: " If only there were more of us! " Infant mortality is 26 per thousand; tuberculosis, with an incidence of 245 per hundred thousand, accounts for 17 per cent of total mortality, with syphilis second at 11 per cent of the total. Those happy serious girls were like a thin line of heroes, knowing they could not win with the forces and ammunition at their command, but gallantly joining the battle anyhow.

After lunch Dr. Gonzales went off to an appointment, and Señorita Flores took me across the street to a splendid hospital. It was like a good hospital anywhere. Scrubbed and polished, smelling of soap and disinfectants; with operating-rooms lighted from above and shining with nickel and glass. In an anteroom women were waiting patiently with babies to be examined. And in long wards sick or injured children lay in bandages or braces, so quiet in their suffering that surely nobody who cannot help should see them. I was ready to go without inspecting other wards where older patients would be more sensitive, perhaps, to intrusive curiosity.

As we walked out to my bus, Señorita Flores was voluble about what she saw in her daily visits among the poor, about what she would do if she could. The homes she knew needed everything: fresh water, good air, screens, space. But above all they needed hope and education, and those she was bringing.

" Our women," she said, and I noted that she spoke not condescendingly as of another class but of Chilean women like herself, " Our women are so intelligent and so willing to learn that we need only show them. If we teach them how to prepare formulas for their babies they do it. When they understand the need for vegetables they get them and cook them, no matter how much trouble. They will give up anything for themselves if they can buy milk for their children. But they are so poor, so poor! "

As my bus carried me away, I thought that as long as they had Rosalba Flores and increasing numbers of her kind, Chilean women were not so poor after all.

XXIII

VALPARAISO AND VIÑA DEL MAR

E

VERY VISITOR TO CHILE SHOULD SAIL EITHER IN OR OUT of Valparaiso. Remote as it now seems from the world's great trade routes, for a very long day Chile's port was on the highway from Europe to the East, from Cadiz to Callao, even from our Eastern to our Western ports. Seamen of every maritime nation knew Valparaiso as the last sight of land before the long sail across the Pacific. Now it is a proud little city with the best bay and the busiest port on South America's long Pacific coast, great wealth, and a long history.

Its name, Vale of Paradise, seems just right for the verdant Quillota Valley, through which the great Aconcagua rolls richly toward the sea. The first white men to see it were on the little ship *Santiaguillo*, bringing supplies for Diego de Almagro, who was exploring southward from Peru along the cordillera. But the ship's captain is said to have named the settlement for his home in Spain. As that was in 1528, Valparaiso is older than Santiago. But throughout the colonial era it was an inconsiderable hamlet, known as Puerto de Santiago, through which the new colony traded with Peru. Agustín

Edwards lists the imports as " sugar, rice, sometimes wheat, jerked meat, tallow, and Negro slaves," and describes Valparaiso's condition as miserable in the extreme.

In 1578 Francis Drake came along in the *Golden Hind*. This first Britisher in the Pacific was so unexpected that he was taken for a Spaniard and he had sailed into harbor and boarded a Spanish ship lying there before the town realized that it was being raided, not revictualed. The inhabitants, stunned with surprise, put up no resistance, and Drake possessed himself of their stores of wine, salt pork, and cedarwood, and some altar vessels.

Thereafter Valparaiso was on the route of England's sea rovers, seeking " beauty and booty " and a share of Spain's wealth. Even then Englishmen were after business as well as adventure and Spain's exclusive policy led to piracy when she and England were enemies, to smuggling when they were at peace. The Dutch vied with the British; among the most horrible sackings of the little village were those of Hollanders avenging Spanish atrocities in the Lowlands. During colonial days Valparaiso, though a preferred port permitted to trade directly with Spain without going through the Portobello fair in Panama, could expect a fleet of galleons only every five or six years. Edwards suggests that Valparaiso has rightly been called the legitimate daughter of the revolution: its importance began only then.

During the War of Independence it suffered the usual vicissitudes of capture and sack and of the earthquakes which in Chile seem to follow hard times of every sort. As is typical of Chile's cities, Valparaiso rebuilt, after every disaster, better, solider, and cleaner than before. Many stone buildings are more than a century old; there are worn red paving stones that O'Higgins laid when he connected the port with the capital by the first carriage road. Valparaiso was seeing another type of Britisher; Irishmen commanded the ships that helped San Martín and O'Higgins defeat the Spanish, and the Scotsman, Lord Thomas Cochrane, in the *Rose*, sailed into the harbor in the nick of time to defeat the great Spanish fleet sent to put down the rebellious colony.

The nineteenth century was Valparaiso's heyday. A free port for the first time, it was crowded with the beautiful swift sailing vessels which linked Chile on a strong, though very long chain with Europe and North America. Many British stayed to found the families whose names now appear on boards of directors and preferred lists of every kind. Yankees were common visitors too, but they did not stay; their own country was too tempting for settlement and exploitation. Thousands of them stretched their legs and their capacity for rum at Valpo (so the British had clipped it) during the Gold Rush and took along hundreds of Chilean miners, whose legend still persists in California.

The end of the century was marked by the one unpleasant episode in the relations between Chile and the United States. It demonstrates how international affairs may be affected by the personal. If our Secretary of State Mr. James G. Blaine had not been wooing the Irish vote, and if an Irish-born citizen, Patrick Egan, who hated the English, had not been our Minister to Chile, Chileans might not today be citing the " *Baltimore* incident " as proof of the overbearing imperialism of the colossus of the north.

It happened like this, according to the sober study, *Chile and the United States,* by Henry Clay Evans:

In 1890 President José Manuel Balmaceda, following a dispute with the Congress, declared himself dictator; and a revolution began. The north and the Navy stood with the revolting

Congress, which was said to be financed by German and British
"Nitrate Kings." Minister Egan supported President Balmaceda with a frankness and fervor more Irish than diplomatic.
He filled the American Legation with adherents of the President and was reputed to be smuggling them out of the country
under diplomatic safe conduct. Accusations and recrimina-
tions spread so widely and feeling against the United States
rose so high that in Valparaiso — which had surrendered to
the Congress party — a sailors' brawl became an international
incident.

The U.S.S. *Baltimore* happened to be in the harbor. Her
crew had been carefully controlled, but on the afternoon of
October 16 some of them had shore leave. Captain Schley,
ashore at half past five, reported them all well behaved. But
at six trouble began. Two sailors, emerging from the True
Blue Saloon, were set upon and mobbed. Or they began the
fight. Witnesses differed. Other rows began in other parts of
the city, so many and so far apart that collusion was suspected.
It ended with thirty-six members of the *Baltimore* in the hoose-
gow and one dead. A Chilean court found fault on both sides
and recommended imprisonment for one American and three
Chileans.

In both countries national pride flared high. In Santiago the
withdrawal of Minister Egan was demanded on the ground
that he had interfered in national affairs. In Washington,
President Harrison devoted most of his message to Congress
to the *Baltimore* incident and asked permission to use force.

Happily cooler counsels prevailed. Chile punished her sailors for their part in the ruction and offered $75,000 in repara-
tion. And President Cleveland issued a statement: " Under no
circumstances can the representatives of this government be
permitted, under the ill-defined fiction of extraterritoriality,

to interrupt the administration of criminal justice in the courts to which they are accredited."

Unhappily Chile has forgotten that statement and remembers only the Minister's partisan interference and the fact that the Chilean flag had been dipped to the *Baltimore*. Chile had never dipped her flag to any foe; the incident is still cited as proof of overbearing *imperialismo Yanqui*. And all, in a manner of speaking, because an Irishman hated the English!

Then imperialismo Yanqui, in its erratic way, went off and dug the Panama Canal, leaving Valparaiso far off the regular highways of the sea. But Valpo has weathered many changes, being remote or near as men's discoveries, stupid laws, and stupider wars have meddled with geography. It is now, as always, the best harbor on South America's Pacific coast. Galleons, clippers, steamers, vessels of every type for four centuries have anchored there. It has been the port of warships, grim submarines, and now of flying defenders. The Panama Canal interrupted Valpo's course, but it teeters precariously on the verge of a new and more dreadful importance. If anything should happen to the Canal . . . !

I planned to sail for home from Valparaiso, but to stay in Viña del Mar, "the paradise of the Pacific," Chile's Riviera, whose casino and racetrack, great hotels and wealthy homes, and golden beaches under a brilliant sky have been advertised as the ultimate dream of bliss. But paradise was full in January, the height of the summer season. No hotel rooms were to be had; even the recommended *residenciales* were crowded. Perforce I went to Valpo and I shall always be glad. For Valparaiso is not " Chile's — anything." It is *sui generis* and has character, strong, attractive, and incomparable. It is like other ports only because one touches there the living fabric which covers the world with trade routes.

The railroad touches the sea at Viña, and it seemed a mistake to pass by its fine buildings bowered in palms, flowering vines, and trees and its gardens. But soon the train was rounding the bay and a strong breeze brought the smell of wet sand and dead fish. It was late evening, and the shore's arc was blinking with colored lights; lights rode ships in the harbor, and a lighthouse swept a long admonitory finger over the hills and out to sea as though reminding landlubbers of men and ships out there. Long before the train stopped in its shed I knew Valparaiso was the place for me. Viña had garden beauty, but Valparaiso, lacking no beauty, has too the thrill of a great port. My taxi crossed a plaza with splendid buildings around a monument and went through busy streets to the Hotel Astur. Even at night I was aware of the heights above the town in a network of twinkles like a spangled scarf.

From my room I faced the long cliff which presses the city into a narrow strip of shore; all along it houses stand on one another's shoulders, crazily, as though there were no way up at all. But there are many: stairways, buses, funiculars, special touring cars, and taxis. First I took a morning stroll along the waterfront with its busy customs house and the bay with tugs and fishing smacks. There was much less shipping than before the war, and the harbor was well guarded. From the Plaza Sotomayor with its monument to the naval hero Arturo Prat, leads a street of his name, the financial and business center. Its solidity is manifest in squared stone banks and import houses with iron-barred windows. Shops showed British leather, wool, and tinned comestibles; more frivolous trinkets and women's clothes from the States; German optical supplies and cameras. There was any port's normal complement of Oriental bazaars. Most of the cars were North American.

On the narrow sidewalks one meets the world: brown sailors

The Light-Spangled Arc of Valpo's Harbor at Night

Grace Line

Viña del Mar Is a City of Gardens

with gold earrings, Yanqui gobs and Yanqui Negroes, ruddy Scandinavians, even turbaned Hindus. Among them go Chileans, seeming a minority among the fresh-faced British matrons with well-disciplined children, and the British business men with their pipes and folded copies of the *South Pacific Mail*. Midday is their hour. Women are homing after shopping, men are going to the British and American clubs for the noon vermouth or Scotch and soda, and stores are putting up shutters for the siesta closing.

Beyond the Plaza Victoria with its fine municipal library, the city takes on a more Chilean aspect, with national goods in the shops, many bookstores, and more and more Chileans as one approaches the municipal market. Subercaseaux complains of these " horribly provincial men who do not perceive the abundance of life which bubbles around them," and insists that only sailors and transients truly know and love the city. To know it one must leave its lower levels and take one of the *ascensores* — the Happy Hill, the Concepción, or the Emerald — to mount the overbearing cliff.

Ascensores are as much fun as Ferris wheels at the fair. You enter a cage hung on wires. It looks too decrepit to make the ascent, but it is irresistible to one who expects death at only the fated hour. Once loaded, the car's doors are closed, creakings and groanings indicate that power is on, and suddenly the thing swings out, leaps upward, causing the stranger to gasp at the unexpected motion, and labors heavily aloft. Natives go quietly on with talk or newspapers. Then suddenly all movement stops with a definite thump, somebody opens the door, and there you are at the top, looking down upon the sparkling bay.

A climb afoot takes one's breath but is worth it. Wide steps form narrow ways between houses, and through slits of masonry one glimpses the far sea shining and a gull dipping. The revealed intimacies are embarrassing, even more so than those seen from the New York El, but may be mitigated by chatting with children during intervals for puffing. These are the conventillos, which Salvador Reyes has described in *Panorama y Color de Chile:*

" There are houses in zigzag with their backbones arched and their walls dislocated, so inlaid one with the other, so superimposed upon others that great effort is needed to determine which roof and which wall belong to which."

I had, besides that, to determine where I was at the moment. Continuing upward is in most situations a fairly safe rule for reaching the top, but not in Valparaiso. I was forever running up against an impenetrable wall or a down-turning path which led into a smelly patio. One could imagine being hexed there and never getting out. After I had passed the same blue façade four times with the same smiling woman hanging out her wash and talking with the resting man with the heavy legs, I begged for help. They laughed with me and summoned a youngster to act as guide.

" Foreign ladies," he told me, as he leapt agilely from step to step, " always lose themselves. They should go in a taxi like the rich."

A taxi ride proved the most comfortable and informing approach to Valpo's heights. A garrulous driver is any town's best informant. This one laid out a course which began with the fine stone buildings of Santa María's technical university. From there he swung up and down, never plumbing the depths of any barranca, but showing me clearly that Valpo's seemingly solid backing was a series of hills, and that each one had a character all its own. On one crest was a playground where children rescued from the conventillos were offered a wading pool, swings and seesaws, and even a place to learn carpentry and other crafts. So wise Chileans combat the threat of foreign ideologies.

Another hill was English, as nobody need be told seeing those brick-walled gardens with lilacs and snowballs along mossy violet-edged walks; uniformed nursemaids with proper children; and an Anglican church. Equally characteristic was Germany's hill. Curious how the slenderly pointing Lutheran spire differed from the less assertive complacency of England's church, how the way houses look out through their windows is expressive of the people inside. We stopped also to gaze across the bay from a terrace in front of the home of Chile's richest man, an Italian. But Valparaiso is not altogether foreign.

On a promontory above the main plaza is the *Escuela Nacional*, the Naval Academy, where two or three hundred youths are being trained as officers. Chile's Navy has a proud record of no defeats; her officers are often men of families who have fought in every war since Independence. From the Academy, which is not open to visitors, one looks along the shining sickle of the shore across the indigo-blue bay, with the vast expanse of Pacific beyond. The breath and the scent of the sea are so strong that one seems to grow almost tall enough to peer over earth's rim at San Fernando, Robinson Crusoe's isle, which lies 350 miles off shore. Excursions go there in settled times; now Chile is most determined that it shall not harbor alien submarines again. During the First World War Count Spee's squadron was based there. The island is a national park now; fishing and lobstering are controlled to protect the supply and also — it is hoped — to prevent photographing of strategic points. Chile's westernmost possession is even more remote than Juan Fernandez. Easter Island, that unread connecting chapter between Orient and Occident, lies 2,200 miles west of Valparaiso. Its weird idols suggest Polynesian habitation, and Polynesian legends bear them out. But no sound archæologist ventures more than a maybe about La Isla de Pascua, alone in the midst of the Pacific.

However alluring Valparaiso, one must know Viña del Mar with its softer enchantments. Friends showed it to me. We drove out of Valpo, dodging the many trucks and buses that almost make the two cities one. But not quite; their characters and functions are too distinct. On the dividing line between them is the University of Santa María, where technicians are being prepared for the new democracy. Poor boys and mature workmen are admitted without pay. When the faculty found that men who came to night school without an adequate meal did poorly, they fed them and the work picked up at once. Boys who live out are also given breakfast, to the advantage of their scholarship. In the new dormitories the best rooms are awarded to the best students. Here too Chile is educating her elite, but by offering food, security, and opportunity Santa María is discovering and developing a new elite.

Beyond that, poverty is not even suggested. Vineyard-by-the-sea is wealth and fashion. We lunched at the Cap Ducal, a restaurant built like a ship and specializing in seafood. From there one sees how the littoral bends inward, giving Viña a suaver climate than Valparaiso. All along are sheltered coves with gold and silver beaches of soft sifted sand. All this is of *la alta sociedad*. Some offer quiet wading pools for children; those nearest the palatial Casino and the great hotels are posed for *Vogue* and *Esquire* photographers with the smartest seagoing and spectator costumes. One sees as many foreigners as Chileans, especially Argentines, who — in peace-times — made a procession of streamlined motor cars across the Andes.

Joaquín Edwards Bello, in his novel *Valparaiso*, describes Viña as " the soul of summering, and straw hats are seen from

January to January. The women are slim, active, and audacious. Don't seek for middle class or meditation. . . . The
men are elegant, given to sports coats, piqué waistcoats, and
Sandow's gymnasium." That neatly dates Señor Edwards's
book, but the rest of it is applicable today.

Viña has everything that every other famous resort can boast,
but in superlative degree. The Casino is stupendous in size,
elegance, and in the sums the croupiers rake in. The racecourse
is equally so. Likewise the hotels. As city regulations require
every house to have a garden, the winding boulevards offer a
continuous flower show. Stately mansions lord it over formal
garden with clipped hedges, rare flowering plants, and tiled
pools where waterlilies float and swans arch their necks. The
simplest homes are overgrown with climbing roses, set apart by
plumbago hedges, and giddy with multicolored flower beds.

Many houses are as streamlined as the automobiles from
Argentina and as daring as the costumes at the O'Higgins, but
conservative Chile is still here. I was asked to tea at a fine old
Victorian home with a conservatory at the end of the garden,
the carriage block still in place, and Grandmother still at the
head of the family. Her house was filled with her children and
her children's children, all of whom spent part of every vacation with her.

Another superb old home, which belonged to the aristocratic
Vergara family, was bequeathed to the city by the last owner.
It is now a public park and its shadowed alleys, moss-rimmed
pools, and sunny grass plots are used all day, and apparently
carefully, by the people and their children. The house, still
containing many of its fine old collections, has been turned into
a school of art. Business has contributed beauty to Viña too.
El Parque Salitre, Nitrate Park, has no explosive intent except

to advertise by startling demonstration what a variety of growing things will reach their perfection on no other food than Chilean nitrates.

From these centers the town goes off in all directions, but always flowers march in the van. The rocky cliffs are dotted with bloom wherever a gardener could climb, and where no gardener could reach, impudent wild flowers spatter the stones with color. They run along the valleys, spill over wet rocks to the edge of the water, dapple the hills with golden yellow and purple magenta. It is like a conspiracy to let no ugly thing intrude on exquisite Viña del Mar.

I spent a radiant Sunday driving on past Viña and along the famous seaside highway which goes north to Zapallar along the shore below the hills. Surely it has a valid claim to being the most beautiful such drive in the world. Others may equal the fine rock formations, with silvery breakers dashing over the crags, the sea's splendor, and the soft white beaches. But only here is there such endless persistence of flowers, which pour out of gardens in floods of vines, burst out of rocks in patches of orange and rose, fill every crevasse.

The resorts are subtly graduated to the social scale. One, with small eating shacks, large signs, and a littered beach is the escape of Santiago's factory workers, who come and go in fleets of buses that cram the roads. The radios are loudest there and boys sell cooked crayfish, parrots in cages, and penguins unhappily drooping in the heat. Another quite as noisy but with more fanciful restaurants built like Dutch windmills or Japanese pagodas attracts office workers and clerks. Government people gravitate naturally to quiet coves where they may own their own houses and gather for meals in clublike centers with tennis courts and dancing floors.

Zapallar, at the end of the road, consists of private homes

so built that each one has a view from its own promontory or hill without even a glimpse of its neighbor. Ambassador Bowers had taken one for the summer, and there Mrs. Bowers and her daughter were happily marooned with no telephone and not even a car except when the Ambassador could come for a few days. " Casa Benoit " had clearly been built by a Frenchman; especially was French taste evident in the garden with its many spots to invite conversation. Smelling pines and the sea, looking straight at the limitless Pacific, and sunned to somnolence, it was hard to remember that our continent, too, was at war; that Ambassador Bowers was spending exhausting hours with Chile's leaders, who could not decide what action to take toward the Axis. Talk in the garden and at lunch was not of war. It was of Chile and Chileans, and every word revealed how deeply and understandingly the Bowerses loved their temporary home.

How perfectly the Bowers family represents the United States! From the middle of our country, they are also from that stock which makes no pretenses, but which is a true aristocracy in that it has for generations been best in its bailiwick, whether the county or the nation. Claude G. Bowers, scholar and historian, is best described as the good old-fashioned Jeffersonian Democrat, he knows with such deep certainty that only through equality and freedom can any country progress. Far too tolerant to be a radical, he seems to wait smilingly on the event with faith that men will work out their salvation in time. Mrs. Bowers is the American mother, whose life in Santiago was so filled with diplomatic and pro-Allied affairs that here she was only reading and enjoying the sun. Even Miss Pat was grateful for a spell of quiet. If I had my way she would be appointed ambassador at large and without portfolio to all Spanish-speaking people. She is the complete American girl, but with such sympathy for the Latin point of view, such limpid and fluent Spanish, and such sound knowledge of history and literature that she should not be wasted on a purely social post.

That day ended, as days at Viña are so apt to do, with dinner at the Casino and a tour of all the gambling-rooms. Returning at last to the Hotel Astur in Valparaiso, our footsteps echoed so loudly between the shuttered buildings that it seemed fearsome even to enter the dark hotel. Down the street one light showed, high up.

"*El Mercurio!* You should meet the editor; he was one whom Ambassador Bowers sent to the States. He is an enthusiast about your country. Come! No sense in going to bed now."

El Mercurio is Chile's solidest, best-edited newspaper, and the Valparaiso edition is older than its Santiago counterpart. The editor courteously disengaged himself from a conference and settled us in his private sanctum as though nothing could be more important than our visit.

" All we need for good neighborliness," he said, " is knowledge. We are bound to like each other, Chileans and Yanquis are so much alike." He thought of something. " Let me show you how *El Mercurio's* friendship with the United States began."

From a safe he extracted a facsimile of the paper's first edition, dated September 12, 1827. Its news of ships, riots, cases in court, and indignant letters from its subscribers were full of interest. But most amazing was its masthead emblem — slightly blurred but decipherable with help. Benjamin Franklin's heirs had sold his type to *El Mercurio,* and as that paper had no device of its own its editor had used Franklin's. So there it stands with the seal of the United States and the American eagle!

Out in the streets again we found a new chill in the last hours before dawn. A stiff wind swirling at the corners picked up crazy papers which gyrated. A few taxis waited with drivers dead asleep. A drunken sailor had stopped for rest against an iron shutter while a mate urged him along. Far away there was music — tinny music. I was reminded that in Valparaiso there is much that does not meet the eye. Again I quote Salvador Reyes:

" Valparaiso, like the world's ports, knows that it must make certain concessions to social formulas. Therefore it stretches along parallel streets with tall buildings and much elegance. But behind these streets appears the true face of the city, a face a little cynical and a little ingenuous, with eyes saddened at times by the music of old electric pianos, with lips which know the expressions of drunkenness, of prayer, and of blasphemy. . . ."

For all that I could not see, as well as all I could, Valparaiso was still more attractive than Viña. It was good to sail for home from Valpo. I should be stopping in northern Chile, but that was Yanqui. I should travel on a Chilean steamer, but bound for the States. Valparaiso was, in a sense, the last I should see of Chile.

XXIV

ANTOFAGASTA AND THE
YANQUI STATE

NTOFAGASTA IS THE CHILEAN PORT THROUGH WHICH
generations of mining engineers have gone up to the mines.
And *Chuquicamata, Estado Yanqui,* is the title of a bitter book
by Ricardo Latcham, son of him who wrote about Indian
dances. Both are important for an understanding of one, perhaps the most important, phase of United States and Chilean
relations.

Mining operations are Chile's greatest source of wealth. The
Atacama Desert in the north, where no rain ever falls, is a vast
nitrate deposit; and underground are endless stores of many
minerals, chiefly copper. It is estimated that for forty years or
so after Chile acquired this region from Peru and Bolivia
taxes on nitrates paid seventy per cent of the government's
expenses. Foreign capital, enterprise, and skill have developed this region into one of the most richly productive in the
world. Today the largest nitrate operations and copper mines
are owned and operated by North American companies: hence
" Estado Yanqui."

The book of that subtitle, published in Santiago in 1926, is a denunciation of Yanqui capitalists. Mr. Latcham, typical muck-raker, also finds Chilean authorities venal, lawyers mercenary, newspapers controlled, and carabineros " forever at the service of the strangers." Clearly only Chile's lack of libel laws has saved him from prosecution. One might dismiss his book, as many Chileans and Yanquis do, as the scurrilous outburst of a dismissed and disgruntled employee. But its significance lies deeper than that. For though his picture may be exaggerated, even untrue in part, it reflects a widely held opinion of Yanqui business men and their manner of doing business. It appears that our mining men have had more influence on international sentiment than all the diplomats.

Mr. Latcham begins by expressing his admiration for the United States, " a great country and worthy of admiration for its exultant nationalism, which we should emulate. . . . The United States, country of Wilson, is other than that of a group of financiers, avid for exploitation. . . ." He goes on with the cry of " Imperialismo! " " The United States looks out confidently over the world, guided by a greedy and reckless oligarchy . . . which thrusts itself blindly over the future with a kind of drunkenness without alcohol." He then lists our sins, concluding: " Tomorrow it will be Chile, our Chile, which today we see menaced by the invincible economic invasion of the Guggenheims and their representatives."

The reason for this economic invasion our author admits very frankly. Faced with many abandoned or unworked mines, he turns his wrath upon his compatriots. " Many of these are reputed to contain great wealth, but most of them lie there abandoned or unknown in the hope that foreign capitalists will awaken them from their lethargic dream.

" When this happens the sons of Chile will again raise their voices to heaven, clamoring that the country's riches are being exploited; but meanwhile nobody does anything to avoid it, preferring to invest their capital and savings in Bolivian mines, Argentine oil, or other speculations which are not national."

Most of the book is concerned with detailed information about what our author saw at Chuquicamata, where he worked for some time. Only an exhaustive investigation could establish the rights and wrongs of what he says. Doubtless the picture he draws could be duplicated anywhere that great operations employ large numbers of laborers. The North American who tries to understand why our two countries, which need each other so much, cannot deal with mutual respect and advantage finds the crux of Ricardo Latcham's book, as of the problem, in a chapter entitled " *Tratamiento*," " Treatment."

" Perhaps . . . most irritating . . . is Yankee self-sufficiency in arrogating to themselves the title of the superior race, and the contempt with which they look upon everything Chilean, except that from which they can extract material gain.

" The natives, as they are disdainfully called, are for them an inferior people, to be kept underfoot without neglecting to exploit them.

" This hatred and disdain are seen in all spheres from the loftiest management to the last Yanqui foreman, with very rare exceptions. They impute to the Chileans all the vices, all the backwardness, all the lack of intelligence, and all the defects of a savage and barbarous people."

Aware of this, I embarked from Valparaiso on the *Aysén*, bound for Antofagasta and the copper mines at Chuquicamata. The *Aysén*, though a small coastwise steamer, was comfortable and clean, and my cabin-mate was a highbred, charming lady, so considerate that sharing a room was no difficulty at all.

The only possible criticism of the *Aysén* was that her cargo of cattle smelled bad.

At every port we loaded fruits, vegetables, and wines. Every tiny verdant valley is tapped for eatables; the Atacama Desert, one of the richest zones on earth, produces nothing to eat. Not a bulb, a leaf, or a blade of grass; scarcely an animal or a bird can live there. Man's life, where he digs out earth's best fertilizer, depends upon food shipped in from poorer lands. It is like a fable of starving to death on a mountain of gold.

The harbor of Antofagasta is backed by arid hills; its whole aspect is so dry-as-dust that it seems even to affect the sea. The water looks glassy, not wet. On the dock a representative of the Chile Exploration Company met me and steered me across the docks where sacks of nitrates and bars of copper awaited shipment to the north.

At the recommended hotel I was given an extensive suite whose bedroom had neither air not light, but whose sitting-room gave on a wide veranda over the main street. It had a bath and a bedbug, which I drowned in the water glass and showed in sour triumph to the maid in the morning.

She was calm, even reassuring. " It is so," she said. " There used to be many in this room, but the Bolivian consul who lived here warred against them, and now they are gone." A dramatic gesture toward my drowned victim did not perturb her. " This," she said firmly, " is the last; clearly they are gone." It was also the last room available in town. Perforce I stayed on for another night and found her right. I had finished the Bolivian consul's war and demolished the last rear-guard bedbug.

Sunday was election day and my escort had warned me not to go out on the streets. " There will be shooting," he said as though it were a regular part of the proceedings. But that hotel would have made shooting electors seem a pleasant relief. Besides, the law was out in full force and attractive guise. Mounted carabineros rode through the streets in detachments, pennons fluttered from their lances, their horsemanship excellent, themselves young and handsome.

No sign of disturbance appeared anywhere. A taximan assured me that only the election of the conservative candidate could save the country; a waiter that only the radical could prevent revolution; the man who sold me a paper foresaw disaster in any case. " *Esos politicos!* (These politicians!) " And the Englishman who lent me the last copy of *Time* averred as Englishmen do: " Your country will have to join us in policing the world and stopping all these wars."

It looked like a Sunday that could have no possible end. By mid-morning I had lived half a century. I found myself quoting to myself a limerick a mining engineer had perpetrated in Antofagasta a quarter of a century ago. It may prove nothing; it may prove that even mining engineers, pushed far enough, will take to triple rhymes.

> A young man of Antofagasta
> At shooting acknowledged no masta
> On tall Llullaillaco
> He shot a guanaco
> And chased him clear up to Mount Shasta.

Then relief appeared. A young vice-consul, homesick for his pretty wife in Cuba, invited me to go to the Auto Club. Driving along, we passed a house in a garden.

" That used to be the place to stay," he said. " German pension. Excellent beds, I'm told, and superlative food. But the proprietor was an ardent Nazi and it got on the British and American black list."

At the Auto Club we found the American and British colonies, plus many Chileans, and all the consuls having a luncheon. Antofagasta, the principal shipping port for copper and nitrates, is a great town for consuls. This affair was a goodwill meeting and felicitation for the Peruvian and Ecuadorian consuls following the settlement of their border dispute.

Their ladies lunched together or with their sunburned children. I noticed that the women fell into groups according to language: English here, Spanish there. The men were speaking Spanish, and the children, released to rush down to the beach, were bilingual and international. Let children follow their natural impulses and international understanding would be the rule in one generation.

The beach was a patch of sand among stern blackish rocks. But pools safe for children had been located there, and even one deep enough for diving. Trellises simulated tree shade, and against the clubhouse a few actual trees and vines struggled to shade the verandas. Antofagasta's society — both foreign and Chilean — has in high degree the quality that is never defeated, or even slightly dashed, by loneliness or desolation. It sunned and swam all morning and lunched in pleasant parties. Afterward many went on to the races, which were quite as exciting as those in Santiago's Club Hipodromo, and later to the vermouth hour at the movies. The ladies appeared each time in different frocks and hats, though generally with the same friends.

"The Yanqui state" has a long history. Chuquicamata's copper mines were worked even before the Incas conquered their aboriginal owners in 1443. The Indians most valued the gold quartz deposits, but they also mined copper, which they could harden into a kind of bronze for ornaments and tools.

When Diego de Almagro was leading the first Spanish expedition along there, in 1543, he came upon the great copper lode and conquered several Indian settlements, which still exist as ruins or adobe hamlets. Almagro made horseshoes of Chuqui copper, and Pedro de Valdivia, who established a supply station at Chiu-Chiu, worked copper in an old Indian smelter on the Rio Salado. Nothing much came of it until the great silver discoveries in Bolivia brought Chuqui to life again. But only high-grade ore was worked, and that desultorily.

Bolivia assumed that the great deathlike Atacama Desert belonged to her, and none disputed her claim. Bolivians shipped their silver out through ports now Chilean — Arica, Antofagasta, and others. But boundaries, as usual, were very hazy. And Chileans were inveterate miners, always seeking the underground fortune. I quote a Chilean historian, Luis Galdames, in translation by Isaac Joslin Cox.

" Years before [1879] some Chilean explorers, crossing the desolate desert of Atacama, had discovered on the shore near Mejillones rich deposits of guano. . . . After exploitation had begun, Bolivia claimed the territory where the deposits lay. . . . The diplomatic debate with Chile . . . became a very heated one. . . . Chile . . . fixed its northern limit on the twenty-fourth parallel (south of Antofagasta).

" Shortly after, other Chilean explorers found deposits of nitrate in the vicinity of Antofagasta, and others, later, found the Caracoles mines in the same region. The explorers petitioned for and obtained from the Bolivian government the right to exploit such wealth; but under very burdensome conditions which, nevertheless, they fulfilled faithfully. To that region, then, went Chilean laborers and capital. They founded the port and city of Antofagasta; they later caused Calama, Mejillones, Cobija, Tocopilla, and other cities to prosper. They performed enormous tasks in opening roads, creating watering places, and making the desert habitable."

(The reader is reminded that this is an account of Chilean capitalists operating in Bolivia, not Yanqui capitalists in Chile. From here on he should bear in mind that a Chilean is quoted.)

" Bolivians did not seem pleased to have the Chileans populate their desert and make it productive. A people still uncultured, shut in by almost impassable mountains and plains, Bolivians despised the foreigner, whoever he might be, just because he was one. . . . And . . . the Bolivian government committed hostilities in various ways, above all by imposing very heavy taxes on the producers of guano and nitrate."

This is enough to indicate the Chilean point of view when the foreign exploiter is Chilean and not Yanqui. Different versions may be read in Bolivian and Peruvian histories. For Peru was also drawn in on the side of Bolivia, claiming for itself the nitrate deposits in the state of Tarapacá. Bad feeling grew apace; all diplomatic overtures failed. Finally Peru " passed a law granting a monopoly of the nitrates of Tarapacá to the state." Bolivia proposed a similar action in Antofagasta. I quote Dr. Galdames again:

" In this manner, the policy of conciliation, of harmony, of almost unlimited compliance which Chile was practicing toward its sister republics . . . suddenly came to a violent end. Its legitimate economic expansion was being checked in a shameful and humiliating manner. It was being cast out of those inhospitable deserts conquered by the brawn of its nationals at the cost of great hardship; and at the same time its most solemn treaties were being violated. To resist these wrongs there was no longer any recourse but war.

"In the middle of February, 1879, and on the very day appointed for the auction of the nitrate plants, two hundred Chilean soldiers under the command of Colonel Emilio Sotomayor landed at Antofagasta, took possession of the city without any resistance, and hoisted the flag of Chile on the public buildings. The entire population, filled with great enthusiasm, gathered to acclaim these men as liberators. There were no Bolivians present except administrative employees and a small garrison. All were allowed to leave without hindrance. The occupation of Antofagasta, thus accomplished, marked the beginning of a war which was to keep the whole American continent in suspense."

Its end gave Chile the "perpetual ownership of the province of Tarapacá and the sovereignty of the provinces of Tacna and Arica for ten years, at the end of which time a plebiscite of its inhabitants should decide to which of the countries they should definitely belong." So was laid the groundwork for the Tacna-Arica dispute.

The War of the Pacific, fought on sea as well as land, had ended with Chile in possession of the copper and nitrate deposits and the ports which had been Bolivia's only outlet to the sea. And Chile owned the property blessedly free of legal complications. According to Bolivian law, a man owned a mine only so long as he worked it. As most Bolivians had abandoned their properties during the war, a Chilean had only to file claim and the mines were his. Thus the vast copper deposits of Chuquicamata came into Chilean hands and were owned by Chileans for thirty years.

Luis Camus tried to work the mines, but as he depended upon water hauled on mules for eighty miles or so, no profitable operation was possible until the British-built railroad reached Calama. Señor Camus was succeeded by his compatriot Antonino Toro, who also shortly retired from the scene.

Chuquicamata is the biggest copper lode in the world, but most of it is low-grade ore, difficult and expensive to work profitably. Two qualities were needed to develop and market its output: inventiveness and money, which included financial daring and access to the world's money markets. None of the Chileans who owned it demonstrated either of these gifts.

The first inventiveness was applied by a Scot, Norman Walker of Antofagasta, who perfected a leaching process which produced copper at £33 a ton. But he could not interest London capital, and several groups of backers in Chile failed. The only pre-Yanqui money-makers were Enrique Vallegas, a Chilean, and his Scotch partner, Walter G. Andrews. They worked the veins east of the great lode at a good profit until they had worked out the accessible veins. Then it was 1910 and time for Big Business. Enter the Yanqui with a new technique for working low-grade ore and enough capital for development.

The first Yanqui was William Burrage of Boston, who heard gossip in London about the great copper hill in Chile. As he was looking for a mine to work with the Burrage-Bradley process, recently developed in Montana for working oxide of copper, he took an option and acquired water and power rights as well. By that time the Guggenheims had a man on the ground too. His report, after he had sunk some test holes into Chuqui's hill, led to a deal by which Mr. Burrage sold his interest for cash and stock in a company formed in New York with a capitalization of fifteen million dollars. The original stock sold for twenty-five dollars a share. The Guggenheims, as a family and as individuals, owned the control. The Chile Exploration Company was formed, and the stage was set for the real play.

In 1912 Fred Hellman was sent down to take charge, and

he and his corps of young engineers — and their women — made a legend old-timers still love to tell. Water, hauled on tank cars to Chuqui station, went up to the mine on two-wheeled carts and finally into the drills in oil cans on burros. Women learned to make a cupful go a long way, but Mrs. Hellman raised a nasturtium on soapy water from her basin, and when they planted the first pepper tree they could have watered it with the tears brought at the sight of so much green. They lived in iron houses on a hill of copper, granite, and shale, ate canned food, and worked. Men now paunchy and graying relate how Mr. Hellman used to reach his office at seven fifteen to be sure no youngster arrived a moment after half past and how he " worked the pants off us." But they speak of him with deep affection and of Mrs. Hellman with tenderness for her way with lads away from home for the first time. As always the rough courage of men's pioneering was topped by the gentle courage of their women, who raised plants in tin cans, hung curtains in tin shacks, and made a family out of a working crew. So the job was done by the technical men and their women.

Representatives of the company state that all profits were reinvested in the company to finance the vast and expensive development of the mine; that no dividends were paid until 1923, though interest on bonds was paid as due. In 1923 the Guggenheim interests sold out to the Anaconda Copper Company for approximately 77,000,000 dollars. It seems likely that nobody really lost. Not even Chile. For the government, watching every move, collected a goodly income through taxes.

During those years of development Chile was in the position of the gentleman owner. Technicians, probably quite unlearned in the humanities, were doing the practical job, a man of business had found the cash, and the aristocratic owner

lived charmingly on verdant plantations or on Parisian boulevards, carefree and tax-free.

It is related that among the Yanqui engineers in Chile during those first hectic days was one from Philadelphia. Not a
Biddle, he was to the Biddles as the Lowells to the Cabots of
Boston. But to Chileans, unaware of social distinctions in the
north's commercial centers, an engineer was not quite a gentleman. So the Philadelphian was blackballed when his name
was proposed for membership in Santiago's most exclusive
club. The affair seems to have had no international repercus-
sions; perhaps the victim was unaware of it.

If Chile had maintained that point of view, perhaps there
never would have been the bad feeling that Mr. Latcham's book
expresses. But two things were to happen. A new class was
arising in Chile which could not see that it profited from the
taxes the Yanquis paid. And that new middle class, untrammeled by concepts of hidalguía and the unworthiness of trade,
was producing technicians and engineers. Even some Chileans
of the bluest Basque blood were choosing engineering as a
career. And the companies were, and still are, paying Yanquis
and other foreigners in dollars and Chileans in pesos. It is a
constant vexation and humiliation which seems to nullify all
official and unofficial efforts to be friends.

A Chilean, who would not be quoted by name, said: " Imagine how a Chilean engineer feels when he is paid 1,500 pesos
a month, which costs the company $77.64, for the same work
that gets a Yanqui $200. The Chilean, mind you, is just as
well trained and efficient. The two sit at the same desk and do
the same job. Often the Gringo needs the Chilean's help in
handling men, especially if the Yanqui doesn't know Spanish
very well. How can there be any equality between them? Naturally the Chilean and his wife can't keep up in dress, in

entertaining, in anything. It causes a galling resentment which often makes the Chilean blow up. Then the Yanquis can say again that the Chilean is unstable."

A Yanqui, also withholding his name, said: " Sounds all right, but we've got a job to do, and your Chilean won't get his hands dirty. The Yanqui will. He understands hard work, he's in the job for life, and he expects to go through the mill before he arrives. The Chilean will leak off after a government job about the time he begins to be worth anything. I tried to get one recently. Offered him 4,200 pesos. The government was paying him 4,000. He said he couldn't afford to come to me."

The company attitude, anonymous too, is that Chileans are paid the prevailing Chilean rate; that Yanquis must be paid the prevailing rate in the United States to get them to go Chile.

To the Yanqui bystander it seems that all these objections could be met by paying the Chilean the same wage for the same work. If he cannot do the work, well and good. But what a splendid patriotic gesture the great companies could make by putting Chilean and Yanqui on the same basis! More than all our diplomats and goodwill representatives our business men make international relations good or bad.

XXV

THE COPPER MINES OF CHUQUICAMATA

THE RAILROAD FROM ANTOFAGASTA TO CALAMA CROSSES a cindery desolation with hills like slag dumps varied by dust traps which a hot wind puffed into the car. No towns, but now and then a huddle of hovels round a mine or a nitrate plant. There men would detrain at a water tower where one spindly pepper tree lived on the drip. In one place there were two poplars, leafless in midsummer, but faintly alive.

" Papá, Papá! " cried the bright-eyed boy across the aisle, " see the little trees! "

" And one big tree," suggested Papá.

The child was a realist. " All little trees," he insisted.

This Atacama Desert, only less extensive than the Sahara, is the apotheosis of deadness. Rusty mortuary brown like California's Death Valley, it shows no sprig of green, not even a hardy cactus. Nothing moves; not a jack-rabbit, snake, or horned toad. No bird slants across the sky.

After hours of that we came suddenly upon wet green, flowing water, trees, and cool dampness on the skin. The River Loa whose wide basin was filled with velvety alfalfa soft enough to roll in, good enough to eat. Then Calama where the du Pont Company has an explosive plant. Ricardo Latcham played upon the word: "*Calama, calamidad.*" But surely it did not look like calamity to him when he came upon it out of the pampa.

Two ladies met me. Fresh in cool summer frocks and wide hats, they made me feel mussy and dirty beyond bearing. I was the guest of the Chile Exploration Company, and in no time they had me comfortable in the guest house and surrounded by that home feeling so good in a foreign land. Some of these Chuqui women have lived in Chile for twenty-five or thirty years, love it, and are sure they could never live in the States again. Their houses are built of corrugated iron and lined with beaver board. They have screens, plumbing, and electricity. Comfort, but no luxury. As Chile produces little handicraft, typical touches are limited to Araucanian ponchos on the floors, and pink copper ash trays. A few zinnias, larkspurs, or sweetpeas on the table testify to devoted care and labor. The whole is the replica of any mining town in the West.

These women have problems. They get lonely and are glad — or make the visitor feel they are glad — to talk with somebody from outside. And they are troubled about their children. The company school is conducted in English, but avoiding a Spanish accent is difficult none the less. Also it is hard to make sound democratic Americans in Chile.

"You see," one mother explained, "the servants treat our children as they do upper-class Chileans. Consequently they get some pretty hard knocks when they go back home, where they find no consciousness of an upper class."

Few Yanqui women learn more Spanish than they need in their kitchens. This makes a real difficulty when Chilean offi-

cials bring their wives to visit. Yanqui women do not read
Chilean history or literature and their knowledge of Chilean
politics is extremely sketchy. Eight women, discussing the election, which was of great importance to the United States, were
unsure of the names of the candidates. Their talk was chitchat
of their own group or of affairs at home. They seemed to live
on an island of the U.S.A. mysteriously transported into a
foreign land. I thought of the fascinating, alert Chilean women,
busy with politics, education, all the arts. What a foreign
legion of good feeling our women could be if they would learn
Spanish, know Chilean women! And what a cure for boredom
and loneliness!

Mr. Matt Sample, assistant general manager of the company, showed me the mine: an outdoor, sunlit mine, as healthful a place as a child's sand pile. A hill a mile and a half long
and half a mile deep has been laid open in long colored terraces. Below the shallow gray top are layers of yellow, terra-
cotta, verdigris, and turquoise. The grayish blue is 1.5 per cent
copper, the green 2.5 per cent. That lovely red is no good
at all.

" The ore in sight," Mr. Sample was saying, " will last a
hundred years at the present rate."

Just then a loud reverberating roar deafened us and raised
a huge dust cloud against the clear blue sky. As it settled I
could see how great electric shovels were scooping up the
shattered rock and swinging round to deposit it in a waiting
car. Electric trains run along the terraces to haul ore to the
plant which I should see later. All this specialized work was
being done by Chileans.

" Most of our workmen are boys raised and trained right
here. . . . Sure they're good, as good as anywhere.

" The government has set no legal minimum wage. Our

pay averages up well with that for the nation. We comply meticulously with all requirements; even lean over backward doing it. We are subject to criticism, you know." He spoke so without rancor that I wondered if he had read Latcham's book.

Then, in answer to questions: " We do a good deal with bonuses too. A bonus split among four men like the crew on that steam shovel keeps them moving right along.

" Our men work an eight-hour day with a twenty-minute interval for lunch, but the shovels never stop. Besides wages and bonuses a man gets his house, water, light, medical and hospital care. And we maintain a store, pulpería, where we sell everything they need. I can say that in ten years there has been no rise in the price of basic necessities. You'll see how they live when you go round this afternoon.

" Yes, the men are unionized; have to be under the law. There is one union for miners, one for the plant, and one for bakers, chauffeurs, and white-collar workers.

" Sometimes they make intelligent demands; sometimes idiotic. We have a strong communistic influence here. Leaders directed from outside stir the men up. We always meet them, hear them, the best we can."

The man who actually manages a mine — or a factory or a plantation — attains a balance seldom seen in a dissentious world. What a feat of equilibrium to be fair between employers demanding fat profits, laborers demanding higher pay and better conditions, and government demanding justice for both — or is it?

A mining man reading this smiled wryly. " And government demanding more and more taxes. Never forget that," he said.

" What would you do, what could you do, if Uncle Sam should suddenly demand more copper of you? "

Chuquicamata is Built on Dry Hills

F. J. Rudershausen

The Mine is Open to the Sun

" Very little. We are running full time now, full capacity, and as efficiently as we know how. It would take years to enlarge the plant, and the new tax the government has just put on copper makes enlargement that much more unlikely."

We drove along the top of that ridge of copper, looking out across the wavering pampa at the pale blue and silver crest of the Andes. From there, I knew, water came: an adequate supply for everything except gardens. Sixty-five miles of pipe bringing pure spring water from an altitude of 14,000 feet. We had stopped at the entrance of a shaft where a rickety trestle was rigged with a bucket. Near by a row of rotting corrugated iron roofs made porches for dugouts. Altogether a most deplorable dump.

" A Chilean mine," he said, " owned and operated by Chileans. They employ about forty men who live in these dugouts. They are working a high-grade vein with a gasoline engine. We swap them water, about 250 to 300 gallons a day, for the right of way for that electric wire.

" Placilla village used to be here. Forty years ago it was a regular Wild West show. A hangout for bandits. Every Saturday night there were shootings and knifings. They said the cemetery's population was seventy-five per cent murderers. We cleaned that out."

He stopped again to point out a man drawing steaming water from a spigot. " Boiling water for tea. Every man carries his tin cup and pinch of tea. They don't like a cold lunch, so we supply electric heat at handy places."

I asked about equal pay for Chilean technicians.

" We have Chileans paid on the dollar scale. Our plant superintendent, Domingo Moreno; our doctors." A little probing brought the admission that the number was few. We returned to the plant superintendent, Domingo Moreno.

" Any number of men like that could get any pay they want. Just show me more like that! He's a graduate of the Colorado School of Mines, and he's tops from any point of view."

The brilliant exception, when we met for a tour of the plant, refused to discuss the matter. Cautious, perhaps, but more likely too absorbed in his job, too enthralled with his engines and wheels to concern himself with extraneous matters. Slim and young, he was Yanqui but Chilean too: a walking, talking example of the American we must produce with all the efficiency of the north, all the grace and charm of the south. My mind whirled as I tried to keep up with his long-legged stride and to understand the technical things I saw.

The cars which I had seen loading at the mine were here running up into a shelter where they were dumped, righted, and allowed to slide easily down again.

" The power of gravity does that."

The dust-filled air prompted me to make one of those dumb would-be-clever remarks which must be so annoying to a man trying to explain a complicated operation to a tyro.

" Why don't you catch all that dust and make use of it? "

Without a trace of irritation he answered: " We do. We save most of it, and we extract some good high-grade ore as dust."

The ore dumped from the cars in great jagged rocks is crushed and crushed again until it is reduced to lumps not more than three eighths of an inch in size. This mass is then passed into great vats like huge swimming tanks brimming with blue-black ink and stained on the edges with brilliant blue-green. Copper is beautiful at every stage.

This is the process technically known as leaching. It consists in washing the crushed rock with dilute sulphuric acid and results finally in pure copper held in solution. This amounts to only 2 per cent of the mass of ore brought from the mine. The 98 per cent of waste residue, known as tailings, is dumped out on the end of a man-made hill which may come in handy some day — if a process is ever invented for extracting more copper in paying quantities.

As we walked along those gorgeously stained vats we were continually meeting men who seemed to be in fancy dress: striped trousers of ugly yellow and black and heavy wooden shoes. Mr. Moreno laughed:

" We provide their work clothes, and that color scheme was my idea. They used to sell the clothes we gave them or save them for Sunday and wear rags in the plant. Especially if a politician came along they'd turn themselves out like ragmen and say: ' Just see how this brutal Yanqui corporation grinds us down.' A great success with our critics! So I got the company to buy good sturdy woolen stuff, but so ugly and so distinctive that nobody else would have it. It worked."

I said: " I've heard Chileans say that Chileans tend to be ' abusadores.' Is that true? Will they take advantage? I've found them honest."

" Of course there are a few who figure it's fair enough to gyp a big soulless corporation. Personally I find them honest, but I have to watch company property all the time."

Then we entered the roofed-in part of the plant: the precipitation tanks where the copper, reduced to solution by the sulphuric acid, is recovered by electrolysis. We looked down long shadowy aisles where men in heavy boots were leaning over open pits and working with sheets of copper, now the true copper color. This process begins with the " starting sheet," a copper plate, paper-thin and about four feet square. It is hung in these tanks and built up by electrolysis to the required thickness: about an inch. The sheet of electrolytic copper is now called a cathode. During this process men are constantly on watch, alert to remove any sheet that needs cleaning or straightening. It is a technical job requiring vigilance and judgment. Most of the men, Mr. Moreno said, were " camp boys "; probably born, certainly raised here and trained for the work.

In one vat the funguslike foam was not quite the right color. It was almost pitch black when it should have been ink blue. Mr. Moreno clicked his tongue in disapproval.

" And won't you stop this dude tour and speak to somebody about it? "

" No. That won't be necessary. Somebody has seen me looking at it. It'll change. You see, this dude tour, as you call it, is not wasting time for me. It's in the nature of an inspection tour too."

The men we passed were Chileans with brown aquiline faces, keen blue or gray eyes, and the nervous though controlled motions of a white man at exacting work. Among them I was aware of a greater creature with a larger frame and heavier features, and slow-moving with quiet inner strength rather than superficial restraint.

" He looks like an Indian."

" He is. A pure-blooded Indian from Bolivia. He's foreman here."

" And how do these white men like working under him? "

" They don't like it, but this work pays better than any other part of the plant, so even if they blow up and leave they usually soon come back."

When the cathodes are thick enough — a matter of days in those midnight-blue vats — piles of them are fed into the refining furnaces. And what an operation that was to watch!

A man, enthroned high on a moving seat and making five

separate motions with levers, caused great cranes to lift a bundle of cathodes, swing it high, back around with it, and approach the flaring, hell-hot, open maw of the furnace. The man, so tiny, but with a trained eye and a calculating brain, could make his monster swing a couple of tons of copper so accurately that it entered the opening without scraping. Once, even more wonderfully, he scraped just enough to push a protruding brick back into place.

Pouring that mass when molten into wires, bars, and ingots for shipping would be done when the heat had finished its work, twenty hours after the cathodes go into the furnace. For that we should come back tomorrow morning.

Meanwhile I learned that oil for the furnaces comes from Peru and even from California. It is landed at Antofagasta and hauled up by train. Electricity, generated at Tocopilla, is wired across eighty-seven miles of desert, because that is cheaper than hauling oil. A little coke is used in the furnaces — just enough to prevent oxidation of the copper — but practically all the fuel is oil, all the power electrical.

I kept thinking about the men working with such accuracy and skill.

" Occupational diseases? No. There is some silicosis from dust, but we check all the men, take only those with sound lungs. And if a man shows any râles we transfer him to another job. One survey of four hundred men showed thirty-five with râles. Not much greater, I imagine, than in any life. But ask the doc in the hospital.

" There is some hazard of blindness to the refiners, due to the ultra-red rays, which may cause cataracts. Oddly enough, it is a preferred job. It pays well and requires a high degree of skill. Originally all refiners were Welsh. Most of them are now Yugoslavs, though we have four or five first-rate Chileans.

In any case it's a hereditary job, a family trade. You'll see the type tomorrow."

Next day the sheets we had seen so accurately shot into that fiery hell pit had melted down into a liquid mass. We stood well back; I had been given a shield to hold before my eyes, but the heat came up in waves. Molten copper is an unbelievable color. Not red, nor orange, nor gold; not flame because there is no flicker. The color of glory perhaps, and like glory it is impossible to gaze upon for more than a split second, because it is blinding to those daring souls who persist in approaching too close. It flowed out through a spout onto a revolving table and into forms. Table and forms were whitened with bone ash and there men in dark clothes moved like inhuman shades. The skill consists in knowing just when to pour. It is done by sight or sound: the color unseen or the hiss unheard by an untrained eye or ear. All along busy lanes we watched those Yugoslav experts — with a few Chileans — pouring streams of glory-colored metal into forms.

Every man was slim, hard, alert, yet at ease and lax between tense moments. One, indeed, having filled a mold with hell-hot liquid, set a tin cup of water on it. "Boiling water for his tea."

In this plant copper is cast into wirebars for drawing into wire, into cakes suitable for sheets, or into ingots for recasting to make brass, for instance. The complete processing is done, that is, in Chile, and the finished product is sold abroad. That most of it goes to the United States is because Chile is not yet ready to use it.

After lunch my hostesses conducted me through Chuqui town, a settlement of twenty thousand workers and their families. In view of the long haul for water a plaza with trees and flowers is no less than a miracle. The playground too had a

The Spanish Conquerors Built a Church at Chiu-Chiu

A Guano Island off Tocopilla

few trees among swings, teeters, and poles. Two large schools
— one for boys and one for girls — are classed as " rural "
and offer the full six years of primary instruction. There are
night schools as well for illiterates and certain technical and
office workers. All are government-controlled but built and
maintained by the company as the law requires.

We went to see the workers' houses. Every dwelling had a
patch of ground big enough to delve in and responsive enough
to flaunt a pepper tree, a vine, or a handful of flowers. The
best-kept homes had potted plants as well.

The worst of them have not improved much since Ricardo
Latcham described them in 1926. " These houses are composed of two rooms and a kitchen. If the family has no children, not too bad; but the majority have children and frequently they are composed of many dependent relatives. One
room serves as dining- and living-room, the other is the only
sleeping-room. One can imagine the unsanitary state which results from this crowding. . . . If we add to this the bad moral
effect of such promiscuity of the sexes in those families which
have grown children, we shall see that the situation is dis-
astrous."

My guides honorably showed me the old houses still remaining. With water piped only to the corner and no sanitary priv-
ies, they are indeed distressing. But the newer ones are better
than workers' houses in most of Chile's cities. We entered one
of a row just finished. The living-room was paneled in pine
to the height of a plate-rail wide enough for many treasures.
There was a sanitary toilet and shower on a tiny patio, and
wide windows opening both on that and on a front porch. With
no closets even an excellent housekeeper might find difficulty
in maintaining perfect order, but cleanliness would be possible. The best of these houses are still too small for privacy,

considering the size of the usual Chilean family and its " *han llegados.*"

The Chilean was amused that I knew the phrase and admitted that even in remote Chuqui few families lack that " dropper-in " who stays on indefinitely.

" But remember," she said, " that this is Chile and not the U.S."

But Chuqui is the United States in so far as a wealthy North American company might build better accommodations for its employees. It is also Chile, wherein a foreign company must conform to good laws, well administered. Much that we saw is the result of Chile's excellent social program.

We visited one of the pulperías, emporiums of general merchandise like any country store in the States. Clerks were busy selling clothes, food, tools, yard goods, furniture, dishes, linoleum, and toys. Everything was immaculate and well displayed, with meat behind screens, perishables on ice, and delicate fabrics under glass. These pulperías meet the competition of private stores which are smaller but similarly stocked. Special shops offer stationery and school books. And here too, in a remote mining camp, were the bookstores so surprising in every part of Chile.

Movie theaters offered lurid horse operas, recent pictures from the United States, Argentina, and Mexico.

Near each movie was a *refrescaría* where soft drinks and ice cream could be had. Liquor is sold only by one concessionaire and by the men's club. A large dull-looking building, the club had rooms for bachelors, an auditorium which served also as a basket-ball court, and rooms for meetings. Also on the plaza were the post office and the *Caja de Ahorros*, that splendid government institution of savings for insurance. Near it was the maternity hospital it supports.

The hospital requires two hundred employees, including ten doctors and nine nurses. All are Chileans except four nurses from the States. Even the so-German young doctor who showed us about was Chilean-born and proud of Chile's health work. He boasted of the well-equipped laboratory with its iron lung and X-ray machine. We walked along the wards where accident cases, maternity cases, and surgery cases lay. And the baby clinic where every child born at Chuqui comes for regular check-ups.

As we crossed the patio Mrs. Sample stopped at a pepper tree. Ferny and seeming so fragile, these trees put up the sturdiest fight for survival on the scanty ration of water they may get in the desert. Wherever it can get a cupful of moisture the pepper tree tries if it does not flourish. This one, taller and leafier than most, was Chuqui's first.

" Planting it was a great ceremony," Mrs. Sample laughed to remember. " Mrs. Hellman had nursed it along for months in a pot and when she thought it was strong enough we all gathered to plant it here." She touched it affectionately. " This is an important tree."

Looking from the tree across the stark grandeur of the desert, wavering now into the pale lilac shadows of evening, and beyond at the Andean peaks flushing pink on silver, I saw the tiny courageous tree as a symbol of all those women have stood in the desert, and stood for.

XXVI

HOMEWARD BOUND

[THE NITRATE DESERT]

RIVING ACROSS THE PAMPA FROM CHUQUICAMATA TO Tocopilla I was reminded of how that desert looked from the air. Burned-out and static it rolled in petrified undulations to the shore, where feathery waves and adamantine cliffs have been battling for all time with no decision yet. But a swift flight shows slashings of emerald where a successful river has won through to the sea and men have planted and built. From an automobile we saw no green after leaving the Loa Valley. Only gray-black, brown-black desert: not dusty, not sandy, just degenerate rock heavily weighing down the earth. Hard silver snow on the peaks sent a cool breeze to cut the sun's heat, and we ran bumplessly along two cement tire tracks on the gravel. We were following a row of shining tall towers which upheld the highly charged wire that carries power to the mine. Now and then we saw a man clinging there aloft; work crews watch this line all the time.

Chile's Atacama Pampa is the greatest known source of nitrate, which so tellingly dramatizes the potentialities of power. As fertilizer it produces food for the multitudes. As high explosives it can blow them to bits. But explosives, too, are capable of good. So man has two chances out of three for decency. The nitrate desert was laid down, geologically speaking, quite recently. As the Andes rose from the sea, these flats rose too, bearing great puddles of sea water which dried slowly, holding all their saline riches in that rainless desert. Caliche, the nitrate-bearing gravel, lies just under the surface rock, which is seldom more than six feet thick and easy to work.

Nitrates, like copper, were well known to Chileans long before Yanqui capital entered the picture. The conquerors made gunpowder from saltpeter; Jesuits and other monastic orders produced nitrates for fertilizer, and for gunpowder to smuggle out to ships in port.

As long as operations were conducted by small owners, they were of the simplest. Indians, employed at piece work, cut the caliche into hundred-pound chunks, rather like a cake of ice. An overseer then ran the flame of a torch across every block. By the way it burned he could gauge the amount of nitrate it contained, and he paid accordingly. Water was then run over it. The insolubles would sink, the water evaporate, and a residue of fairly pure nitrate remain. Even this rudimentary process was not feasible until the British railroad to Bolivia began to haul water down from the Andes.

The first foreign investors in Chilean nitrates were British and German, and the greatest nitrate fortunes were made before 1914. During the war Germany developed synthetic nitrates and soon afterward all countries were making them. Chile, from having been the greatest source of supply, dropped to producing only twenty per cent of the world's need in 1929. But after the minor crisis of 1926, the du Ponts had begun to buy up small investors; and improved mechanization and marketing brought Chile's exports up again.

We passed two of the du Pont plants, at a distance. Far away across the dim desert, where shimmery mirage water reflected imaginary trees, ghostly white buildings seemed just as insubstantial. But no, they were real; and the puffs of white were nitrates, not smoke. Nitrate too were the occasional whirlwinds idling across the flats.

The road crossed a depression where long-dried mud had cracked into cakes, demonstrating perfectly how the pampa was made. Yet those cracked cakes looked so recent that I asked:

" *Agua?* "

" Yes," the driver answered, " water when it rains."

" Every century? "

" Three years ago it rained. I'll show you later."

Beside one dry wash we came upon two tombstones shaded, marvel of marvels, by two small but flourishing pepper trees.

" People passing," the driver explained, " bring water for the trees. They light candles too."

Candles and prayers are familiar at the sites of accidents in any Catholic country, but I had never seen such flaming banners of faith and brotherhood as those fresh green sprigs kept alive by unknown friends bringing water across a desert.

Far away an oasis shimmered, and sailing out of it came a sailboat. But the sailboat was no mirage. Actuality on that mystical desert seems stranger than visions. It was a flatcar on a railroad track, rigged with a sail and taking workmen home from the nitrate works.

Then we scented the sea and were soon traveling down a stony canyon. Here the flood of three years ago seemed to live again in violently tumbled rocks, devastated roadbeds and retaining walls. Many people lost their lives in a cloudburst whose like nobody was old enough to remember. A turn

Antofagasta Is between Salty Sea and Barren Hills

Loading Nitrates

showed us the shining-white sea and Tocopilla, a boxlike brown town under brown cliffs. Beyond the smoke blossoming out of the plant, oil tankers rode in the harbor, and a fleet of boats and barges. The only white spot in town was a large apartment house, government-built for workmen.

" It's like a Los Angeles real-estate development, isn't it? That's what our Frente Popular has spent 14,000,000 pesos on." My Chilean companion was soured on Chile's New Deal. "Three-, four-, and five-room apartments with electricity, kitchen, and bath with running water." He chortled harshly. " The only slip-up is that the people won't live in 'em. I think there are three apartments rented out of 167. And not to workmen. No workman can afford 350 pesos, and that's the minimum. A good workman makes 700. Calculate it for yourself.

" Besides, workmen like ours don't want to live like that; don't know how to live like that. They're not house-proud. Their pride is expressed in clothes; their extravagances are in drink and gambling."

" But isn't this an effort to raise their standard of living? "

" Claro! And very admirable. Just badly thought out, as so many of our efforts to imitate you are. That's our national vice, trying to emulate the United States. A little thought would have resulted, I believe, in something a laborer would like and could pay for. For 3,500,000 pesos the government could have built many two- and three-room houses with patios where a man could raise a few vegetables and get his feet on the ground. That's what he likes, you know: to touch the earth and see a plant grow."

I was sorry when the frank Chilean left me in the plaza where the reliable little pepper trees and a few eucalyptus shaded cement walks and a bandstand. Tocopilla reveals itself without reservations. Old: many houses show the style and trimming of the nineties. British: pith helmets enter heavy stone offices or bungalows with green and white verandas. A port: Hindu turbans and stores with Chinese, Greek, and Norwegian names. Yanqui: the great gray plant behind tall wire fences where the last tower delivers the last length of charged wire we had followed across the desert. A cheap restaurant named O-Key and a company house for bachelors called the Barking Dog Kennel. Tourists: *The Grace Line,* discreetly announced on an elegant bronze plaque on a stately edifice. And among the oil tankers two trim white launches waiting for the fishermen who would be lacking now for the duration.

The Grace Line, purveyor of the most luxurious South American seagoing, has begun to develop fishing grounds off Ecuador and Chile. The fish, perhaps, needed little development. They are there; the biggest, most plentiful, and gamest in the world. Also the most fun because they will take bait and need not be harpooned as off the Florida coast. Off Tocopilla "the world's top ranking Broadbill Swordfish have been caught." The tiptop was an 860-pounder. "Of all the Swordfish taken in the world weighing over 600 pounds, all but two have been caught off Tocopilla." . . . Less strenuous angling is offered by Yellow Fin Tuna, the Pacific Albacore, Dolphin, and Oceanic Bonitas, which are used for Swordfish bait and are so numerous that no bait problem is ever offered. Indeed, the prospectus suggests that no problem of any sort ever faces the Grace Line's sportsman. In the launch he is attended by an expert crew: one to steer the boat, one to cut bait; the third "takes care of the fisherman's needs, does all the gaffing and is the number one lookout in trying to locate fish." The fisherman himself is seated in a comfortable chair, "complete with foot bracing and adjustable turning gear, also heavy duty gimbel rod socket." Below he finds a "beautifully appointed cabin with washroom, galley, etc." The " etc." includes hot or cold luncheon as preferred and afternoon tea. Nothing is said about a folding bar — an oversight the Grace Line should rectify immediately after the war.

Ashore no oversight is discernible. An old residence has been adjusted to Yanqui taste by removing all plants from the patio and installing a badminton court. Bedrooms have been cut up to provide " and bath," and supplied with Simmons beds and thermos bottles. Tackle-room, photographers' dark-room, and electric refrigerator remove some of the horrors of roughing it; and butler, house boy, two chambermaids, chef, assistant chef, and laundress stand ever at the weary angler's shoulder.

All this was shown and told by the Grace Line's two young representatives. Clean-cut, college-bred, and with cultivated accents they were, perhaps, the type that prompts some Chileans to consider us a race of softies — especially as they appeared against that background of luxury for the sportsman. But both young men were chafing to get home and into service. How quickly, I thought, a national need will crack that smooth finish and lay bare the true and tough American stuff that underlies it!

At the guest house where the hospitable company put me up I too reveled in Yanqui softness. The woven-wire fence was covered with flowering vines, and beds of zinnias outlined a wide veranda shaded by reeds laid on beams. No need to guard against rain here. Inside was everything Yanquis delight in: screens, ice, spotless table linen, gravy for dinner, biscuits for breakfast, bedrooms opening all round for the breeze, and a smiling " China boy " to supply every want.

I spent a morning seeing the electric plant. It is the largest in the world; surely nowhere could the world's interrelated-

ness be more strongly felt. The water it uses comes a hundred
and fifty miles; its fuel oil thousands; the power it generates
travels a hundred miles to Chuqui; and the copper it makes
there will go — we hope — to Japan. The place is guarded
like a jewel. No stranger is allowed even to approach the high
barbwire-topped fence; all night guards patrol the lighted
premises. Many doors we passed were opened by a key or by
a guard summoned by a bell.

Mr. Art Boynton, the manager, was quite as interested in his
garden. He had planned the flower beds around the guest
house, and his own house has a tiny green dingle to catch the
view and the breeze. But his pride is the company garden.
Though water comes far and is precious beyond all price, he
has proud rows of lettuce, radishes, tomatoes, and melons.
Six thousand heads of lettuce a month go into the pulpería,
where the company takes a loss in order to supply the workers
some green stuff.

"If we didn't do that," Mr. Boynton explained, "they
simply couldn't buy. Prices are prohibitive. Green stuff comes
from Coquimbo, over 300 miles down the coast. The farmer
may have hauled it 30 or 40 miles from his place to the dock.
There he sells it to someone who has rented space on a ship's
deck and who pays first-class transportation to Tocopilla. By
the time he has paid a couple of stevedores, and sold to a mer-
chant here, every tomato might as well be a ruby. I figured once
that a shipment has been handled by seven middlemen. . . .
What this country needs more than anything is roads."

We passed the workers' houses, much like those at Chuqui.
Mr. Boynton chuckled: "We once had water piped into every
house, but we had to give it up. We found that every Sunday
relatives would come in for miles and use water by the barrel."

"Week-end bathing parties?"

" Bathing, nothing! Washing clothes! They'd bring clothes sixty miles and do family washings for the whole northern desert. So we took out the taps and now they have to carry the water."

In the afternoon I drove to Antofagasta, where I should embark for home. Off shore stood a sentinel island, ivory-toned and far too beautiful to be the guano island it is. The desert persisted to the very beach, relieved only here and there by a creeping vine with purplish flowers. We passed one abandoned town after another: places where mining operations had been discontinued and people had been left clinging like bats to empty houses. They showed themselves, forlorn and ragged, and the driver took time to convey messages or news. Every place reminded him of something.

Here a German had arrived with trucks and workmen and informed the caretaker that the company had commissioned him to remove all scrap metal. His manner was so assured, even overbearing, that the poor employee suspected nothing wrong. Weeks later it developed that the whole scheme had been a steal.

Another collection of gaping, roofless wall had been a resort when all this was Bolivian territory. "They say," the driver said, "that honeymoon couples driving down from La Paz used to arrive about the time the baby was born."

Off a promontory where the sea and sky met, melting into a blue mist, an old man saw the *Caleuche* once. " She was very clear. He saw the masts and spars. The sails drooped in the calm, but he could hear metal scraping as the anchor was lowered and even voices faintly." I marveled that that ghost ship of the austral seas had come so far north, but there could be no doubt, the driver said. The man who saw it had told him so.

As we drove into Antofagasta we passed the airport.

" I tried to get work there." The chauffeur was steadily talkative now. " I want to be an aviator. In your country I could be. I've heard that there a poor man can work and study, better himself. Here they won't even let you try. When I asked for a job, any kind of a job just to learn, they only laughed at me."

On the edge of town he pointed out the Catholic industrial school where his son was doing so well. " It will be better, I think, when he is a man. He will be able to better himself." It was the universal Chilean plaint; all the way from the lovely Emerald Lake in a dripping southern mountain forest to this stark and barren port on the desert I had heard Chileans say that all they needed was a chance such as my country offered. It is good to know that one's country typifies that to a people whose strength and intelligence ask only opportunity.

[THE ACONCAGUA]

I sailed for home from Antofagasta. The *Aconcagua*, a Chilean ship, sailed late; she had been delayed, they said, loading copper. But ships were being deliberately delayed by that time. The war news was bad; Japanese or German submarines might, for all anybody knew, be based on San Fernando or the Galapagos Islands, or even hidden in mainland coves. Chile was neutral; her flag with wide red and white bands and a single white star on a blue field was painted on the *Aconcagua's* sides and floodlighted at night. But her cargo was copper and nitrates and her destination was New York. In this war one could not count on neutrality. But the Chilean steamer rode proudly through: neutral, but doing her part to aid the Americas.

XXVII

CULTURAL RELATIONS

CULTURAL RELATIONS BEGIN BETWEEN ANY TWO COUNtries when two of their nationals come face to face for the first time. A shipwrecked sailor accepting a banana or a skin garment is partaking of the culture of the savage who succors him. A ship's captain or a trader ingratiating himself with beads or whisky is offering his culture as surely as the missionary setting up the cross or translating the Bible into an unwritten language. In every case the two cultures meet to clash or to fuse. It is a cultural relationship whether its results are good or bad.

Perhaps it is typical of the idealistic United States to use the phrase as connoting only good and of our gift for organization that we have set up a division under the Department of State to foster more and better cultural exchange with the whole world. It always seems to us that anything well done by individuals could be better done on a large scale by trained and organized groups. This may be true, though it would be truer if the original man-to-man aspect of human relations were never lost sight of.

The title Cultural Relations was first applied to our association with Latin America by Hubert Herring, who was studying Mexico back in the twenties. He heard a member of our Embassy describe his obligation as limited to protecting American business. It occurred to Mr. Herring that our diplomats might better serve us if they, and we in general, knew more of the countries with which we dealt. So he — typical Yanqui — organized groups of students to study Mexico in Mexico. This began a series of " seminars " which first introduced many United States Americans to the history, present problems, and future hopes of the other Americans. For the scheme was rapidly expanded to include the whole hemisphere. It made good friends and more understanding from the Rio Grande to the Bío-Bío.

The title Cultural Relations was too apposite to supersede. So when our government went into official interchange of culture with the whole world, the phrase went too. In 1938 the Division of Cultural Relations was created under the Department of State " for the purpose of encouraging and strengthening cultural relations and intellectual co-operation between the United States and other countries."

Its program includes the exchange of professors, teachers, and students; co-operation in all the arts and other cultural activities; supervision of radio broadcasts and dissemination of informative and educational motion pictures, and of publications of many kinds; and encouragement of closer co-operation between unofficial cultural organizations in the different countries.

None of this was virgin territory. The new division found that it must collaborate with many private organizations, with the Pan-American Union, which was hoary with age and experience in the field, and finally with the Office of Co-ordinator of Inter-American Affairs, which was created in 1941 to do just what its title indicates.

This office, under Mr. Nelson Rockefeller, concerns itself with every aspect of our complicated relationships with the governments of Latin America from the development of rubber production in Brazil to sponsoring a tour of the Yale Glee Club; from strategic highways to the translation of novels; from the training of librarians to the consideration of erosion in its effect on Andean Indians. The Co-ordinator's office has sent movie stars south, brought professors north, built up good feeling, and caused at least one diplomat to threaten that if he had to face one more goodwill delegation he would declare war on the United States. With our usual determination to make a clean sweep we have discommoded many conservative people, upset many scholarly minds, offended many sensitive souls. But we have also released many millions of dollars for projects in health, education, industrial development, and a hundred other public benefits which our neighbors have requested and approved. As usual our successes have been in the material or organizational field; our failures because we neglected or did not sense the personal implications of what we did.

It is clear that as we strive to learn more about our neighbors and to help them intelligently, they are learning even more about us. Laughing at our blunders, offended by our clumsinesses, they are learning too that the fearsome colossus of the north is not bad at heart; that Uncle Sam is really trying to help. Understanding is beginning to work both ways. But there is real need for a steadying influence, one that will know how to make human relations easy and comfortable. This is where the Division of Cultural Relations comes in.

331

It is headed by Charles A. Thomson, a judicious and tolerant man who spent years of study in Mexico, Central America, and the Caribbean area. This gave him a specialized knowledge of Latin America, and later experience as a staff member of the Foreign Policy Association widened the base of his interests and his knowledge. In the Latin-American field his familiarity with Spanish and Portuguese and their literatures, an instinctive sense of the Latin-American point of view, and *simpatía* have given him hosts of friends and the confidence of intellectual leaders. His staff sees as he does the problem of making a dignified and friendly approach to fine people whom we need quite as much as they need us. His office should and does provide lubrication for the whole vast and complicated machinery of our dealings with our hemispheric neighbors.

Nothing about our now highly organized program is new; it is merely a standardization of what has long been going on through private efforts and personal contacts. This probably means that it is a sound program. Our contacts with the Latin-American countries during our existence as a sovereign state fall easily into classification. Diplomacy first; and who can deny personalities are often the dominant factor? Then through our missionaries, who enter the most intimate personal fields. Even business, though it is concerned with hard economic facts, is aided or hampered by personal considerations. Besides this we have a shorter but, on the personal side, perhaps more successful history of dealings in all that may be classed as science, including medicine and the control of epidemics and running through the entire alphabet of ologies from anthropology to zoology.

Our diplomatic approach has occasionally earned criticism for an excessive zeal to meddle in our neighbors' domestic politics. Even now an articulate group in the United States would have us declare, in certain countries, for the radical pretender as against the conservative incumbent. These same critics, of course, deplore the times when we have supported the other side.

With Chile our diplomatic relations have been, on the whole, excellent. Only the *Baltimore* incident has marred more than a century of pleasant dealings. That resolved itself into an Irishman's hatred of England. Our government accepted the decision of the Chilean court, our President expressed disapproval of the Minister's partisanship and recalled him. Yet that episode of more than fifty years ago still rankles and is useful in Nazi propaganda. One can only conclude that what individuals do is ultimately more important than what governments intend.

Missionaries, who make an overt attempt to supplant one culture with another, present a very special problem in our relations with Latin America. Europeans, so conscious of racial and religious superiority, have overspread the world with their faiths, trying to do good. To their recipient these ministrations may seem only insulting. Often he does not recognize the missionary's good as for him. Few people appreciate having their beliefs upset, their children weaned away from them, their social scheme disrupted by alien ideas. One who believes that all peoples make their own best adjustment to the vicissitudes of life and find their own best expression of awe before the inscrutable forever marvels at the disrespect with which evangelists will uproot long-established beliefs, deride customs hallowed by ages of devotion, and split tribes and families. True, Jesus said: " Go ye therefore and teach all nations, baptizing them in the name of the Father, and of the Son, and of the Holy Ghost." So perhaps Christians must always proselyte.

But Jesus did not say: "Go into countries already Christian and coax people away from their ancestral church into yours." Perhaps He did not mean it. Yet Latin America is filled with United States citizens trained and financed to combat the Catholic faith as fervently as though Southern Methodists, Anglicans, or Seventh-Day Adventists were bringing the first glad tidings of Jesus. That the missionaries are devoted, often consecrated men and women does not alter the fact that the effect of their presence is often most unfortunate.

This is true in spite of the facts that individual missionaries have made devoted friends in South America, and that their non-religious work is generally much admired. Their schools, hospitals, and social centers often serve as models. Even Catholics have, in some cases, paid them the sincere, though covert compliment of imitation. Here again it is not what the Yanqui does that is criticized, but his manner of doing it. One could wish that we might aid our neighbors in their fight against ignorance, disease, and poverty without opposing their preferred — and Christian — faith.

Business, on the face of it, should offer the sanest basis of interchange, and the one freest of bad feelings. Latin-American countries need our capital as we needed European capital in the nineteenth century. They need the machinery and the technicians we produce in quantity and of high quality. Because our country was geographically easier to occupy and to develop than any of theirs and because we caught the great waves of European immigration, we are a few years ahead of them in industrialization — and we have what they need. We are equally in need of what they have: undeveloped resources and a limitless potential market. By supplying them with what we have we shall help them to produce what we lack. Yet too often and in too many places one hears complaint of Yanqui business men socially and in industry. Absorbed in the exacting detail of getting out the oil or the copper, developing the plantation, holding down costs and increasing profits, the industrialist is apt to forget the international implications of what he does. How he does it is often even more important. Such matters as treating native customs respectfully, and especially the general and generally resented policy of paying Yanquis more for the same work than nationals, may seem minor; but they are major factors in Latin-American opinion of the United States in every country where we have large-scale operations.

Our best representatives, as a class, have been scientists: men of objective interests with no faith to spread and no profits to increase. A stranger studying any aspect of a country — its folk, flora, or fauna — may seem queer to the natives, but the simplest of them are flattered by his interest and he generally inspires confidence and makes friends. Moreover, he comes into contact with the country's own scientists and establishes a mutually respectful and helpful association with them. It would be impossible to overrate the goodwill built up by the Carnegie Institution, the Rockefeller Foundation, many museums and universities and other organizations financed in the United States.

Their most important contribution, perhaps, has been in health. Charles Morrow Wilson, in *Ambassadors in White*, presents a thrilling summary of what United States organizations have accomplished in Latin America. He calls those countries " a sick man's society," where people are dying of diseases which are preventable and have been or are on the way to being eliminated in our country. These diseases are also communicable; they are plagues. Until the International Health Board, financed by Rockefeller, cleaned up the port of Guayaquil, everyone who stepped ashore there was menaced by yellow fever or bubonic plague. The equatorial jungles of the Amazon, where our men are now developing rubber plantations, are rife with malaria and even more virulent (and communicable) diseases. Malaria is rampant everywhere south of the Rio Grande. Trachoma is everywhere. For the most selfish reasons it behooves us to help our neighbors in their fight against disease. And they have not waited for us. The earliest Spanish expeditions included physicians; Spanish colonial capitals had hospitals; and all the new republics have done what a few well-trained and poorly financed physicians could to combat disease. Our contribution has been to finance and to expand programs already begun.

It is significant and important that our contacts with Latin-American nations have previously suffered from one-sidedness. Their citizens have found little reason to come to the United States; what they sought was in Europe and they went there for education, culture, and widened social horizons. The few who came to the United States — generally as official representatives or as students — usually reacted and reported favorably. But they have been too few to make much impression either on their countries or on ours. They have known us best not as seekers after knowledge, but as missionaries, teachers, or employers. This has given us both false impressions. They have seen us as interfering busybodies or as tyrannical bosses. We — in the position of teacher or hirer — have inclined to see them only as children or as laborers. This at worst. At best, of course, these personal contacts have resulted in much individual understanding and good feeling, enduring friendships, and happy marriages. But the general picture has been bad enough to impel the American governments to try officially to improve understanding.

Government action has two outstanding advantages over the uncoordinated and personal undertakings of the past. The first is that government financing can reach a wider field than the most generous private endowments have done. Our awareness of how much we need the other Americas is measured by the size of our loans to them. Nor is this a cynical observation. Friendship is a give-and-take affair on the international as well as on the personal plane. If we finance the building of ships and shipyards, steel mills and armament factories, it is because we may need well-equipped allies. If we make funds available for better communications, for electrification, and for surveys of strategic materials, it is because we need neighbors better developed industrially than they are yet able to become alone. If we seek to improve their fisheries, agriculture, and stock-raising, it is because we of the Western Hemisphere suddenly must produce what we used to import from other parts of the world. Moreover, well-fed, healthy, and prosperous friends are more reliable than the poverty-ridden and undernourished.

The second advantage of official co-ordination of inter-American affairs is that a well-planned approach will undoubtedly remove many silly and baseless prejudices. We of the Americas enjoy cultures founded on the same Hebraic-Greco-Roman base. We got ours via England while theirs came from Spain and France, but the heritage is the same; and their love of independence, inspired by the French, is quite as fundamental as is ours, coming from the English. All the American nations broke with Europe at about the same time and for the same reasons. Our governments are on the same model. We are the oldest and most enduring democracies. That none of us have fully realized our ideals should make us mutually tolerant, not unsympathetic. If they have their dictators, we have our labor czars; if they have peonage, we have Negroes, both as slaves and now. In a sad world we had better look toward our similarities rather than toward our differences.

This is where the Division of Cultural Relations comes in. Its office, though not precisely so stated, is to increase mutual respect and understanding by increasing knowledge. Its policy of bringing north as many distinguished leaders and promising students as it sends south is rectifying the former one-sidedness. They generally like us even at our simplest in our own homes. Many of us are learning for the first time that the other Americas have vigorous thinkers in many lines. And technicians, scientists, and artists whose preoccupations preclude racial discrimination or religious prejudice go far toward making them non-existent. If a woman sings magnificently, what musician cares what color her skin may be? If a full-blooded Indian archæologist digs up a bone that provides an important link, what Spaniard or Swede of purest Caucasian strain would hesitate to honor him? Who stops to ascertain the church affiliations of the doctor who isolates a germ and saves thousands of lives? These things are in a realm far above our primitive prejudices.

What we are doing is sound. Is our way of doing it again at fault? The " cultural attachés " in some of our embassies make one wonder. By what standard have these handsome, energetic young college men and women been selected? Their youth is engaging, their assiduous efforts to learn primary Spanish commendable. But one fears that they have been better fitted to get a job than to cope with the difficulties of serving as liaison officers between two cultures.

A professor in the University of Chile, in answer to a query, suggested the qualifications for a cultural attaché:

"First, a working knowledge of our language. How can one be a cultural link who can neither speak nor understand? A knowledge of our literature and of our colloquialisms would be endearing, though perhaps not indispensable. Given the right state of mind and the language, anyone could acquire that as he went along. But really essential is a thorough familiarity with our history and that of diplomatic relations between our countries. Often this is lacking, and its lack causes curious and embarrassing situations." Then he laughed and concluded: "*Ojalá que no se sienta* superior! (God grant that he should not feel himself superior!)"

This is a modest enough list, even including the final requirement, which implies only a fair amount of culture and good manners. One might add others without demanding too much: A knowledge of social forms in the United States and sufficient adaptability to conform to foreign customs without complaint or criticism. Better yet would be an unconscious understanding of Latin-American social attitudes and standards because of long association with them. People, for instance, of French blood from Louisiana or of Spanish blood from the Southwest would have a great advantage over anybody (barring extraordinary aptitude) of Nordic heritage from other sections of our country. This would be especially true of Catholics. A woman — and women should be very successful as cultural attachés — should be mature enough to assume a dignified position in a society where girls do not play a leading role.

Do these criticisms seem trivial? They are not. In final analysis sound and fruitful international relations depend upon a respectful attitude one toward the other, and that depends upon the persons concerned.

A Nazi-inclined professor in Santiago riffled the pages of

two magazines designed for South America — one from Germany, the other from the United States. " See," he sneered, " the trivial stuff those Yanquis send us in comparison with this excellent review conducted and written by really learned men. Compare the half-formed children the United States sends us with the distinguished scholars who occupy similar posts in the Germany Embassy. Why should we choose the people who look down upon us, who give us their second-best? "

This is an extreme point of view, but salutary to look upon.

Surely it is evidence of a world growing always more aware of its interrelatedness that a great country like ours should study friendliness and set up a government agency to promote it. And wisely. Our interdependence with Latin America is so great and so sure to grow greater that it would be only stupid not to strive for better methods of dealing. Here, as in every phase of democracy, the attitude of the individual is of paramount importance. We are learning that in international as in personal affairs the greatest monetary gift, the most disinterested offer of aid, gain or lose value according to the manner of the giver. In all essentials all Americans hold the same beliefs. We all want national independence, personal liberty, equality of opportunity, and continual material development toward better living for all. We are willing to work for that end; even to fight for it. The barriers which have held us apart in misunderstanding and ill feeling have been largely personal and removable by personal effort.

But we, the American nations, have a greater obligation than to get along well together. We led the world in establishing democratic states which — in spite of heterogeneous populations representing every race, creed, and degree of civilization — have endured for well over a century. Now that war has violently severed the ties which held us to Europe and hence apart from each other, we must perforce weave a new pattern, north and south. This is sure to have incalculable importance for the post-war world which rightly concerns us all so deeply. For here we have the American model for an international democracy on which the world might build a stable future. It is not perfect. None of our democracies has been perfect. But they have worked. Now it is our obligation, even as we are fighting to win the war, to make sure that in this hemisphere — so blessedly saved from the more immediate horrors of invasion — we are perfecting a workable international democracy. The all-America Simón Bolívar visioned is in process of realization. May it lead us out of a global war into a global democracy of nations!

INDEX

i

PRINTER'S NOTE

This book was set on the Linotype in *Bodoni Book,* a printing-type so called after Giambattista Bodoni, a celebrated printer and type designer of Rome and Parma (1740–1813). *Bodoni Book* as produced by the Linotype company is not a copy of any one of Bodoni's fonts, but is a composite, modern version of the Bodoni manner. Bodoni's innovations in printing-type style were a greater degree of contrast in the " thick and thin " elements of the letters, and a sharper and more angular finish of details.

The book was composed, printed, and bound by The Plimpton Press, Norwood, Massachusetts.

each other and revealed to me were ugly, old, snaggle-toothed.
Their clothes were poor and dirty, their shoes ill-fitting. It
was a mean travesty of love-play. Yet they danced with vigor
and fine rhythm. They delighted their audience, who bought
them drinks and egged them on with cries: " Catch her, she's
a star! " " Go to him! " " Arr-rr-rro! "

As people left the grandstand the crowds grew in size, in
noisiness, and drunkenness. When a man said to a woman:
" A turn with me? " they turned first to the bar and downed
a glass or two of chicha or fragrant *mistela*. Between turns
he offered more, or their admiring friends did. Now and then
a seated drinker toppled over and was hauled out, but the
dancers only waxed more vigorous and suggestive in their
gestures as they drank. All along that line of arbors, however, the dancers were middle-aged or more. It was not that
no young people were there. Girls, many of them pretty and
dressed in modern print frocks, sat at tables, beating out the
rhythm, tapping their toes, looking hopefully at the guasos.
But those caballeros, handsome and young, kept their horses'
bridles in hand, or entered only to drink. It was as though
only the aging knew that the way out of life's misery was to
assume a gaiety if they had it not. Youngsters may be growing self-conscious about the old peasant dance if not ashamed
of it.

But the oldsters were artful and inventive. They varied
the endless circling, dodging, and overtaking until they made
every dance seem individual. The men made loops of their
waving handkerchiefs, the women postured provocatively.
Men forced their bodies against their partners, making them
spread their skirts like a fan to evade the kiss which must
have been very alcoholic against the face. They ended always
with a fast and furious clicking of heels on the board floor,

the mounting tempo of instruments and voices, the whoops of excited observers. The woman was shyly overcome at last and the man, leering and strutting, was the conquering male. And all, mind you, with misshapen bodies and feet, ugly old faces, poor and often dirty clothes. If the stranger cannot see the happy carefree Chileno, but only sad-seeming people drinking and letting off the fumes of drink as they sweated in the dance, one sees the invincible spirit of the Chilean.

Once, as we stood at a booth's entrance, I was roughly pushed aside by a man running. Another followed, reeling with drink. Then we heard cries; men pushed out to look and in again, telling each other that one had stabbed the other. Immediately carabineros were on the spot and in command.

"It's time to go," advised Boleslo at my back. "The drinking will get worse. More shootings, knifings too. The police are here, and it is never well to be around when men are killed and the police ask questions."

I was ready to go too, but I made it a lingering stroll along the arbors in vain search for the young and pretty dancers that appear on all the postal cards and in the tourist guides. I could only hope, as we drove off into the reddened dust cloud of sunset, that the pretty girls would show up at the *baile social* that night. Lush enticing young things with flashing eyes, rounded figures, and dainty feet under full skirts. They would be the partners for those handsome guasos who had all afternoon been too assiduously attending their horses.

Later, looking for photographs to illustrate the cueca, I found the very girls I had missed, but looking somehow only palely posed, too stagy in their rippling skirts, shoulder shawls, and heeled slippers. Even the guasos, all correct in leggings, spurs, and ponchos, were characterless in contrast with the real cueca dancers I had seen. In dull clothes, ugly